REFLECTIVE HISTORY SERIES

Barbara Finkelstein and William J. Reese, Series Editors

WHEN SCIENCE ENCOUNTERS THE CHILD

EDUCATION, PARENTING, AND CHILD WELFARE IN 20TH-CENTURY AMERICA

EDITED BY

Barbara Beatty, Emily D. Cahan, and Julia Grant

TEACHERS COLLEGE PRESS

Teachers College, Columbia University
New York and London

Published by Teachers College Press, 1234 Amsterdam Avenue, New York, NY 10027

Library of Congress Cataloging-in-Publication Data

When science encounters the child : education, parenting, and child welfare in
  20th-century America / edited by Barbara Beatty, Emily D. Cahan and Julia Grant.
     p. cm. — (Reflective history series)
  Includes bibliographical references and index.
  ISBN 0-8077-4691-6 (pbk. : alk. paper)
    1. Education, Elementary—United States—History—20th century. 2. Parenting—
United States—History—20th century. 3. Child welfare—United States—History—
20th century. 4. Child development—United States—History—20th century.
I. Beatty, Barbara, 1946– II. Cahan, Emily D., 1956– III. Grant, Julia, 1953–
IV. Series.

  LA219.W44 2006
  372'.973090—dc22

                                             2006040456

ISBN-13:   ISBN-10:
978-0-8077-4691-2 (paper)   0-8077-4691-6 (paper)

Printed on acid-free paper
Manufactured in the United States of America

13 12 11 10 09 08 07 06   8 7 6 5 4 3 2 1

To the good food and conversation we had along the way,
and to the patience of our authors

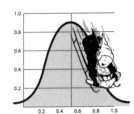

Contents

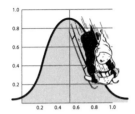

Acknowledgments

THIS BOOK BEGAN as a panel we did at the History of Education Society, a project that our enthusiastic discussant Barbara Finkelstein encouraged us to turn into an anthology. It evolved at a meeting of the Society for Research in Child Development, at which our discussant Sheldon H. White gave us insightful advice. Some of these chapters were presented as papers at these and other professional meetings. We are very grateful for the beneficence of the Spencer Foundation, both personally and collectively. With the foundation's assistance, three scholars from the fields of education, psychology, and history were afforded the opportunity to work on a collaborative project that, we hope, stretches the endeavors of each of our fields. We appreciate the support of Wellesley College, Wheelock College, and James Madison College at Michigan State University. We are also grateful for the patience of our authors, who uncomplainingly responded to the seemingly endless commentary of three different editors. We want to thank Brian Ellerbeck and the staff of Teachers College Press for their expertise; Doug Meyer for his copyediting; and our families and colleagues, who saw us through various revisions. Like children, edited volumes take a while to mature and pass through interesting stages along the way. Like science, the outcome is open to interpretation, but hopefully is useful and contributes to future research.

WHEN SCIENCE ENCOUNTERS THE CHILD

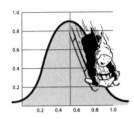

Introduction

Barbara Beatty, Emily D. Cahan, and Julia Grant

IN 1919, VERA BROWN and Bertha Schrader, two girls who had been refused admission to the Seattle public schools, were caught up in a professional dispute among child scientists. Nelly Goodhue, a teacher with training in mental testing who was the principal of the system's new special schools, stood by her diagnosis that the girls were too severely mentally retarded to attend. Dr. Ira Brown, the school medical inspector, thought otherwise and argued that as a physician he should have the final word on the girls' placements. In the ensuing controversy, teachers, principals, truant officers, police officers, juvenile court officials, probation officers, school nurses, school doctors, state hospital administrators, the director of the state institution for the feebleminded, the director of a mental hygiene bureau, university psychologists, the superintendent, the school board, and the state supreme court were all directly or indirectly involved. The superintendent decided in favor of Goodhue and psychology. Dr. Brown and medicine lost this round. Vera Brown and Bertha Schrader were permanently excluded from the Seattle public schools. But as Stephen Woolworth shows in his chronicle of this episode, the jockeying for power among children's experts did not subside.[1] And all of the parties involved in the dispute over Vera Brown and Bertha Schrader used the language of science to buttress their arguments about what should happen to the two girls.

THE RISE OF THE SCIENCES OF CHILDHOOD

At the beginning of the twentieth century, science was beginning to encounter the child. The number of new fields of professional expertise relating to children grew rapidly. As they grew, a seemingly endless series of turf disputes erupted over who was qualified and had the right to guide education, parenting, and child welfare practices. In most of the training given to children's professionals and parents, the sciences of childhood, or "child sciences," a term we borrow from historian Hamilton Cravens, overlapped. The outcomes of these disputes and overlaps were rarely stable. Alliances formed and shifted. Status hierarchies developed and were challenged. Although there was considerable skepticism about the role of science, by the end of the twentieth century, most school districts, child welfare organizations, and parental advice-givers drew upon scientific rationales and expertise. The sciences of childhood became firmly entrenched in policymaking in the numerous new federal, state, and local agencies vying for authority over aspects of children's lives. Yet there were always questions about the legitimacy of the research guiding policy and even more questions about the level of funding allocated to children's programs.[2]

Science did not win all of the many encounters with children in which it was invoked, but it had an enormous influence on most children's lives. Vulnerable children were shuffled in and out of different institutions as others fell through the cracks. Fortunate children were more protected, but all were exposed to the variability of psychological treatments, educational approaches, and child-rearing advice, not to mention the questionable competence of individual practitioners. Some children resisted and refused to participate in the programs designed to alleviate their supposed, troublesome, and sometimes very real problems. For all of these children, shreds of autonomy remained, if only because childhood is ultimately unknowable to adults, no matter how well intentioned, caring, and expert they may be.[3]

The rise of the child sciences was implacable. The authors of the chapters in this book show many of the varying ways that the child sciences were used and ask how these uses served children. Our answers vary. The verdict was often mixed. Often there was no way to really know. Our chapters document the growth of an empire of child servers, the growing role of science in this empire, and the growth of concerns about the well-being of children—all of which, in turn, fueled the growth of the child sciences. Along the way, we document the reactions of some dissenters who doubted the usefulness of science and how it was being used with children. Although these dissenting voices were often muted among the advancing claims, and may be infrequently heard in these pages, we want to underscore their continuing existence.

CHILD PSYCHOLOGY AND ITS METHODS

We use Craven's term *child sciences* to refer to any one of a number of natural and social sciences that appropriate children as objects of inquiry. There is no one science of childhood; there are many. A small sample would include psychology, medicine, sociology, economics, anthropology, and political science. Scientists study children in ways that vary wildly in terms of motive, method, and analytic tools. The "data" or "vocabulary" for each of the child sciences reflect different phenomena that are analyzed in different ways and interpreted using different analytic frameworks. We focus primarily on psychology in its many forms. While medicine has had equally profound effects and sociology has been of great consequence, psychology has arguably become the dominant paradigm for understanding children, and indeed ourselves.[4]

Child psychology was never a unified field. Psychoanalytic theory represented the child as caught between instinctual drives and the civilizing processes of society; behaviorism made the child an infinitely malleable bundle of habits and seeker of rewards; educational psychology and testing measured individual differences and defined children by a set of particular mental abilities. Developmental psychology looked at the child as an evolving being who changed in different ways at different points over time.[5]

Psychological findings about children were as variable as the methods that scientists employed. Mental testers studied the number of correct or incorrect responses on sets of standardized questions and calculated intelligence on the basis of age norms, assuming that intelligence could be defined as that which the intelligence tests test. Beginning in the 1920s, in a synthesis of philosophy and biology, Jean Piaget defined intelligence very differently, as a form of adaptation to the world, and used observation and interviews with children at home, in school, in the laboratory, and on the playground in order to develop his theories. Experimental child psychologists began pursuing their work primarily in laboratories, where infants and children were expected to respond to particular stimuli, learn connections between events as a result of repeated experience, and demonstrate patterns of attention and learning that could be quantified. Clinical psychologists studied unconscious emotional conflicts by observing play and listening to children for indications of "Oedipal conflicts," sibling rivalry, or sexual inhibition. Each specialty had its own location in time and space and had what psychologist Sheldon H. White called its own "social proof structure"—a set of agreed-upon analytic tools and procedures for collecting, analyzing, and interpreting empirical findings.[6]

THE USES AND USERS OF CHILD PSYCHOLOGY

We have adapted David Olson and Jerome Bruner's concept of "psychology in use," the idea that as psychology is applied by practitioners and loosed from its academic moorings, it changes and becomes "folk psychology," the psychology that practitioners cobble together, invent, and reinvent in their daily lives and work. We examine how these sciences were used for different purposes, in different environments, with different kinds of children, and by whom.[7]

Psychologists, though perhaps most visible, were far from alone in the child sciences. Reformers and child scientists of the late nineteenth and early twentieth centuries confronted dependent, delinquent, different, and "defective" children, to use the argot of the period, on teeming city streets, where children hawked newspapers, cared for small babies, and harassed passersby. At the turn of the century these confrontations resulted in the creation of a new field—social work—and inspired a generation of sociologists and settlement house workers, most notably in Chicago, but in other cities, too. Teachers in urban schools at the turn of the century encountered students with foreign voices, dirty clothing, oozing ears, and a daunting range of academic skills. The realities imposed by twentieth-century immigration, industrialization, and urbanization spurred the development of the school clinic, psychological testing, and special education movements, among other phenomena. The many young people clogging the juvenile court founded in 1899 in Chicago sparked the formation of the first child guidance clinic in 1909 for the diagnosis and rehabilitation of delinquents. These populations and their needs and problems pushed child scientists to respond in various ways and influenced agendas for research.[8]

In the first decades of the twentieth century, H. H. Goddard's and Lewis Terman's adaptations of Alfred Binet's school diagnostic test evolved into a normalizing project of vast dimensions, the IQ testing movement. Other psychologies were used in all manner of ways in all the institutions and places where children were educated, treated, housed, and reared.[9]

THE CHILDREN'S INSTITUTES

Child psychologists rapidly became the superstars of a new advice industry. With dubious claims to expertise, some capitalized on their new prominence as problem solvers for the American public, while others sought to acquire scientific knowledge on which to base their pronouncements. Public demand for more knowledge about children generated funding opportunities and initiated the establishment of institutes, sometimes called child development or child welfare institutes, where an eclectic program of basic and applied research on children was pursued. Supported by both state and private monies, children's institutes were founded at major universities throughout the country. Arguing that there had been an overemphasis on children who were "abnormal"—a code word for poor, racially different, orphaned, abandoned, abused, or differently abled—researchers at the new institutes began mapping the contours of normality. In the process, the meanings of "normal," "average," and "ideal" merged in a confusion of empirical data, descriptive statistics, and values.[10]

Researchers at the new children's institutes charted both urban and rural children using both cross-sectional and longitudinal designs. However, southern, southwestern, and immigrant children, as well as members of nonwhite ethnic-racial groups, were underrepresented, because most research centers were located in the Northeast and the Midwest. This underrepresentation was compounded by the view that the developmental trajectories of children from "other" groups were thought to be so abnormal or statistically aberrant as to cloud the vision of normalcy that the studies sought to reveal. As early as the 1930s, sociologists were documenting the dire effects of prejudice, segregation, and unequal opportunity on African American children. But it was not until the 1950s, when Kenneth Clark published his famous doll studies, that research on black children and their development began to have a significant impact on the child sciences. In the 1960s, a headlong assault was made on the idea that African Americans were genetically inferior intellectually, with the Head Start program making valiant efforts to ensure that African American children were provided with the educational experiences necessary for academic success.[11]

GENDER

An interest in gender differences arose in tandem with the child development movement. Girls' education received a boost from the findings of early psychologists such as Edward L. Thorndike and Leta Hollingworth, and later Eleanor Maccoby, who demonstrated that there was little differentiation between males and females in terms of intelligence. Nevertheless, many sociologists of the 1920s and 1930s contended that traditional gender roles were essential to the healthy functioning of the family. Meanwhile, psychoanalysts defined mental health in terms of the development of heterosexuality, and social-learning theorists of the 1940s and 1950s emphasized the role of rewards for learning gender-appropriate models and behaviors. In the 1960s and 1970s feminists capitalized on this research and argued that if gender roles were learned, they could and should be unlearned, opening the floodgates to a new generation of research on the acquisition of gender roles in children.[12]

EDUCATION

Of all the arenas in which psychology held sway, education was the largest. Driven by immigration and the population explosion that began in the second half of the nineteenth century, public schools experienced unprecedented growth. Between 1890 and 1930 the number of pupils in the public schools doubled, from more than 14 million to more than 28 million. By 1960, 99.5 percent of seven- to thirteen-year-olds were in school, along with 90.3 percent of fourteen- to seventeen-year-olds. By 1990, more than 46 million students were attending K–12 schools, more than triple the number of a century earlier. As schools expanded, so did the number of teachers, from around 364,000 in 1890 to some 2,357,000 in 1990—an almost 700 percent increase. Urban school systems experiencing an enormous influx of children from very different backgrounds especially demanded and used psychology, for many purposes.[13]

With this huge growth in schools and teachers in an age in which science was seen as the solution for almost all societal needs, professional educators launched an ambitious project to create a science of education and raise the status of education as a profession. Given the broad mandate of their field and higher status within academia, psychologists were natural allies in this undertaking and rapidly assumed the role of creating a new psychology of education. With a tenfold increase in the number of professional psychologists between 1919 and 1939, from a few hundred to some three thousand, and exponential jumps to more than thirty thousand by 1970 and nearly a quarter of million by 1995, there were plenty of psychologists to take on the task.[14]

PARENTING

Unlike education, the study of parenting did not have a disciplinary home. Instead, it inhabited departments of family ecology, psychology, sociology, social work, home economics, and pediatrics, to name just some of the arenas in which research related to parenting has been conducted. Nineteenth-century literate parents could have access to a wide-ranging literature on raising children, much of it written by ministers and educated women. Parent education programs grew exponentially in the 1920s, some conducted in conjunction with the child welfare institutes, and others sponsored by women's clubs, schools, and churches. Magazines, books, and government-sponsored pamphlets offered advice on feeding, sleeping, and disciplinary tactics, inundating parents with a profusion of information. Parents of different racial, class, regional, and ethnic backgrounds responded differently to this wealth of conflicting expertise. Some eagerly embraced it. Others rejected it. Some parents were never exposed to it. Child-rearing advice kept shifting, from an emphasis on routines and habit training in the 1920s to the softer, more developmental approach of Benjamin Spock's 1946 *Baby and Child Care*, though in retrospect there seems to have been little scientific research to show that either type of disciplinary regime contributed to healthier, better-adjusted children.[15]

CHILD WELFARE

Child scientists were also involved in the first major child welfare event of the twentieth century, the White House Conference on the Care of Dependent Children, which took place in 1909. Convened by President Theodore Roosevelt, the gathering brought together child welfare workers from throughout the country—heads of orphanages, settlement house workers, and social scientists—who unanimously endorsed a set of concrete and far-reaching recommendations for the president to consider. Their findings combined sentiment, politics, and science: sentiment because the group determined that homes were more fitting places for children than were institutions, a conclusion based more on reverence for motherhood than on science; politics, because the group held the government responsible for ensuring that poverty did not stand in the way of keeping parents and children together; and science, because of the group's recognition of the need to create a central agency that could acquire information to guide child welfare practices.[16]

Founded in 1912, the U.S. Children's Bureau embodied the conference's aim to approach child welfare more scientifically, beginning with gathering statistics and publishing research on such phenomena as child labor, maternal and infant health care, and unwed motherhood. Moving children from institutions to boarding or foster homes was a slower process, because there were no federal mandates or any central national authority for accomplishing that mission. And pursuing the goal of providing mothers' pensions to "worthy" single mothers proceeded on a regional basis only, before the implementation of the Social Security Act in 1935, which never attained the goal of providing assistance to all women, or of providing adequate coverage to any women.[17]

The problem of children in the custody of the state, or children who were without parental care because of abuse, neglect, or delinquency, sporadically compelled attention. Although the movement of dependent children from institutions to boarding homes predated the research, studies by Dorothy Burlingham, Anna Freud, Rene Spitz, and John Bowlby during the 1940s and 1950s on the damage inflicted on English war orphans by parental separation and institutionalization made institutions a last resort for troubled children. But many African American children continued to languish in reform schools and other public institutions. The publication of *Beyond the Best Interests of the Child* in 1973 by attorney Joseph Goldstein, psychoanalyst Anna Freud, and pediatrician and psychiatrist Albert Solnit set forth concepts of the "child's sense of time" and the "psychological parent" that would influence child custody decisions in the years to come. Throughout the course of the century the disciplines of medicine, psychology, education, and sociology all offered up research with significant implications for child welfare. Whether they were implemented depended on a plethora of factors, including the degree of mass-media attention; economic factors; tensions between parents' rights and children's best interests; and, perhaps most important, whether Americans had the political or moral will to devote themselves to the improvement of children's lives.[18]

"BRAIN SCIENCE"

All the contributors to this volume address issues that have important implications for child scientists and children's professionals today. Despite critiques from researchers, practitioners, and philosophers of science who espouse humanistic approaches and doubt the existence of a value-neutral, deterministic relationship between science and children, applications of laboratory research have sharply increased.

The new "brain science" permeates schooling, parent education, and child welfare. The mass media, politicians, and some practitioners working in schools and parent education would have one think that we know much more about how children's brains operate than we actually do, and that this knowledge can be put to immediate use. For instance, one organization, the Learning and the Brain Society, sponsors annual conferences at which, in 2005, for $495 teachers and clinicians could listen to prominent neurobiologists, cognitive scientists, and pediatric neurologists talk about how to use "brain plasticity" to "raise achievement for all learners." In 1998, the state of Georgia distributed a classical-music tape for every newborn baby. Distribution of the tape, which was titled *Build Your Baby's Brain Through the Power of Music*, was justified by limited and preliminary research on the impact of classical music on college students' cognitive performance on particular tasks.[19]

In preschool education in particular, perhaps because young children and preschool curricula are thought to be more malleable, the science of child development has been especially influential. Developmental psychology has been enshrined in the preschool bible, the National Association for the Education of Young Children's guide *Developmentally Appropriate Practice in Early Childhood Programs*. Exaggerated claims about the importance of early brain stimulation have fueled public support for quality preschool and childcare programs for disadvantaged children. Meanwhile, serious, sophisticated research by economists, psychologists, and others on the costs, benefits, and effects of early childhood care and education receives much less attention.[20]

Policymakers like quick, cheap fixes. The idea that we can inoculate children from the vicissitudes of poverty and other social ills through early intervention has resulted in myriad short-lived programs that produce mixed results. We have yet to try what psychologists Michael Lewis and Richard Weissbourd suggest, providing "vulnerable" children with a platform of services throughout childhood.[21]

"SCIENTIFICALLY BASED RESEARCH" IN EDUCATION AND TEACHING

In elementary and secondary education, the 2001 No Child Left Behind Act's 111 references to "scientifically based research," now referred to by some simply as "SBR," has become the topic of heated debate. The core philosophy of No Child Left Behind—accountability through the use of supposedly valid and reliable, scientifically designed achievement tests—has become ingrained in American education, despite much sharp criticism, some from educational psychologists. The Education Sciences Reform Act of 2002 and the new Institute of Education Sciences in the Department of Education recommend that only research based on randomized controlled field trials be funded. In its 2002 report *Scientific Research in Education*, the National Research Council set out broad principles that strike a middle ground, as did its 2004 follow-up *Advancing Scientific Research in Education*. The federal What Works Clearinghouse, sponsored by the Institute of Education Sciences, recommends that schools adopt "evidence-based" curricula that meet the standard of "randomized controlled trials" and "regression discontinuity designs." Its reports rating curriculum models by these standards provoke much controversy, because of disagreements over methodology and the appearance that the federal government may be impartially ranking specific curricula and because the gap between "scientifically based research" studies that easily lend themselves to statistical analysis and "research-based" practice is vast.[22]

With promises of breakthroughs in cognitive science, the hope for a "real" science of education is stronger than ever, despite the glaring disparities between what schools can actually provide and growing polarities in what students from poor and upper-income backgrounds experience. Qualitative research on the benefits of programs such as Geoffrey Canada's Harlem Children's Zone, which gives children and their families much-needed social services in conjunction with their schools, seems sidetracked in the race for better test scores.[23]

Ideas about the child brain have had mixed effects on child welfare practices. Widespread assumptions that children with histories of trauma or neglect are irrevocably damaged have resulted in a range of frightening medical labels and the creation of specialized services for troubled children. Research on the long-term consequences of early abuse and neglect, in combination with our failure to provide safe care for children in state custody, has led to a reversal of earlier child welfare policies that combined an emphasis on family reunification with often protracted foster care placements. With the passage of the Adoption Assistance Act in 1997, adoption was promoted as the government's best response to the problems of the thousands of children from poverty-stricken and disproportionately African American homes, most of whom were removed from their parents for the nebulous crime of "neglect."[24]

IMPACT OF THE SCIENCES OF CHILDHOOD TODAY

We focus most intensively on the first half of the twentieth century, when the research, organizations, and relationships that formed the framework of the empire of the child sciences and child servers were laid out. Once these structures were formed, we argue, the outline of the modern sciences of childhood and child serving was in place. If anything, faith in the ability of science to serve children has only become stronger as the reach and numbers of child servers has grown, and the number of encounters between science and children has increased.

We ask questions about these encounters and about the impact of this empire on the daily lives of children and families. Disproportionate numbers of children from low-income and minority families, with disabilities, and for whom English is not the first language, continue to fall behind in school, experience poor health, and languish in the child welfare system. Parents seem more anxious than ever about their children's health, safety, and hopes for achieving economic success. Of course, relative to children in many other parts of the world, many American children lead extraordinarily comfortable, if not overprotected, childhoods. But child poverty and its consequences, the "unequal childhoods" that sociologist Annette Lareau describes, are seemingly intractable problems in this political universe. We know more than ever about child development but seemingly less than ever about how to fix the unequal consequences of differential childhoods.[25]

In Chapter 1, Emily Cahan focuses on the history of developmental psychology, beginning with the child study movement of the 1890s that originated under G. Stanley Hall, whose influence on education, parenting, and child welfare was so pervasive that he appears in almost every chapter in this volume. In Chapter 2, Barbara Beatty shows how Hall, John Dewey, and Edward L. Thorndike applied their quite different theories of learning to "psychologize" arithmetic teaching in the Progressive Era, and speculates about how teachers use psychology. In Chapter 3, Carlos Kevin Blanton discusses how Hall adapted French linguistic methods, which progressive educators in the 1920s and 1930s transformed into the monolingual methods of the "English-Only" approach. In Chapter 4, Roblyn Rawlins analyzes changing views on precocity from the nineteenth century to the twentieth, and shows how the rise of intelligence testing influenced advice to parents on how to raise "gifted children." In Chapter 5, Stephen Woolworth describes conflicts that took place among physicians and psychologists in the Seattle public schools in the 1910s and 1920s, when intelligence testing gave psychologists more power over decisions about children with special needs. In Chapter 6, David Wolcott and Steven Schlossman describe the Chicago Area Project of the 1930s and juxtapose sociologist Clifford Shaw's innovative ethnographic methods, aimed at understanding and remediating juvenile delinquency, with the power of adolescent peer culture. In Chapter 7, Diana Selig uses the 1930 White House conference to demonstrate the way in which social science and psychology competed to define child welfare, and the way in which both disciplines could be employed to develop a better understanding of the environmental and psychological hazards facing African American children. In Chapter 8, Jonna Perrillo shows how clinical psychology influenced the intercultural movement in New York City schools in the 1940s and early 1950s, when teachers who were attempting to address racial prejudice ran up against the realities of white and black students' identities and experiences in segregated schools and communities. In Chapter 9, Christopher Schmidt analyzes how lawyers and justices involved in the *Brown v. Board of Education* Supreme Court school desegregation case of 1954 used psychological research on the damage of racism to black children but ignored evidence on the psychological harm inflicted by prejudice on white children. In Chapter 10, Rima Apple surveys parenting literature in the first half of the twentieth century and documents why many mothers reacted favorably to prescriptions from psychologists and physicians to begin toilet training early and to feed children according to strict schedules. In Chapter 11, Julia Grant examines psychological research on boys and masculinity, gender-related practices in child guidance clinics and nursery schools, and the responses of parents and children themselves to attempts to instill proper masculine behavior. Finally, in a coda, Barbara Finkelstein places in a larger social perspective the growth of the child sciences throughout the twentieth century and comments on the uses of science and its relationship to child welfare.

We do not pretend to have answers to the many troubling questions our authors raise. What we do know is that there are no simple scientific solutions to the problems that confront us in educating and raising children both individually and collectively. The attempt by psychologists to define and, in effect, produce the "normal" child was an enterprise with mixed success, often ambiguous and misleading results, and unintended consequences. There is no standardized child, no average child, no ideal child. There are only children, children who embody difference not only through race, class, gender, and nationality, but also through a multitude of other variables, including age, personality, and types of bodily and mental abilities. Yet those serving and rearing children require a knowledge base upon which to construct their practices and want to know how to differentiate between merely troublesome behaviors and those that augur more serious trouble down the road. All of us who care for children want to know how we can best facilitate their learning, health, and happiness. We all want to do everything we can to ensure that our encounters with children have positive outcomes. If science can help us to better serve children, so much the better. But we should be wary of attempts to substitute technical solutions for answers to social problems that are essentially moral and political. The demand for knowledge too often outstrips supply, and oversimplification of complex findings is employed in order to reach an army of practitioners—teachers, child welfare workers, and parents. Perhaps a better understanding of the history of the uses of the child sciences will help us to unravel this troubled legacy and heighten our awareness of both the promises and limitations of science in helping us to rear, teach, treat, and understand those wonderfully complex beings known as children.

NOTES

1. For this professional competition, see Andrew Abbott, *The System of the Professions: An Essay on the Division of Expert Labor* (Chicago: University of Chicago Press, 1988).

2. Hamilton Cravens, "Child Saving in the Age of Professionalism, 1915–1930," in Joseph Hawes and N. Ray Hiner, eds., *American Childhood: A Research Guide and Historical Handbook* (Westport, CT: Greenwood Press, 1985), 415–488. On skepticism about science and children and the uses of science in public policy,

see, among many others, Ellen Condliffe Lagemann, *An Elusive Science: The Troubling History of Education Research* (Chicago: University of Chicago Press, 2000); David L. Featherman and Maris A. Vinovskis, eds., *Social Science and Policy-Making* (Ann Arbor: University of Michigan Press, 2001); and Hamilton Cravens, ed., *The Social Sciences Go to Washington: The Politics of Knowledge in the Postmodern Age* (New Brunswick: Rutgers University Press, 2004). On the history of children generally, see, among many others, Paula S. Fass and Mary Ann Mason, *Childhood in America* (New York: New York University Press, 2000); the Twayne History of American Childhood Series edited by Joseph M. Hawes and N. Ray Hiner; and Steven Mintz, *Huck's Raft* (Cambridge: Harvard University Press, 2004).

3. On children's resistance to scientific advice, see Kathleen W. Jones, *Taming the Troublesome Child: American Families, Child Guidance, and the Limits of Psychiatric Authority* (Cambridge, MA: Harvard University Press, 1999).

4. Martin Gross, *The Psychological Society: A Critical Analysis of Psychiatry, Psychotherapy, Psychoanalysis, and the Psychological Revolution* (New York: Random House, 1978).

5. Cravens, "Child Saving in the Age of Professionalism"; David N. Livingston, *Putting Science in Its Place: Geographies of Scientific Knowledge* (Chicago: University of Chicago Press, 2003). See also Ellen Herman, *The Romance of American Psychology: Political Culture in the Age of Experts* (Berkeley: University of California Press, 1995); Donald S. Napoli, *Architects of Adjustment: The History of the Psychological Profession in the United States* (Port Washington, NY: Kennikat Press, 1981); and Joel Pfister and Nancy Schnog, eds., *Inventing the Psychological: Toward a Cultural History of Emotional Life in America* (New Haven: Yale University Press, 1997).

6. Sheldon H. White, "Social Proof Structures: The Dialectic of Method and Theory in the Work of Psychology," in *Life-Span Developmental Psychology: Dialectical Perspectives on Experimental Research*, ed. N. Daton and H. Reese (New York: Academic Press, 1977).

7. David R. Olson and Jerome S. Bruner, "Folk Psychology and Folk Pedagogy," in *The Handbook of Education and Human Development*, ed. David R. Olson and Nancy Torrance (Cambridge, UK: Blackwell, 1996), 9–27.

8. Roy Lubove, *The Professional Altruist: The Emergence of Social Work as a Career, 1880–1930* (Cambridge: Harvard University Press, 1965); Anthony M. Platt, *The Child-Savers: The Invention of Delinquency* (Chicago: University of Chicago Press, 1969); Jones, *Taming the Troublesome Child.*

9. On IQ testing, see, among others, Paul Davis Chapman, *Schools as Sorters: Lewis M. Terman, Applied Psychology, and the Intelligence Testing Movement, 1890–1930* (New York: New York University Press, 1988); Stephen Jay Gould, *The Mismeasure of Man* (New York: Norton, 1981); and Leila Zenderland, *Measuring Minds: Henry Herbert Goddard and the Origins of American Intelligence Testing* (Cambridge: Cambridge University Press, 1998).

10. On the institutes, see, among others, Steven L. Schlossman, "Philanthropy and the Gospel of Child Development," *History of Education Quarterly* 21 (Fall 1981): 275–99; Hamilton Cravens, *Before Head Start: The Iowa Station and America's*

Children (Chapel Hill: University of North Carolina Press, 1993); Julia Grant, "Constructing the Normal Child: The Rockefeller Philanthropies and the Science of Child Development," in *Philanthropic Foundations: New Scholarship, New Possibilities*, ed. Ellen Condliffe Lagemann (Bloomington: Indiana University Press, 1999), 131–50.

11. Cravens, *Before Head Start*; Grant, "Constructing the Normal Child"; Barbara Beatty, *Preschool Education in America: The Culture of Young Children from the Colonial Era to the Present* (New Haven: Yale University Press, 1995); Edward Zigler and Susan Muenchow, *Head Start: The Inside Story of America's Most Successful Educational Experiment* (New York: Basic, 1992).

12. Rosalind Rosenberg, *Beyond Separate Spheres: Intellectual Roots of Modern Feminism* (New Haven: Yale University Press, 1982); Julia Grant, *Raising Baby by the Book* (New Haven: Yale University Press, 1998); Elaine Tyler May, *Homeward Bound: American Families in the Cold War Era* (New York: Basic Books, 1988); Joseph H. Pleck, *The Myth of Masculinity* (Cambridge, MA: MIT Press, 1981); Eleanor Emmons Maccoby and Carol Nagy Jacklin, *The Psychology of Sex Differences* (Stanford: Stanford University Press, 1978).

13. Lagemann, *An Elusive Science,* 8. On urban schools and the use of science, see, among others, David Tyack, *The One Best System: A History of American Urban Education* (Cambridge, MA: Harvard University Press, 1974); and Herbert M. Kliebard, *The Struggle for the American Curriculum* (New York: Routledge, 1986).

14. James H. Capshew, *Psychologists on the March* (Cambridge: Cambridge University Press, 1999), 1.

15. Grant, *Raising Baby by the Book*; Ann Hulbert, *Raising America: Experts, Parents, and a Century of Advice about Children* (New York: Alfred A. Knopf, 2003); Peter N. Stearns, *Anxious Parents: A History of Modern Childrearing in America* (New York: New York University Press, 2003).

16. *Proceedings of the Conference on the Care of Dependent Children* (Washington, DC: GPO, 1909); Kathleen W. Jones, "Sentiment and Science: The Late Nineteenth Century Pediatrician and Mother's Advisor," *Journal of Social History* 17 (1983): 79–96.

17. Molly Ladd-Taylor, *Mother-Work: Women, Child Welfare, and the State, 1880–1930* (Urbana: University of Illinois Press, 1994); Linda Gordon, *Pitied but Not Entitled: Single Mothers and the History of Welfare, 1880–1935* (New York: Macmillan, 1994).

18. Anna Freud and Dorothy Burlingham, *Infants Without Families: The Case for and Against Residential Nurseries* (New York: International University Press, 1944); Rene Spitz, "Hospitalism: An Inquiry into the Genesis of Psychiatric Conditions in Early Childhood," in *The Psychoanalytic Study of the Child*, vol. 1, ed. Anna Freud, Heinz Hartmann, and Ernst Kris (New York: International University Press, 1945), 53–74; John Bowlby, *Mental Care and Mental Health: A Report Prepared on Behalf of the World Health Organization as a Contribution to the United Nations Program for the Welfare of Homeless Children* (Geneva: World Health Organization, 1951); Joseph Goldstein, Anna Freud, and Albert J. Solnit, *Beyond the*

Best Interests of the Child (New York: Free Press, 1979). And see especially LeRoy Ashby, *Endangered Children: Dependency, Neglect, and Abuse in American History* (New York: Twayne, 1997).

19. Electronic announcement for "Learning and the Brain: Using Brain Plasticity to Raise Achievement for All Learners" conference, organized by Public Information Resources, Incorporated, Cambridge, MA, April 28–30, http://www.quinncom securestore.com/edupr/secure/ccbrainreg.html. See also John T. Bruer, *The Myth of the First Three Years* (New York: Free Press, 1999); Alison Gopnik, Andrew N. Meltzoff, and Patricia K. Kuhl, *The Scientist in the Crib: Minds, Brains, and How Children Learn* (New York: Perennial Currents, 2001).

20. Sue Bredekamp and Carol Copple, eds., *Developmentally Appropriate Practice in Early Childhood Programs*, rev. ed. (Washington, DC: National Association for the Education of Young Children, 1997).

21. Michael Lewis, *Altering Fate: Why the Past Does Not Predict the Future* (New York: Guilford Press, 1997); Richard Weissbourd, *The Vulnerable Child: What Really Hurts America's Children and What We Can Do about It* (Reading, MA: Addison-Wesley, 1996).

22. Number of references in NCLB and "SBR," from Michael J. Feuer, Lisa Towne, and Richard J. Shavelson, "Scientific Culture and Educational Research," *Educational Researcher* 31 (November 2002): 4; James W. Popham, *The Truth about Testing* (Alexandria, VA: Association for Supervision and Curriculum Development, 2001); House Education and the Workforce Committee, H.R. 3801: The Education Sciences Act, March 20, 2002; National Research Council, *Scientific Research in Education*, ed. Committee on Scientific Principles for Education Research, Richard J. Shavelson and Lisa Towne (Washington, DC: National Academy Press, 2002); National Research Council, *Advancing Scientific Research*, ed. Committee on Research and Education, Lisa Towne et al. (Washington, DC: National Academy Press, 2004); Institute of Education Sciences, What Works Clearinghouse, "WWC Evidence Standards," http://www.whatworks.ed.gov/reviewprocess/study_standards_final.pdf; Debra Viadero, "Math Programs Seen to Lack a Research Base," *Education Week*, 24 (November 2004): 1, 17.

23. Paul Tough, "The Harlem Project," *The New York Times Magazine* 20 (June 2004): 44–49, 66, 72–73, 75.

24. Dorothy E. Roberts, *Shattered Bonds: The Color of Child Welfare* (New York: Basic Books, 2002).

25. Annette Lareau, *Unequal Childhoods: Class, Race, and Family Life* (Berkeley: University of California Press, 2003). See also Judith Sealander, *The Failed Century of the Child: Governing America's Young in the Twentieth Century* (Cambridge: Cambridge University Press, 2003); Steven Mintz, *Huck's Raft: A History of American Childhood* (Cambridge, MA: Harvard University Press, 2004); and Paula S. Fass and Mary Ann Mason, eds., *Childhood in America* (New York: New York University Press, 2000), among many others.

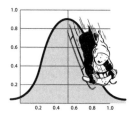

Toward a Socially Relevant Science: Notes on the History of Child Development Research

Emily D. Cahan

THOSE WHO CARE FOR and educate children often rely on the results of contemporary science to inform their practices and policies. Teachers, parents, child-care providers, and legislators routinely turn to developmental psychology to help guide them through the complex and sometimes perplexing details of dealing with children in a highly complex society. Courses in developmental psychology serve as foundation courses for teachers, social workers, and child-care providers. The traditional boundaries between "basic" and "applied" research have blurred as developmental psychologists can be found working in any one of a variety of research settings, including the laboratory, hospital, home, school, clinic, playground, or office of a member of Congress. The different kinds of questions posed in these different environments have demanded new methods and means of data analysis. In short, contemporary developmental psychology consists of multiple endeavors. On the one hand, it is an eclectic blend of technical and scientific inquiries into "basic" processes and sequences of growth in the child. On the other hand, it explores the possibilities of application to the practical and political problems of child management, education, and welfare.

The application of the child sciences to practical and policy questions is not easy, obvious, or objective. The connections between knowledge generated in unnatural laboratory environments and that garnered from the natural environments of children are often tenuous at best. Dangers, both technical and ethical, hover over attempts to apply a science constrained in time and place to the practical and political needs of children—what William Kessen once called "the arrogance of an ethic based on current findings."[1]

ORIGINS OF RESEARCH IN CHILD DEVELOPMENT

The roots of developmental psychology were many but at the very least include (1) a nineteenth-century tradition in which speculative histories of human evolution and progress were given sanction by evolutionary science and projected onto early theories of child development; (2) a concerted child welfare movement set into motion by the poverty and class conflict resulting from urbanization, industrialization, and immigration; (3) the emergence of a new scientific psychology distinct from its intellectual parentage in philosophy; and (4) a systematic philanthropy aimed at finding the causes of disease, social misfortune, and disorder and promising to improve the general welfare of humankind. The first is important in establishing developmental psychology's rich intellectual foundations; the second is meaningful in establishing the social role and relevance of the field; the third provides an understanding of the struggles of the field within the broader scientific community; and the fourth is critical to understanding the financial infrastructure of the discipline. Organized developmental psychology did not spring forth from either philosophy or science; it emerged out of a matrix of scientific, social, and humanitarian ideals.

The institutional history of developmental psychology is typically divided into three periods of active and cooperative empirical inquiry. Each period is distinct for its notion of what a science of childhood should look like and what it can and cannot do for children and society. As leader of the child study movement (1883–1910), G. Stanley Hall and his colleagues built up a reasonably coherent theory of development grounded in evolutionary theory and a program of questionnaire studies. Hall's vision was a prophetic one in which he recognized the potential role of a science of child development in addressing practical and political questions. The child development movement (1917–1935) formally ensconced child development as a scientific specialty, one replete with journals, meetings, and public and private sponsorship. This was an era when the social sciences were hardening and becoming more quantitative, leading to a largely apolitical and atheoretical science of child development. The center of the field retreated from social relevance and concentrated on the normative construction of the child by means of testing and measuring indices of growth and development. A generation later, in the 1960s, the rapid social and scientific changes of that period drew developmental psychologists into designing programs and policies for children; among these programs was the paradigmatic Head Start. Today, there is a substantial presence of developmental psychologists situated both in universities and at all levels of government working at the intersections of science, practice, and policy.

THE CHILD STUDY MOVEMENT

Dorothy Ross aptly subtitled her biography of G. Stanley Hall *The Psychologist as Prophet*. Hall was prophetic in his vision of what the systematic study of children might look like and what it might offer to society. Early in his career Hall realized that he would be unable to make a living, because "neither philosophy nor psychology would ever make bread." Aware of the groundswell of interest in children, Hall turned his vast energies away from administration and began developing a major research program in child study, centered at Clark University. Hall rapidly became one of the most important figures in organizing and promoting American psychology and established a "first cooperative program in developmental psychology." His research program relied not so much on the physiology and experimental methods of the "new psychology" he learned in Germany but rather on the questionnaire method used by German pedagogues.[2]

Drawing largely from evolutionary theory and the data collected from questionnaires, Hall wrote tirelessly and prescriptively. He moved easily from description to prescription and warned, for example, of the dangers of premature exercise of the fine-motor muscles. He also cautioned against rote exercises for young children and the physical confinement of grade-school children, and he drew attention to the dangers of precocity and masturbation. The potential for improving the prospects of humanity, Hall argued, lay in modernizing education and child rearing so as to conform to the principles of human development. Hall was especially popular with mothers and teachers, who became zealots not only for child study but also for a host of other progressive reforms related to children. At their very first meeting in 1897, the National Congress of Mothers, a powerful network of mothers' clubs, embraced Hall as their spokesperson.[3]

Between 1894 and 1903, Hall and his associates distributed 115 questionnaires on various aspects of child life and mentality to thousands of mothers, teachers, and others associated with children. In 1891, Hall began publishing the journal *Pedagogical Seminary* as an outlet for child study. In its first issue, he appealed to a wide audience that included "prominent laymen," school administrators, professors of pedagogy, and teachers in normal schools. Hall and his colleagues published some two hundred research reports based on the results of questionnaire studies called "topical syllabi." Studies focused on sundry topics related to children and their worlds at home, kindergarten, church, and school and among peers. Studies of young children's instincts, attitudes, beliefs, and ability to control emotions; investigations of the development of the higher faculties of reason and morality; and research in teacher training and the kindergarten filled the many pages of *Pedagogical Seminary*. Hall began to build a new and public picture of what we might expect from a "typical" child. Shared knowledge about the characteristics of "ordinary" children was sparse and child study helped to give people a sense of what an "average" child is like and what society's commitments toward children should be. All told, the wide range of topics reflected an eclectic composite of philosophical, scientific, professional, and popular interest in childhood. Child study was exploding and gaining visibility and influence.[4]

By 1900, Hall's vision began to fade. With increasing force many educators, psychologists, and social welfare advocates found fault in his questionnaire work. Philosophically strong psychologists such as James Mark Baldwin and John Dewey longed for a better integration of theory and data. Hugo Münsterberg, a professor and the director of Harvard's Psychological Laboratory, openly claimed that child study was not psychology. In 1898, he declared that "we cannot indeed doubt any longer that most of so-called child psychology is partly history, partly economics and ethics, partly physiology, partly nothing at all, but decidedly not psychology." Münsterberg spoke for many (mostly young) proponents of the new laboratory-based experimental psychology. Psychologists were eager (perhaps overeager) to separate themselves from their philosophical parents and establish their status and autonomy as experimental scientists. The child study work was scattered, heterogeneous, often speculative, and sentimental. In his *Talks to Teachers*, William James criticized Hall for enlarging the already too-large burden placed upon teachers. Nonetheless, teachers and other child workers gravitated toward Hall in their efforts to modernize practices with children. While Hall "lost" in academic psychology he very much "won" in the classroom and on "the streets." The research was methodologically weak, to be sure, but the public and professional momentum for child study reached beyond the scientific possibilities of the day.[5]

In 1904, Hall published his most infamous work—a two-volume treatise titled *Adolescence: Its Psychology and Its Relation to Physiology, Anthropology, Sex, Crime, Religion, and Education*. More than twenty-five thousand copies were initially sold, and while *Adolescence* was poorly received by academic psychologists, it was quite popular outside the academy. The crusade for children was advancing on many fronts and pursuing many strategies, including legislative lobbying, political campaigning, casework, and the strategic use of social statistics in directing attention and resources to children. Increasing numbers of child professionals and bureaucrats began to draw upon Hall and child study for guidance.

EARLY ATTEMPTS TO ALIGN SCIENCE, PRACTICE, AND POLICY

In early 1909 Hall circulated a proposal to organize a permanent conference on child research and welfare to begin meeting that summer at Clark University. Having received favorable responses, he forged ahead and held conferences in July 1909 and in 1910. For a few days, psychologists, social workers, child welfare advocates, teachers, and others associated with the well-being of children gathered at Clark to explore the interface between research in child development and research in child welfare. Conference papers were a composite of reports on research, practices with children, and questions about society's ethical commitments to children.

Hall's "prime motive" for the conferences was to unify what he recognized as the scattered efforts of child welfare and child study. Recognizing the growing number of child professionals and helping agencies, Hall was struck by how little coordination existed between them and scientific child study. He wrote, "[T]here was often duplication and waste" and "each society goes its own way" without reference to other similar societies. The time had come, Hall claimed, to consider a "society of societies that might pool knowledge, organize endeavor, and thus increase efficiency." The leader of the child study movement's second motive for the conferences was to "establish relations between scientific study and practical work for children." Hall was anxious to bring child study to the attention of those who worked with children and observed that the burgeoning science had produced too many technical works that were inaccessible to practitioners. He deeply believed that child practitioners should make use of the growing scientific literature on the child, a literature represented by a proliferation of journals, in order to make their work more effective and rational. Hall also hoped that a "society of societies" around children would coordinate the work of child scientists, practitioners, and social reformers. His efforts were short lived. By 1912, when the Children's Bureau was established, there existed a "female dominion" in American reform. Bureau leaders such as Julia Lathrop paid little if any heed to Hall, despite his desire to funnel child research in their direction.[6]

A third conference, independent of both Clark University and the child study movement, was held in 1914 under the auspices of the National Congress of Mothers. Hall had hoped that the work of the conferences would continue and become embodied in a "Children's Institute" at Clark University. He attributed the demise of his effort to the fact that child researchers and child welfare workers had little interest in each other. Hall had already alienated scientists and advocates alike. Scientists continued to assault Hall's methods and extravagant claims; furthermore, many child welfare leaders did not trust Hall's science, sincerity, or conservative politics. Hall's own private attitudes toward child welfare were ambivalent at best and vacillated between concern and contempt. Critical of social reform, he wrote a stinging critique of the well-known photojournalist Jacob Riis. For Hall, the subjects of Riis's studies, "the vagrant, itinerant vagabond, gadabout, hobos, and tramps," were "arrested degenerate[s] or perverted being[s] who abhor[red] work." Writing for *Cosmopolitan* in 1910, Hall remarked that "the children of the poor . . . thrive well under a certain degree of neglect." With such attitudes, Hall was blindsided in his hopes for support from progressive child welfare reformers. In spite of his own scientific and personal limitations, his vision for a socially relevant science of child development was prophetic. He recognized the strategic role that a science of child development could play in the design of practices and policies for children. However, by the mid-1920s, the strictures on method that psychology subsequently put in place would severely limit the chances of his vision ever coming to fruition.[7]

PHILANTHROPY, RESEARCH IN CHILD DEVELOPMENT, AND THE NATIONAL AGENDA

Aided by Carl Seashore, an early student of Hall's and a flourishing researcher at the State University at Iowa, Cora Bussey Hillis, a member of the fledgling Iowa Child Study Society and a friend of Iowa's governor, persuaded the Iowa state legislature in 1917 to establish the Iowa Child Welfare Research Station. Subsequent support, orchestrated by Lawrence K. Frank, an economist at the Laura Spelman Rockefeller Memorial Fund (LSRM), brought to life a network of institutes for research in child development, child welfare, and parent education. Institutes were begun or enlarged at Columbia University in 1924; at the universities of Iowa, Toronto, and Minnesota in 1925; at Yale in 1926; and at Berkeley in 1927. The cooperative output of this network would come to be known as the child development movement.[8]

This child development movement was not only larger and better supported than Hall's child study movement, but also oriented toward basic research on child development in a way that was fundamentally different, with altogether new methods and goals. Whereas Hall's program suffered from little or no academic or governmental structure, by the mid-1920s the child development movement enjoyed ample amounts of both. Additionally, while Hall's theoretical reach often stretched further than his data, the child development movement was more data oriented; less theoretical; and, like many of the emerging social sciences, driven by the pursuit of a value-neutral, positivistic conception of science. The social scientific disciplines and practices were only beginning to form professional and disciplinary societies in Hall's time; thirty years later they were firmly in place with journals, associations, and university departments. Basic research in child development was reconstituted as a strictly scientific endeavor modeled on the biological and medical sciences and isolated from the broader social sciences. Eschewing questions related to practice and policy, developmental scientists removed themselves from their roots in the social and practical needs of children. Tensions existed between the more powerful psychologists who sought to create a true "natural" science of childhood and weaker groups who sought to create a more inclusive "social" and applied science of development.[9]

In this interwar period, researchers in child development established themselves in an academic niche that was allied with but distinctly separate from the disciplinary structure of the modern university. Two distinct but entangled sources of support facilitated the project: first, a major philanthropic foundation supported child study and parent education; and second, the federal government recognized the importance of child development research to the nation's welfare. Serious conflicts emerged between the interests of philanthropy and the demands of academic researchers.

Wearied by the traditional philanthropic interest in charity and alms, Beardlsey Ruml, director of the LSRM, urged a fundamental change in LSRM priorities. Ruml desired to see the LSRM shift away from practical social amelioration toward basic, but practically useful, social science research. Like other progressive thinkers, Ruml hoped that the social sciences would yield more enlightened "measures of social control" that would reduce such "irrationalities" as "poverty, class conflict, and war between nations."[10]

ORGANIZING A NEW SCIENCE OF CHILD DEVELOPMENT

The National Research Council (NRC) was founded in 1916 in order to make more effective its parent organization, the National Academy of Sciences (NAS), in responding to the nation's research and defense needs. The NAS Division of Psychology and Anthropology was organized in October 1919. In April 1920, in the middle of President Woodrow Wilson's Children's Year, the division recognized the need for the "scientific investigation of basic facts and principles in the field of child welfare" and established a Committee on Child Welfare to advise the government on matters concerning children. By choice or by design, the committee did little. Division leaders questioned whether the orientation toward "welfare" was appropriate for a scientific committee, and in 1925 the Committee on Child Welfare was renamed the Committee on Child Development (CCD).[11]

In 1924 Lawrence Frank made clear the committee's turn away from welfare toward science in a letter he wrote to Robert S. Woodworth, a distinguished experimental psychologist from Columbia. Frank worried that Grace Abbott, then director of the Children's Bureau and a pioneer in sociological studies of children, was "more interested in social work and the remedial child welfare activities than she is in research." The NRC had stipulated that, while there was widespread demand for information about child welfare, the demand should be met by the Children's Bureau and not by the CCD. An unfortunate mutual antipathy grew between the bureau and child development researchers. Lois Meek, who combined research and reform in her work on nursery schools, described Frank's efforts to influence Abbott. Meek remembered Abbott as "an autocratic, brilliant woman who knew just what to do and what the Children's Bureau should do. And that was that. . . . There had been efforts to get the Children's Bureau into the child development movement with no success." The bureau's work in social statistics and applied sociology, work rooted in the settlement house tradition of Lillian Wald and Jane Addams, was not of central interest to those seeking to establish a basic science of child development. G. M. Stratton noted in 1925 that the NRC gave "cordial recognition" to the broader social sciences and "appreciates their value, but it does not feel that its own best effort can be directed in their field."[12]

Consistent with the mandate of the NRC, the new CCD would steer clear of child welfare. Throughout its life great care was taken to confine its function to research and to ensure that its status "was not tainted by association with child welfare or parent education activities." John Anderson, director of the Institute at the University of Minnesota, wrote to Woodworth that child welfare would be appropriate for a new series of abstracts in child development "were it not for the unfortunate connotation of the word welfare" with "uplift." Woodworth warned Anderson that the NAS would only accept a "hard-headed" experimental child development program, rather than child welfare in its traditional sense.[13]

RESEARCH GOALS OF THE COMMITTEE
ON CHILD DEVELOPMENT

Between 1925, when the CCD was founded, and 1933, when the Society for Research in Child Development (SRCD) was created, the new CCD held four meetings to assess the possibilities of and shape the realities for a new kind of child development science. The leaders of these meetings were scientific men. As such, they deeply identified with the sort of scientific objectivity that was untainted by "values" or "sentiment." At the heart of the program was a devotion to an experimental science modeled after the biological and medical sciences.

Prior to the first meeting, Woodworth surveyed members of several scientific societies, including university-based psychologists, physiologists, chemists, anatomists, zoologists, and pediatricians, in order to assess the extent of existing research on child development. Survey results indicated that a variety of research on child development existed in several fields. Woodworth self-consciously directed his surveys toward the natural sciences and later admitted that "some lines of work such as psychology were more completely circularized than others such as home economics." Woodworth's exclusions from the survey were undoubtedly intentional and consistent with the goals of the CCD and the NAS.[14]

Convinced that current scientific knowledge was an inadequate guide to the thriving child welfare movement, the committee took a position of pristine purity and maintained that science must precede reform. In his opening address to the 1925 conference, Woodworth, couching his language in aggressively masculine and militaristic imagery, reiterated that the mission of the NRC was to uphold the ideal of research. "Adopting a military phrase, we may say that it aims to mobilize the scientific workers of the country for an attack upon fundamental problems." Meanwhile, Bird Baldwin reported on the progress of experimental research at his Iowa Station. Researchers at Iowa were not only interested in gathering data on children's psychological and physical development, but also wanted "to learn how far children from 2 to 6 years old could serve as subjects for psychological examination and experimentation, how far their behavior could be observed and objectively checked, and what particular types of motivation could be relied upon." These were not trivial issues. In order to establish a viable science, questions concerning children's capacities to sustain attention, motivation, and their capacity to cooperate as subjects needed to be settled.[15]

Amid the roar for experimental science, less powerful proponents for a broader-based developmental science argued their case. Edward Bott from the University of Toronto commented that while some problems "can be worked out on campus," there were many, and "perhaps the most interesting and important . . . can only be studied in the actual situations in the community in which the children are living." Bott argued for the scientific validity of clinical case studies. Others sought to explore the possibilities of using habit and child guidance clinics as research sites, thus broadening the "geography" of developmental psychology beyond the laboratory. Such advocates also proposed that a "closer coordination of field and laboratory methods should be made in the study of the child."[16]

While the CCD maintained its commitment to science, the LSRM generously supported its undertakings and in 1926 pledged an annual appropriation of ten thousand dollars for four years. Consistent with Ruml's insistence on practical, useful research, Frank initiated an ambitious program of parent education in conjunction with the research initiative and persuaded CCD members to serve as an advisory body to the LSRM in administering awards for graduate work in child study and parent education. These fellowships were initially designed for and almost exclusively awarded to women, and (perhaps inevitably) this bias led to quarrels between the CCD and the LSRM. Once the orientation of the fellowships toward practice and "women's work" was made clear, the CCD withdrew its help in administering the fellowships. The practical goals of the LSRM did not sit easily with the CCD.[17]

The CCD brought with its existence a modicum of organization, communication, and some feeling of community and shared ideals among researchers. With information about people and research, the first volumes of *Child Development Abstracts and Bibliography* and a *Directory of Research* were published in 1927. The second, 1927 conference focused on appropriate methods with which to study children. Anderson again made the case for experimental methods. In spite of deep historical precedents he paid questionnaire studies little heed. Together, the observational biography and the questionnaire "can be dismissed without a word. . . . [They] do not solve problems, but put problems." In his drive to dismiss the case history Anderson cited numerous difficulties, including sampling errors, observational bias, and the errors of retrospective reasoning. He called for other methods "essentially scientific in nature" such as testing, measuring with "instruments of precision," and controlled experimentation. He argued for paring down the complex and admittedly "more appealing" (and more complicated) questions of child development to those that could be addressed using experimental procedures to quantify aspects of child growth and development.[18]

Meanwhile, William Blatz, from the University of Toronto, argued that longitudinal studies "have all the advantages that statistical treatment of cross-sections lack." Herman Adler, from the Illinois Institute for Juvenile Research, urged the committee to study the child in all of his or her humanity. The "mental scientist," argued Adler, "can no longer confine himself" to the laboratory or even to the clinic, but must be equipped to deal also with the "social problems of the individual." Cooperation, he insisted, must ensue between the different child sciences and professions. Leslie Marston, executive secretary for the CCD, urged caution in prematurely applying research to humanitarian ends, while at the same time agreeing that "research should discover the child in the home as well as in the clinic, the laboratory, or the nursery school."[19]

Knight Dunlap, from Johns Hopkins, opened the third CCD conference in 1929. While celebrating the march of science, Dunlap warned against the dangers of "propaganda" and "exploitation" in the field. Bemoaning the persistence of such "propaganda," Dunlap added that "hordes of normal school and university students are being solemnly stuffed with dope about the child." In a 1931 progress report to the LSRM, the CCD reiterated that "we confine ourselves to the promotion of constructive investigation" and leave to "organizations better fitted for the promotion of human betterment in general, the more technical and practical application of these principles to the community."[20]

The fourth and final conference in 1933 concluded with the formal founding of the Society for Research in Child Development (SRCD). While the conference was held jointly with a meeting of the Social Science Research Council (SSRC) and its Committee on Personality and Culture, the committee's emphasis on the social and cultural factors in child development failed to move the more powerful proponents of research in child development. Frank, ever the mediator and the consensus builder, wisely and presciently suggested that if child scientists take seriously the contributions of anthropologists to child science "a theory will have to be developed that will take cognizance of the cultural patternings that have been imposed upon the child by the family." In retrospect, the apprehensions held by Frank and others who questioned the compass of the emerging science were more than justified.[21]

THE REALITY: *CHILD DEVELOPMENT*, 1930–1934

While the CCD conference reports represent a set of visionary statements, the reality of a science of child development began to unfold in the pages of *Child Development*. This flagship journal of the SRCD began abruptly in 1930, without even a greeting or a statement of editorial intent. Buford Johnson, professor of psychology at Johns Hopkins, served as editor. He was assisted by the psychologist John Anderson and a group of academics that included a professor of pediatrics, a professor of biochemistry, the director of research at the Washington Child Research Center, and a professor of anatomy. In keeping with the CCD conferences, the editorial staff drew heavily on biology and medicine. At the same time, research in child development continued to receive generous support through both private and public funds. In 1928 child development research received more than $450,000 of the total amount of gifts for psychological research, leaving a mere $50,000 for all other fields of psychological research. The aid was substantial enough to help launch the first *Handbook of Child Psychology* in 1931, beginning a series that continues today.[22]

With the journal *Child Development* and a network of university-based institutes, those involved in the child development sciences belonged to a scientific movement housed and funded in a way that was quite different from that of the antecedent child study movement. Curiously, despite the rhetoric on methods, one looks in vain for a theoretical program or an explicit scientific agenda that would organize the bustling empiricism of this young science. There appears a considerable amount of careful and substantial work of lasting value but nothing like the kind of theory-driven empiricism that drives real scientific progress.[23]

A survey of 174 articles published between 1930 and 1934 in *Child Development* identified several overarching themes. Central to the journal's mission at that time were attempts to find quantitative indicators or scales of various aspects of a child's health and mentality and to identify natural sequences of child development. The spirit of tests and measurements was alive and well as the institutes at Iowa and Minnesota squared off on the heritability of intelligence. Individual and group differences were explored on such specialized topics as distractibility, ocular-motor differences between black and white babies, and preschoolers with high- and low-muscle tension. The nursery schools that were present at the institutes served as "laboratories" for observation and testing and facilitated studies of preschool practices and consequences. Papers appeared on food preferences, the incidence of colds and illnesses in nursery school, and personality changes as a function of preschool experience. Studies of normative sequences of physical growth and psychomotor development included reports on skeletal maturation, age-related changes in weight and height, age changes in sleep patterns, and the development of motor control. Studies of the "natural" development of stages and sequences included reports on perceptual, linguistic, cognitive, and emotional development, and there were stirrings of what would become the great longitudinal studies. Importantly, though there was a fair amount of applied work published in *Child Development*, mostly by women, other professional journals carried the load for applied child science.[24]

Still, one looks in vain for theory. By 1930 the methodological and ideological positivism that had already conquered other areas of psychology claimed child development. In 1934, Frank reviewed the work at the institutes and concluded that they suffered from isolation and narrowness. In his view, the requirements for the doctorate "perpetuate[d] the short, discrete study" that only rarely contributes to theory-building. In 1935 Frank wrote an editorial, "The Problem of Development," in which he gave a long and complicated definition of what we should look for in a theory of child development. Ultimately, Frank saw the study of child development not only as a scientific endeavor but also as an extension of preventive medicine and "as an outline for larger social welfare." He hoped that child development would do for politics what preventive medicine had done for disease and characterized parent education as a form of "preventive politics." We would be wise to wonder just what Frank meant by this ambiguous and highly charged term.[25]

Ironically, there was a plethora of developmental theory for researchers to draw upon. By 1930, all the great theorists who have had a lasting influence on developmental psychology had made their major statements, though none had done so by using strictly experimental methods. Sigmund Freud was a force in some universities and, through William Healy, in child guidance. In 1940, the English translation of Heinz Werner's *Comparative Psychology of Mental Development* was published. The great Russian psychologist Lev Vygotsky died in 1934, closing off a short but brilliant career. Between 1923 and 1932, Jean Piaget published his first and "famous five" books on cognitive development. Frank knew about Piaget and supported his work. Even so, American child psychologists did not welcome Piaget's theories until the 1960s. In a survey of reviews, replications, and critical commentary on Piaget in twenty-two psychological journals—including *Child Development*—between 1921 and 1941, Piaget's work is conspicuously absent. Although research psychologists judged Piaget's quasi-clinical methods for probing the contents of children's minds to be insufficiently rigorous, outside of psychology, both early childhood educators and psychoanalysts more fully embraced the influential researcher on children's cognitive development.[26]

The CCD conference proceedings, coupled with the early volumes of *Child Development*, represent efforts to establish a science of child development modeled on the biological and medical sciences and consistent with the goals of the NAS. The commitment to maintaining a positivistic science of child development, compounded by a pronounced reluctance to engage in broader humanitarian efforts for children, resulted in a narrow and unsentimental science limited in both theoretical and practical import. It would take another generation, a call to service, and a broadening of the meaning of *science* in child development research to return to something like Hall's prophetic developmental psychology.

THE REAWAKENING: DEVELOPMENTAL PSYCHOLOGY AND PROGRAMS FOR THE GREAT SOCIETY
SCIENTIFIC CHANGES

In the early 1950s reviewers for the *Annual Review of Psychology* reported that research in child development was thin, at best. One reviewer declared the field near death. "Child psychology," he wrote, "lacks vigor" and, by nearly every index available, "shows little life."[27]

Within a decade, child psychology came back to life. Beginning in the late 1950s and continuing into the 1970s, a revived discipline, now centered in departments of psychology and at first focused on children's cognitive development, sprang forth. The behaviorism that had long held the scientific high ground of psychology gave way to a reconsideration of cognitive processes in a broad movement in psychology known as the "cognitive revolution."

In June 1959, the SSRC formed a Committee on Intellective Processes and held a stream of conferences that brought forth influential monographs on how young children thought. American developmental psychologists rediscovered Piaget and people began to assume that "everything is bent toward Geneva." In 1962, one conference participant noted that something like a "Piaget revival" was occurring and added that "it is surely the workings of the Zeitgeist with a vengeance!" The 1962 conference brought together mathematicians and psychologists for dialogues on mathematical learning. In those anxious years following the launch of Sputnik, worry mingled with hope that a new cognitive developmental psychology would help in the design of innovative curricula in science and mathematics.

The conference reports were landmarks in their day. They breathed life back into developmental psychology, turned the field in new directions, and helped break the stranglehold that behaviorism had held over much of research psychology. More broadly, a constellation of scientific, social, and political change would soon crystallize around children and economic opportunity.[28]

SOCIAL CHANGES IN THE 1960S AND THE ROLE OF DEVELOPMENTAL PSYCHOLOGY

In a message to Congress in 1963, President John F. Kennedy called for new standards of excellence in education and equal educational opportunities. Once again major foundations, such as the Carnegie Corporation, the Sloan Foundation, and the Ford Foundation, lent their support. Like the progressive social scientists *cum* reformers of the late 19th century, social scientists such as Michael Harrington and Oscar Lewis wrote influential books documenting in detail the extent of poverty in America. As our foreign policy tilted increasingly toward a cold war against communism, a domestic war against poverty was launched, the battle for civil rights pushed forward, and the nation turned its attention toward children in new ways.[29]

The Economic Opportunity Act proposed by President Lyndon Johnson gained congressional approval in 1964 and opened the war against poverty on several fronts. Community Action Programs enabled communities to plan and administer their own assistance programs. Later that year a panel of pediatricians, child development researchers, educators, and psychologists recommended to the Office of Economic Opportunity (OEO) that preschool programs be implemented so that poor children would be able to develop to their full potential. Many believed that compensatory programs for poor young children who were presumably deprived of the kinds of the learning opportunities experienced by their more affluent peers would help break the cycle of poverty. In 1965 the OEO created Project Head Start— a program of comprehensive services for children of poor parents that included health-care and family services as well as preschool education. Under the mandate for maximum feasible participation, parents were empowered to manage and staff Head Start classrooms. Despite various critiques and political challenges Head Start remains an integral part of child and family services today.

Throughout the 1960s and continuing into the 1970s, institutions for the preschool-aged child changed dramatically. In order to address issues around design and evaluation, developmental psychologists steeped in the traditions of experimental research were forced to rethink their science and their place in society. With little preparation or policy experience, university-based developmental psychologists were called to Washington, DC, and given large tasks to do in little time. Urie Bronfennbrenner, from Cornell, spoke for many when he commented, "I had not thought of myself as one who either had or should be engaged in delineating directions for science, let alone policy affecting the nation's children."[30]

Fundamental knowledge in the design of programs for young children was wanting. Jule Sugarman, executive secretary of the Head Start Planning Committee, found significant gaps in the knowledge of the "expert." Sugarman lamented, "No one could tell us, based on real evidence, what the proper child-staff ratios or length of the program should be." The demands on developmental psychologists consulting in the design of these programs required a new kind of child development research.[31]

NEW ALIGNMENTS BETWEEN CHILD DEVELOPMENT RESEARCH AND SOCIAL POLICY

By the mid-1970s a series of innovative institutions were created to better realign child development research and social policies. In 1977, SRCD established a standing Committee on Child Development and Social Policy and in the following year, a continuing program of Congressional Fellowships in

Child Development. Responding to proposals from leading developmental psychologists, in 1977 the Minnesota-based Bush Foundation established four centers at prominent universities to train developmental psychologists to work at the intersection of developmental science and policy. While the journal *Child Development* remains the voice of SRCD and the gold standard for scientific rigor, it too has changed. Policy-related research, as well as research reports based upon children in their socially designed environments, has increasingly peppered the journal in recent years.

There seemed to be a reciprocal influence, not seen since perhaps Hall's awkward efforts, between research in child development and the design of social programs. Within a rejuvenated field, some developmental psychologists began to move away from regarding the laboratory as the only or even the best environment in which to study children. Research based on data collected in nonlaboratory environments was demanded by the new alliance with policymakers. On the heels of Piaget's massive influence on research in children's cognitive development, the field moved toward questions of social development, and some have embraced a broader cultural view of child development. Like Piaget's work in the 1960s, Vygotsky's sociocultural psychology was rediscovered in the 1970s.

In concert with the research needs for these new programs and policies, a fresh sensitivity to the social and cultural contexts of child development worked its way into research questions and designs. For many, the effects of family, school, community, class, race, and culture were no longer ignored or discounted as merely "noise in the data" (i.e., annoying sources of variance in experimental studies), but rather as important agents themselves in a child's development. Prominent psychologists such as Donald Campbell and Bronfennbrenner echoed John Dewey's arguments from six decades prior and urged their colleagues to consider interventions as experiments in the possibilities of human development. Legislatively mandated evaluations of public programs pushed people to define their ideals for programs and to design appropriate instruments for assessing progress toward those ideals.

Not all developmental psychologists are comfortable doing research related to questions of social design and social policy. Furthermore, such research is not always well regarded by universities and tenure committees, and it is important to note that many remain content doing basic research in the laboratory and maintaining an arm's-length distance from questions of practice or policy. There will always be tension between the demands of academic science and the needs of children, and child development scientists will always need to stand guard against fads that exaggerate and distort the practical and political possibilities of such science.

DEVELOPMENTAL PSYCHOLOGISTS TODAY:
THE ROLE OF VALUES IN DEVELOPMENTAL SCIENCE

In this chapter I have reviewed the shifting relationships between science, practice, and policy in the child developmental psychology that has evolved over the past century. Hall's child study movement was brought to life by social relevance at the beginning of the twentieth century. In the interwar period, practitioners continued to apply psychology to children's affairs while a narrowly conceived science of child development, shaped by the academic elite, assumed form and power. By midcentury, basic research in child development was thin, void of theory or relevance. Social, scientific, and political changes contributed to the rebirth of the field in the heady 1960s and generated a renewed sense of social relevance.

Developmental psychology began by offering secular and scientifically grounded ideas about child nature. Inevitably, such questions lead to value-laden issues related to the best interests of the child—what constitutes good care and education, good parenting, good TV, humane child welfare, and good development itself. The field addresses both basic questions about children's nature and capacities and the dilemmas that ordinary people face in their dealings with children. Sheldon H. White argued that "the idea of development arrived at in a systematic analysis becomes the idea of the Good in practical affairs" and "is very likely to be treated as an ethical ideal."[32]

When challenged to provide answers to such vexing questions as the effects of child care on the attachment between a child and his or her caregiver, the developmental psychologist cannot hide behind a veil of objectivity. The "answer" depends upon how we construe such value-laden issues as "good" child-caregiver relationships and the social place of mothers. Developmental psychology can be a reconstructive force in society (no less an eminence than Dewey said so explicitly). In being such a force, developmental psychologists can lend technical assistance in the design of environments and so help in the realization of values.[33]

NOTES

1. William Kessen, "The American Child and Other Cultural Inventions," *American Psychologist* 34, no. 10 (1979): 818.

2. Dorothy Ross, *G. Stanley Hall: The Psychologist as Prophet* (Chicago: University of Chicago Press, 1972); Alexander Siegel and Sheldon H. White, "The Child Study Movement: Early Growth and Development of the Symbolized Child," *Advances in Child Development and Behavior* 17 (New York: Academic Press, 1982): 233–238; Sheldon H. White, "Child Study at Clark University: 1884–1904," *Journal of the History of the Behavioral Sciences* 26 (1990): 131–50.

3. G. Stanley Hall, *Educational Problems*, vols. 1–2 (New York: Appleton, 1911).

4. Siegel and White, "Child Study Movement."

5. James Hendricks, "The Child-Study Movement in American Education, 1880–1910: A Quest for Educational Reform Through a Scientific Study of the Child" (PhD diss, Indiana University, 1968); Hugo Münsterberg, "Psychology and Education," *Educational Review* 16 (1898): 112.

6. Conference for Research and Welfare, *Proceedings of the Conference for Research and Welfare (1909–1910)*, 2 vols. (New York: G. E. Stechert, 1910), 1: 9–10; G. Stanley Hall, *Life and Confessions of a Psychologist* (New York: Appleton, 1923), 215; Robyn Muncy, *Creating a Female Dominion in American Reform, 1890–1935* (New York: Oxford University Press, 1991).

7. Hall, *Life*, 401; Hall, quoted in Jane Mulligan, "The Madonna and Child in American Culture, 1830–1916" (PhD diss., University of California–Los Angeles, 1975), 611; G. Stanley Hall, "What Is to Become of Your Baby?" *Cosmopolitan* 47 (April 1910), in Ross, *G. Stanley Hall*, 362.

8. Robert Cairns, "The Emergence of Development Psychology," in *Handbook of Child Philosophy*, ed. Paul Mussen, 4th ed. (New York: Wiley, 1983), 41–102.

9. Sheldon H. White, "Child Development, 1930–1934: Organizing a Research Program," Society for Research in Child Development (SRCD), Indianapolis, 1995; Robert Bannister, *Sociology and Scientism: The American Quest for Objectivity, 1880–1940* (Chapel Hill: University of North Carolina Press, 1987); Dorothy Ross, *Origins of American Social Science* (New York: Cambridge University Press, 1991).

10. Martin Bulmer and Joan Bulmer, "Philanthropy and Social Science in the 1920s: Beardsley Ruml and the Laura Spelman Rockefeller Memorial, 1922–1929," *Minerva* 19 (1981): 347–407, 363; Beardsley Ruml, *Laura Spelman Rockefeller Memorial Final Report* (New York: Rockefeller Foundation, 1933), 10.

11. "Quadrennial Report of the Committee on Child Development," 1925, SRCD Archives, box 30, MS C387, National Library of Medicine (NLM), Washington, DC.

12. "Quadrennial Report of the Committee on Child Development;" Lawrence K. Frank to Robert S. Woodworth, 20 December 1924, SRCD Archives, box 30, MS C387, NLM; "Lois Meek Stoltz: An American Child Development Pioneer," interview by Ruby Takanishi, Palo Alto, CA, 1978, Schlesinger Library, Radcliffe College, Cambridge, MA, 18; Committee on Child Development (CCD), *Conference on Research in Child Development*, Washington, DC: National Research Council (NRC), 1925, SRCD Archives, NLM, 10.

13. Alice Smuts, "The National Research Council Committee on Child Development and the Founding of the Society for Research in Child Development," in *History and Research in Child Development*, ed. Alice Smuts and John Hagen (Chicago: University of Chicago Press, 1985), 112; John Anderson to Robert Woodworth, 19 June 1925, SRCD Archives, box 30, MS C387, NLM; Robert Woodworth to John Anderson, 25 January 1925, SRCD Archives, box 30, MS C387, NLM.

14. Robert Woodworth, "Present Status of Child Research," SRCD archives, MS C387, NLM, n.d.

15. CCD, *Conference on Research in Child Development*, 1925, 3, 11, 13, 14.

16. CCD, *Conference*, 1925, 20, 31; David Livingston, *Putting Science in Its Place: Geographies of Scientific Knowledge* (Chicago: University of Chicago Press, 2003).

17. Steven Schlossman, "Before Home Start: Notes Toward a History of Parent Education in America, 1897–1929," *Harvard Educational Review* 46, no. 3 (1976): 436–67; Emily D. Cahan, "Science, Practice, and Gender Roles in Early American Child Psychology," in *Contemporary Constructions of the Child: Essays in Honor of William Kessen*, ed. Frank Kessel, Mark Bornstein, and Arnold Sameroff (Hillsdale, NJ: L. Erlbaum Associates, 1991), 225–50.

18. CCD, *Conference on Research in Child Development*, 1927, 56, 58.

19. CCD, *Conference*, 1927, 80, 81, 95.

20. CCD, *Conference on Research in Child Development*, part 2, 1929, 9, 228; CCD, "Progress Report," 1931, box 36, Laura Spelman Rockefeller Memorial Archives (LSRM), Rockefeller Archives Center (RAC).

21. CCD, *Conference on Research in Child Development*, 1933, 9

22. NRC, *Conference on Experimental Psychology* (Washington, DC: NRC, 1931).

23. White, "Child Development."

24 White, "Child Development"; Barbara Beatty, "The Rise of the Nursery School: Laboratory for a Science of Child Development," in *Developmental Psychology and Social Change*, ed. David B. Pillemer and Sheldon H. White (New York: Cambridge University Press, 2005), 264–87.

25. Lawrence K. Frank, "Present Situation in Child Research," 26 March 1934, General Education Board Archives, General Education Board Archives, box 369, RAC; Frank, "The Problem of Child Development," *Child Development* 6, no. 1 (1935): 7–18; Milton J. Senn, interview with Lawrence K. Frank, 1972, Milton J. Senn Oral History Collection, NLM, MS c280a, box 1, n.p.; Frank, "Forces Leading to the Child Development Viewpoint and Study," 28 November 1939, Lawrence K. Frank Papers, NLM, MS c280.

26. Emily D. Cahan and Yeh Hseuh, "American Educators and Psychologists Encounter Piaget's Early Works," the Jean Piaget Society, Montreal, 2000.

27. Roger Barker, "Child Psychology," *Annual Review of Psychology*, vol. 2, ed. Calvin P. Stone and Donald W. Taylor (Stanford, CA: Annual Reviews, 1951), 1–22.

28. John Flavell, "Historical and Bibliographical Note," in *Cognitive Development in Children: Five Monographs of the Society for Research in Child Development*, ed. Roger Brown (Chicago: University of Chicago Press, 1962), 13.

29. See Michael Harrington, *The Other America: Poverty in the United States* (New York: Macmillan, 1962); Oscar Lewis, *Children of Sanchez* (New York: Vintage, 1963).

30. Edward Zigler and Jeanette Valentine, *Project Head Start: A Legacy of the War on Poverty* (New York: Free Press, 1979), 78.

31. Zigler and Valentine, *Project Head Start*, 119.

32. Sheldon H. White, "The Idea of Development in Developmental Psychology," in *Developmental Psychology: Historical and Philosophical Perspectives*, ed. Richard Lerner (Hillsdale, NJ: L. Erlbaum Associates, 1983), 55–78, 74.

33. Sheldon H. White, *Developmental Psychology as a Human Enterprise* (Worcester, MA: Clark University Press, 2001).

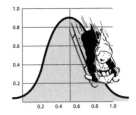

Psychologizing the Third *R*: Hall, Dewey, Thorndike, and Progressive Era Ideas on the Learning and Teaching of Arithmetic

Barbara Beatty

THERE WAS CONSIDERABLE DEBATE around the turn of the nineteenth century about whether and how psychology could be helpful to teachers. William James, the founding father of American psychology, was notoriously skeptical. In 1892 James told a group of teachers that he did not think that "methods of instruction for immediate classroom use" could be derived directly from psychology; an "intermediary inventive mind" was necessary to make the application. James predicted that psychologists stood to gain the most from applying psychology to education and that teachers might be disappointed when psychology could not give them "radical help." James's warning did not stop teachers from looking to psychologists for help, nor did it deter psychologists from offering it. James's student G. Stanley Hall was much more sanguine. In 1885, Hall, who had begun giving lectures to teachers in Boston before James, called pedagogy "applied Psychology," and said that the "application is not hard to make."[1]

As there were many different types of psychology, there were many different applications. G. Stanley Hall, John Dewey, and Edward L. Thorndike, the three best known of the Progressive Era psychologists whose research focused on education, each took a stab at applying his type of psychology to arithmetic. Like other progressives, Hall, Dewey, and Thorndike have been categorized in various ways, often with an eye to how they viewed education and social reform broadly. For my purposes, Hall was a maturationist who believed that knowledge developed organically; Dewey was a constructivist who believed that knowledge developed through social construction; and Thorndike was an associationist who believed that learning took place through the formation of situation-response bonds. Their thinking changed over the course of their long careers, especially Dewey's, so it is important to note that some of the works under discussion here are early ones. [2]

How did Hall, Dewey, and Thorndike explain how children learned arithmetic? What advice did they give teachers about how to teach arithmetic? Were Hall's, Dewey's, and Thorndike's ideas about how arithmetic was learned consonant with their advice about how arithmetic should be taught? How were their ideas translated into teacher education and school texts? And what do these applications of psychology to arithmetic suggest about relationships between the child sciences, teachers, and children?

PSYCHOLOGIZING SCHOOL SUBJECTS

Hall, Dewey, and Thorndike were convinced that psychologizing school subjects would improve education, but they had different ideas about what this psychologizing meant. For Hall, who began doing research in the 1880s on young children's knowledge before they entered school, it meant that teachers should understand how children's knowledge developed naturally. For Dewey, who stated explicitly in his 1902 classic *The Child and the Curriculum* that school subject matter needed to be "psychologized," it meant that teachers should connect subject matter with the child's experience. For Thorndike, as he argued in his 1906 *The Principles of Teaching*, using the results of psychological research experiments would make teaching more effective and efficient. [3]

Of course Hall, Dewey, and Thorndike did not psychologize arithmetic in a vacuum. With the growth of science, industrialization, and market economies in nineteenth-century America, arithmetic, which had initially been taught primarily as bookkeeping, became a full-fledged school subject. Hall, Dewey, and Thorndike might have learned arithmetic themselves from any number of older texts. The first American arithmetic text to use the new national currency, Nicholas Pike's 1788 *A New and Complete System for Teaching Arithmetic*, subtitled *Composed for the Use of the Citizens of the United States*, was still in use well into the nineteenth century. As did other early texts, Pike taught arithmetic through definitions and memorization of rules, followed by laborious calculations, and included extensive tables of annuities, simple and compound interest, and other types of business arithmetic.[4]

In 1821, three decades after the introduction of Pike's text, Warren Colburn's *First Lessons in Arithmetic* revolutionized the teaching of arithmetic in the United States. Building on the methods of the Swiss educator Johann Heinrich Pestalozzi, Colburn had children solve problems using physical objects. He also instructed students to do "mental arithmetic" before they memorized rules or worked out problems on paper. As Barbara Finkelstein describes in her book *Governing the Young*, this was the beginning of the "math wars" between older and successively newer methods of teaching arithmetic.[5]

While Hall, Dewey, and Thorndike clearly thought that psychology could help teachers and children, professional reasons also propelled the psychologizing of school subjects. With psychology course enrollments booming in the late 1890s and early 1900s, psychologists needed jobs. In 1898, Harvard University psychologist Hugo Munsterberg wrote to Columbia University psychologist James McKeen Cattell that Munsterberg had 360 students in his elementary psychology course. What, he asked, would "this country do with all these psychologists?" The answer was that many, if not most, psychologists would find employment in teacher education. In the 1890s, almost three-quarters of the recipients of doctorates in psychology from Clark University, where Hall was president, found work in teacher education colleges, teacher-training programs, or child study departments.[6]

As a historian of education and a teacher educator who has taught courses in educational psychology and has supervised student teachers, I can attest to how deeply psychology has influenced teacher education. One look at a program from an American Educational Research Association or Association for Supervision and Curriculum Development conference shows the extent to which psychological theories and research have become the putative knowledge base for education. It would not be an exaggeration to say that psychology "colonized" education, though not without some resistance.[7]

PSYCHOLOGY AND TEACHING

The relationship between psychology and education was never a simple, one-way street, however. There was always much back-and-forth between teachers' practical needs and academic theorizing, with many intermediaries in between. In fact, many psychologists were teachers before they became academics, as the careers of Hall, Dewey, and Thorndike document. Hall taught for a term in a rural district school in western Massachusetts before going to Williams College in 1863 and then eventually to Harvard, where he received the first American doctorate in psychology, in 1878. After graduating from the University of Vermont in 1880, Dewey taught high school algebra, Latin, and science in Pennsylvania and then in a rural district school in Vermont, before going to graduate school at Johns Hopkins. Thorndike tutored high school Greek, Latin, chemistry, and French while attending Wesleyan College in the early 1890s, and would have become a high school English teacher had he not received a scholarship to Harvard in 1895. Hall, Dewey, and Thorndike all had jobs in teacher education for a while; Thorndike was at Teachers College, Columbia University, for most of his career. All three produced some of their best scholarly work during or soon after periods of direct observation or involvement in classrooms.[8]

As William James foresaw, psychologists profited in many ways from the psychologizing of school subjects. With the expansion of psychology into teacher education, growth of public school enrollments, and demand for new texts for schools and teachers, psychology was "commodified" into a variety of education products. Textbook publishers acted as intermediaries between psychologists and teachers and solicited psychologists to develop texts. Psychologists themselves initiated textbook projects. Some of Hall's books sold well to popular audiences; Dewey surely profited from the sale of his texts; Thorndike was remunerated handsomely by his textbook royalties and helped found the Psychological Corporation, which marketed tests and other applications. As a psychologist's views became well known, larger course enrollments, more graduate students, and more resources for research might ensue, all of which could help strengthen that brand of psychology.[9]

Psychologizing school subjects could have benefits for school administrators and teachers as well. Collaborating with psychologists in the production of school texts could bring monetary and professional rewards. Using psychologized methods might make school systems and schools appear more modern and principals and teachers seem and feel more innovative and up-to-date. And there was the hope that using psychologized methods would make teaching easier and make it easier for children to learn school subjects.

HALL'S "ARITHMOGENESIS"

Origins

Although Hall's book *Educational Problems*, with a chapter titled "The Pedagogy of Elementary Mathematics," did not appear until 1911, Hall began collecting data on arithmetic in Boston kindergartens in the 1880s. He thought that young children learned arithmetic naturally, through a process of "arithmogenesis," in the historical sequence in which arithmetic had evolved from primeval times. He picked up pieces of this organic view while studying in Germany in the 1870s and 1880s. The notion of "culture epochs," the idea that school curricula should repeat the stages of cultural history, came from Tuickson Ziller and Wilhelm Rein; the idea that ontogeny recapitulates phylogeny came from the German physiologist Ernst Haeckel and others. Hall combined these concepts to create what he called "genetic psychology" and began applying it to the study of children and education.[10]

Hall's thinking about arithmetic teaching reveals traces of these German origins, along with older, humanistic views. Although he expressed his ideas in romantic nineteenth-century prose, Hall loved the hard, unchanging objectivity of mathematics. As he wrote in his chapter "The Pedagogy of Elementary Mathematics," the "processes and conclusions" of mathematics were "right or wrong, with no middle term," and were thus less affected by the changing fads of "pedagogical fashion" than were other subjects. For Hall, mathematics was the essence of moral, male, scientific thought. Influenced by his experiences in Prussia and keenly anxious to protect masculinity, Hall stated that mathematics should be taught "authoritatively, magisterially, with a kind of masculine military rigor." Arithmetic was "a moral discipline," Hall said, and noted correctly that for "a long time" it "was not taught at all to girls," who took sewing instead.[11]

Natural Teaching Methods

Despite his attraction to the formal rigor of mathematics, Hall thought that arithmogenesis was a developmental process that occurred naturally in young children, the "direct product of the counting instinct." Like "savages" who lacked formal concepts of number and kept "tab on fingers, by pebbles, by notches," young children developed number consciousness through "tapping, nodding, beating time, rocking," and manipulating common objects. Most children, Hall argued, passed "through a stage of counting with almost no reference to the things counted" and then progressed to visual symbolism in which they personified numerals figuratively. Hall described how some children might imagine that the numeral 4 was "a fat duck," for instance, "7 a tall man," and "5 a pigtail." In this youthful numerology, some numbers were bad or good and had magical powers. The number 7 was "usually bad," and "11 may be happy-go-lucky, 13 is mean," and so on.[12]

Hall was opposed to premature academic pressure and what he saw as artificial teaching methods. He criticized teachers who constantly badgered children about numbers and did not recognize that "the counting stage" was a "paradise" of knowledge that they themselves had lost. In a flight of psychoromanticism, Hall, who had brought Freud to America for a conference at Clark University in 1909, warned of the dangers of pushing young children into formal arithmetic too soon. If "we applied psycho-analysis to the teachers," Hall wrote, "we should doubtless find that the reason they so insist upon this triviality of application is because of a deep unconscious instinct in their own souls that prompts them to atone to childhood for the outrage of snatching the child away from the number series and pushing him out so soon beyond his depth, where he is utterly helpless and only does blindly what he is told." "Premature ciphering methods," Hall said, were harmful and wrong. They left the child to sink or swim, instead of "keeping him near the shore till the dim mystic sense of the infinite sea of number begins to murmur like a seashell echo in his ears and draws him on naturally by its own unique charm." It was time to return to natural teaching methods, to "turn back the bookmakers and look again at the child and let him lead us."[13]

After reviewing German and American theories, including those of Dewey and Thorndike, Hall declared that arithmetic teaching lacked developmentally appropriate methods. He recommended that formal teaching of arithmetic be postponed for "perhaps two years," until second or third grade or the age of eight or nine. "Man did not begin to add and then learn to subtract and then perhaps multiply." These were artificial abstractions and, "like all abstractions," were "ghastly" to children. Real advances in arithmetic teaching would come when teachers understood the parallelism between the history of mathematics as a subject and the development of the child and the human race.[14]

When arithmetic was taught, Hall recommended using concrete materials and graphic, tangible methods. He approved of the German approach, which he said was Socratic and required less homework and drill, and described diagrams and materials found in European schools. Because anthropological research showed, in his view, that primitive peoples were fascinated by geometrical figures, he suggested that different shapes be hung in classrooms, so that children could acquire and test geometrical ideas by themselves. He strongly encouraged teachers to use paper folding, puzzles, crystals, mazes, the abacus, and chess to stimulate children's mathematical abilities. Taught in this natural manner, Hall concluded, arithmetic was the subject in which children, "in a far more rapid and effective way than in other domains of thought," repeated the history of the human race.[15]

Hall did not write a school arithmetic text, which would have been antithetical to his notion of naturalistic learning. His ideas were influential among teachers, however, especially in the kindergarten movement and with other teachers of young children. Arithmogenesis was an extreme example of a maturationist version of developmental psychology in which children were thought to learn naturally through organic development. The notion that pushing children to learn arithmetic before they are ready was ineffective and harmful became one pole in a continuing debate.

DEWEY'S CONSTRUCTION OF NUMBER

Origins

John Dewey collaborated with James McLellan of the Ontario School of Psychology to write *The Psychology of Number*, which came out in 1895. Although McLellan is listed as the primary author, the book provides an interesting glimpse of a young Dewey struggling with the psychology of a specific school subject, a topic notably absent from most of his later work in which he talks about curriculum and education more generally. In McLellan's and Dewey's theorizing, children constructed concepts of number by mentally acting upon numbers and using them in everyday life. Number was "not a bare property of facts," they wrote, but "a certain way of interpreting and arranging them—a certain method of constructing them."[16]

Social Construction of Number and Constructivist Teaching Methods

Like Hall, McLellan and Dewey thought children's concepts of number developed gradually. In opposition to Hall, however, they emphasized that this occurred socially, in response to real-world problems. Measurement was use oriented. It developed in stages, from measuring undefined things such as apples, to measuring definite, comparable units such as yards and acres. If there had been enough free land in the world, McLellan and Dewey argued, the concept of measurement would not have evolved, because it would not have been necessary. "Arithmetic" brought "home to the pupil the realities of the social environment in which he lives" and grew out of practical needs.[17]

For McLellan and Dewey, understanding the concept of number was a rational process involving the measurement of limited quantities. Numbers were based on "definite measurement, the definite valuation of a quantity falling within a given limit." But simply having children measure objects was not enough. Number was "not impressed upon the mind by objects even when they are presented under the most favorable of circumstances." Number was "the product of the way in which the mind deals with objects in the operation of making a vague whole definite," they wrote. Numbers were not merely a "set of symbols"; that was "old fashioned." Older texts taught that arithmetic was something done with rules that produced right answers; McLellan and Dewey argued that it was something more complex, that it was learned through the "activity of the mind in dealing with objects." Number, McLellan and Dewey stated emphatically, was "not (psychologically) got from things, it is put into them." The key was to employ "things in a constructive way."[18]

McLellan and Dewey saw numbers as ratios or part-whole relationships and thought that numerical operations should be taught by inducing "a mental operation of parting and wholing." Unlike Hall, McLellan and Dewey did not think that learning numbers was a completely natural process, though they did think that natural rhythmic activity could help. Like Hall, they urged teachers to rely upon "the principle of rhythm, the regular breaking up and putting together of minor activities into a whole; a natural principle, and the basis of all easy, graceful, and satisfactory activity." The trick to teaching arithmetic well, according to McLellan and Dewey, was to form the "habit of parting and wholing." Here McLellan and Dewey credited kindergarten founder Friedrich Froebel's positive influence. Kindergarten activities, including playing with Froebel's "gift" materials, the wooden blocks that kindergarten children used to copy complex geometric patterns, were a good way for children to see part-whole relationships. Some kindergarten methods, however, such as using tables with inch-square grids, introduced bad habits, McClellan and Dewey thought, because children became used to counting three inches in from the edge and became dependent on counting things one-by-one.[19]

McLellan and Dewey saw addition, subtraction, multiplication, and division as correlated processes, ones that should be taught with frequent examples for simultaneous practice. Because multiplication and division were harder and more advanced, McLellan and Dewey thought that they should be taught later than addition and subtraction. Although this reasoning may seem self-evident now, the sequence in which arithmetic was taught was a matter of great debate at the time. Unlike Hall, McLellan and Dewey believed that this sequence was based on psychological evidence, not evolutionary history. The "old-time arrangement—Addition and Subtraction, Multiplication and Division," was the psychological order in which these processes developed cognitively, "the order in which they appear in the reflective consciousness of the child; the order of increasing growth in psychological complexity." Having accepted this "old-time arrangement" as psychologically accurate, McLellan and Dewey recommended some relatively traditional methods for teaching these processes. Children were to memorize the multiplication tables up to twelve "perfectly," for instance.[20]

Like Hall, McLellan and Dewey thought that learning numbers was naturally interesting to children. They described a first-grade class that loved arithmetic more than recess and had become "so thoroughly interested in arithmetic under a sympathetic and competent teacher, as to prefer an exercise in arithmetic to a kindergarten song or a romp in the playground." Like Hall, they thought that if children disliked arithmetic it was a sign of bad teaching, which could cause arrested development. When the "native aptitude for number" was "continually baffled" and "artificial" activities were "forced upon the mind," then "arrested development of the number function ensues," McLellan and Dewey argued. They estimated that "nine tenths" of those who disliked arithmetic and thought that they were bad at math actually suffered from being badly taught.[21]

Dewey continued to work out his ideas about arithmetic at the University of Chicago Laboratory School, which he and his wife, Alice Chipman Dewey, directed from 1896 to 1903. There he became even more convinced that children learned academic subjects best by doing "hands-on" problem solving and meaningful real-life projects. He became less sure that learning the multiplication tables perfectly was important. In fact, as he told the Pedagogical Club in 1896, children learned more through practical occupations such as constructing a pencil box, the activity entering children did on their first day at the Deweys' school, than by traditional study of "paper and pencil" arithmetic. Although a "child may not learn as much of number as by the study of the multiplication table" through projects like this, Dewey conceded, the child would "get an idea of what number really is, instead of the mere technique of number as is the case at present." Arithmetic was integrated throughout the curriculum of the laboratory school. Children were taught to count, measure, and do more sophisticated calculations through such activities as cooking, sewing, and carpentry. They spent very little time in direct instruction in arithmetical skills. Out of a total of twenty hours a week, the seven- and eight-year-olds spent only two hours a week in "techniques" of reading, writing, and arithmetic, though of course they used these techniques in other activities.[22]

Dewey's Arithmetic Texts

At least three arithmetic series were developed based on Dewey's ideas, two of these series apparently coming out shortly after the publication of *The Psychology of Number*, with the third arriving twenty-five years later. In 1921, Indianapolis public schools superintendent Georgia Alexander worked with Dewey to produce The Alexander-Dewey Arithmetic Series. Published by Longmans Green and Company and edited by Dewey, the series was targeted for use in elementary schools. According to the preface, Dewey and his wife had read the full text and made suggestions for activities and exercises, which Alexander had then tested in classrooms in Indianapolis.[23]

The texts' general methods seem Deweyan in their emphasis on the social context and purposes of learning. Children were to be introduced to arithmetical concepts through "socialized recitation," followed by "scientific practice" and then "application to new concrete situations." The preface states that the main purpose of arithmetic was to foster "clear and independent thinking as a preparation for business, science, and industry." "Skill in mathematical computation" was listed as the second purpose, followed by "[c]ivic responsibility which will carry into action whatever is needed for the welfare of the community." Here Alexander and the Deweys echoed the progressive rhetoric of the *Cardinal Principles of Secondary Education*, the controversial curriculum guidelines that had come out three years earlier, in 1918, and that prioritized vocational preparation and citizenship and deemphasized traditional academic study.[24]

The Alexander-Dewey series was a compromise between older and newer methods. In what sounded like an innovation, "[f]ully fifty per cent of the work" was "to be performed without pencil," when in fact, Colburn had stressed doing mental arithmetic instead of paper-and-pencil work a century earlier. The series contained lots of "real-life" problems, including some with racialized content typical of attitudes of the day, about which Dewey and some other progressives were notably silent. There was a problem on fractions, for instance, in which a caricature of a black "mammy" gave white children a watermelon to be divided. The first lesson, which began with Mary and Fred's trip to the grocery store to buy some laundry soap for their mother, was more typical of the banality of most of the examples, however. As in McLellan's and Dewey's earlier work, the upper-level texts in the series included standard arithmetic problems and formal instructional techniques. So although Dewey thought that arithmetic was learned and should be taught through progressive psychological methods in which children constructed knowledge, his arithmetic texts combined progressive approaches with some quite traditional ones.[25]

THORNDIKE'S THEORY OF ARITHMETIC LEARNING

Origins

More than any other psychologist, Edward L. Thorndike propelled the movement to psychologize school subjects. It was at Harvard during the late 1890s, while studying under William James and conducting animal experiments on chickens (kept in the basement of the James's house, to the delight of their children and dismay of Mrs. James), that Thorndike began to develop his associationistic theory of learning.[26]

As a graduate student at Columbia, Thorndike began doing work on human abilities. He collaborated with his colleague Robert S. Woodworth in numerous experiments on learning, including on how adults ascertained accurate weights and added numbers. At the time, the prevailing theory of mental discipline held that mental effort in one area was supposed to exercise the mind and aid in the learning of other subjects, but Thorndike and Woodworth's research discredited these notions. Moreover, it had huge implications for education and spurred much research on the learning of specific academic skills and subjects. If there was relatively little transfer of training from one discrete mental ability to another, as Thorndike and Woodworth argued, then each school subject needed to be specifically and systematically taught.[27]

Thorndike explained his theory of how knowledge was acquired in the 1903 and 1913 versions of his magnum opus, *Educational Psychology*, which contained his measurements of individual differences and "laws" of learning, the experimentally derived rules that he argued described how associations were learned. Thorndike wrote that learning was "essentially the modification of connections between actual situations and the responses of the individual to them." Teaching, Thorndike stated in his 1906 *The Principles of Teaching*, written for Education A, the largest course at Teachers College, should be based on this psychology of individual differences and associations. While "present knowledge of psychology" was "nearer to zero than to complete perfection," he admitted, "other things being equal," teachers who could "apply psychology" would be "more successful."[28]

Psychology of Arithmetic and Direct Teaching Methods

Despite the nascent nature of educational psychology, Thorndike confidently began applying the discipline to school subjects. He founded the journal *Educational Psychology* in 1910 and in its first issue laid out an agenda for how psychology could help education. Many of Thorndike's books, of which there was a sizeable output, were filled with examples of learning taken from his own research and from work done by his graduate students at Teachers College. He focused in particular on the effects of practice. After reviewing numerous studies on different types of arithmetical skills, and on the amount, rate, and improvement of mental functions, he arrived at the conclusion that arithmetic was taught inefficiently in most American schools. Teachers' and children's time was being wasted on overly lengthy, ill-timed, inappropriately sequenced, poorly designed drills that did not produce commensurate amounts of achievement.[29]

Based on his theory of learning, Thorndike set out to improve the teaching of arithmetic. In his 1922 book *The Psychology of Arithmetic*, he listed seven aspects of arithmetic that elementary schools should teach: numbers; decimals; addition, subtraction, multiplication, and division; measurement; fractions; problem solving; and percentages and interest. He described four competing concepts of number: the "*series meaning*," that two is more than one, for instance; the "*collection* meaning" of being able to correctly identify a group as containing six objects; the "*ratio* meaning" that three is three times one; and the "*relational* meaning" of knowing that six is more than five and less than seven. Practical and eclectic, Thorndike knew that each of these ways of conceiving of number had its proponents and that because individual children learned differently, children needed to be taught all these ways of using numbers. The problem, in Thorndike's view, was "the narrow vision of the extremists," who advocated only one method.[30]

In a very modern-sounding recommendation, Thorndike said that arithmetic teachers needed to do a better job of introducing children to the language of arithmetic. Children needed to know what words such as "both, all, in all, together, less, difference, sum, whole part, equal, buy, sell, have left" and "measure" meant. Thorndike thought that schools should teach children how to do actual problem solving, instead of forcing them to do boring, artificial problems with no relevance to things that they would ever actually do. As an example, he included a page "taken almost at random from one of the best recent textbooks, filled with problems involving people buying quantities of things, working for so many hours on this and that, and so on." Instead, he argued, children should do more immediate things, such as keeping score in classroom games, computing costs at a real or play store, mapping out a school garden, measuring their own achievement in a school subject, or figuring out costs of things in mail order catalogs. He also recommended using lots of concrete materials.[31]

Like many other progressives, Thorndike wanted to help teachers make their students' learning more efficient. He listed desirable bonds and "wasteful and harmful" bonds and suggested that students be introduced to equations with unknown variables well before their instruction in formal algebra. He summarized his recommendations for what bonds should be formed, stressing that no bonds that later would "have to be broken" should be taught, that the least number of bonds necessary should be formed, and that bonds should be formed "in the way that they are later required to act." It was a waste of time, Thorndike said, to learn "arbitrary units," "multiples of eleven," "least common multiples," "greatest common divisors," "misleading facts and procedures," "trivialities and absurdities," "useless methods," or "problems whose answers would, in real life, be already known."[32]

Thorndike thought that schools needed to improve the teaching of arithmetical reasoning. To do this required understanding of the principles of habit formation and training. Thorndike argued, for instance, that adding a column of two-place numbers involved at least seven hierarchical processes, each of which was "psychologically distinct" and required "distinct educational treatment." He proceeded to break down other common arithmetical tasks into their component steps and showed how many specific habits needed to be formed for children to be able to solve arithmetic problems. There was not any "special time when the human animal by inner growth" was "specially ripe for one or another section or aspect of arithmetic," Thorndike stated. In a vigorous dissent to Hall, he said that there was no "arithmogenesis" or "arithmetic instinct," that "man's original nature" was "destitute of all arithmetical ideas," and that "the human germs do not know even that one and one make two!" Arithmetic did not develop naturally. Each step had to be specifically and directly taught.[33]

Individual Differences

Thorndike thought that teaching arithmetic had to take into account individual differences in learning. Because there were so many specific bonds and individual differences, he did not think that psychology could offer a "single, easy, royal road to discovering" the "dynamically best order" for teaching addition, subtraction, multiplication, and division. The traditional order was fine, he said, but this was based on convention, not on how the subjects had evolved over the course of human history or on psychological development. He agreed with Dewey that it was "justifiable" to sacrifice optimal order in teaching arithmetic concepts so as to increase children's interest. But relying on interest was tricky because there was so much variation among individual children. "Thirty children, half boys and half girls, varying by five years in age, coming from different homes, with different native capacities," would not "in September, 1920, unanimously feel a vital need to solve any one problem, and then conveniently feel another on, say, October 15!"[34]

Luckily, Thorndike's surveys showed that most children enjoyed learning arithmetic and found it interesting, as Hall and Dewey thought as well. The only subjects children liked better, Thorndike reported, were shop, cooking, drawing, gymnastics, and history. Children liked arithmetic because it was definite and objective and because they could see clear results. Arithmetic "more than any other of the 'intellectual studies' of the elementary school," Thorndike said, ". . . permits the pupil to see his own progress and determine his own success or failure." Arithmetic had "intrinsic interest" as a subject because it was like a game that children wanted to win. "Pupils like to learn, to achieve, to gain mastery." "Success is interesting," Thorndike declared, speaking from personal experience. If arithmetic was well taught, there would be little need "to sugar-coat it with illegitimate attractions."[35]

As testing was the sine qua non of Thorndike's educational psychology, he measured all manner of arithmetical abilities, including speed, accuracy, and difficulty. The achievement tests he developed showed a wide range of individual variation in arithmetic skills, which he thought was largely the result of inborn differences in children's original nature. Interestingly, however, nowhere in his vast body of work did Thorndike suggest that arithmetic achievement was correlated with gender, a view consonant with his overall opinion on the insignificance of sex differences in academic ability and their irrelevance for differentiation of curriculum and teaching methods.[36]

Thorndike's Arithmetic Texts

Even before the publication of *The Psychology of Arithmetic*, Thorndike had begun translating his theories into practical applications. His 1917 school arithmetic series, *The Thorndike Arithmetics*, was explicitly designed to apply "the principles discovered by the psychology of learning, by experimental education, and by the observation of successful school practice." His texts differed from older arithmetic books, Thorndike wrote in the preface, because nothing was included "for mere mental gymnastics." Like many modern proponents of curriculum standards, of whom he is the forebear, Thorndike set a high bar for school achievement, but one bounded by individual differences in ability. He expected students to be able to "approximate 100 percent efficiency with the thinking of which they are capable." Like modern proponents of testing, Thorndike was criticized for focusing only on basic skills. University of Chicago psychologist Charles Judd, who also studied mathematics teaching, argued that Thorndike ignored higher-order mental processes, to which Thorndike retorted that reasoning was important because it was the organizing principle that governed the rest of learning. But for Thorndike, reasoning was a concrete process that could be described, measured, and taught, not "a mythical faculty which may be called upon to override or veto habits."[37]

Carefully sequenced with an exactly calculated number of required drills and practical problems, Thorndike's arithmetic texts became very popular and soon captured a large share of the market, thanks in part to the new policy of statewide textbook adoptions. In 1919 California adopted his series; by 1921 a half million copies were circulating in print throughout the state. It was also adopted in Indiana, even though that state was where the Dewey series had been developed. By 1924, Thorndike was earning fifty-eight thousand dollars a year in addition to his Teachers College salary, mostly from textbook royalties.[38]

Promising empirical, effective, and efficient methods, Thorndike's widely used texts and achievement tests helped categorize children into the academic levels and tracks in which they supposedly belonged. A legacy of progressive education, this categorizing and sorting was another reason for the popularity of his associationist approach.

PSYCHOLOGIES OF ARITHMETIC IN THE CLASSROOM

At the level of formal theory, there were clear differences in Hall's, Dewey's, and Thorndike's ideas about how knowledge of arithmetic was learned. Hall thought that children acquired knowledge of arithmetic naturally, and he rejected the direct teaching of arithmetic to young children. Dewey thought that children constructed arithmetic concepts in social contexts. Thorndike thought that direct teaching of specific subject matter was the only efficient approach. At the level of advice and materials for classroom teaching, however, there were a surprising number of similarities in their recommendations about how arithmetic should be taught. They all agreed, though for different reasons, that addition, subtraction, multiplication, and division should be taught in the traditional order. They all recommended using practical, real-life problems. They all encouraged using concrete materials. And both Dewey's and Hall's texts included some quite traditional teaching methods.

My point is not to minimize the differences in Hall's, Dewey's, and Thorndike's ideas, but to show that historically the psychologizing of arithmetic was a more complex process with more intermediaries and influences than academic discourse reveals. When theories of arithmetic learning were transformed into school and teacher education texts and other classroom applications, they came up against what David Tyack and Larry Cuban call the "grammar of schooling," the conforming pull of the realities of teaching large numbers of children in institutional settings and resistance of some teachers to change. Conflicting educational goals and organizational convenience also contributed to the conflation of curricular approaches, as David Labaree suggests. The traditions and subject matter of mathematics as a discipline had a unifying influence, too, as did the demands of the publishing industry for products that could be sold in a wide range of markets.[39]

So whose psychologizing of arithmetic "won"? Ellen Lagemann argues that Thorndike's methods triumphed in American education and that Dewey lost, as Thorndike's and Dewey's relative textbook sales might be seen to attest. David Labaree argues that Dewey prevailed in schools of education, which may help explain why many mathematics education texts for teachers seem so Deweyan.[40]

I would elaborate on Lagemann's and Labaree's positions. Aspects of Hall's maturationism returned in force in the new developmentalism of Jean Piaget: witness the numerous calls for "developmentally appropriate practice," especially for younger children. It would be more accurate, I think, to characterize these pedagogical disputes as a standoff, with Hall, Dewey, and Thorndike each enjoying heydays and comparatively more influence within different niches and populations.

THE "MATH WARS" TODAY

Hall's, Dewey's, and Thorndike's psychologizing of arithmetic were round two in the "math wars," after Colburn. Piaget's and Jerome Bruner's psychologies were influential in round three in the "new math" of the 1960s, as were the ideas of mathematicians at the Universities of Iowa, Chicago, and elsewhere. The Deweyan, constructivist National Council of Teachers of Mathematics Standards that came out in 1989 signaled round four. Salvos in 2004 from the U.S. Department of Education's What Works Clearinghouse, which released a list of five middle-school math programs "for increasing K–12 math achievement" based on randomized field trials, and the National Research Council's 2005 report, *How Students Learn Mathematics in the Classroom*, which draws from a variety of types of research, herald that the math wars are ongoing. And in each round, more intermediaries joined the fray.[41]

Strains of Hall's maturationism, Dewey's constructivism, and Thorndike's associationism can be seen in arithmetic texts and methods today. To simplify quite a bit, *Everyday Mathematics,* the series that grew out of research begun by the University of Chicago School Mathematics Project in 1983, states on its website that children learn best when they "develop an understanding of mathematics from their own experience" and that mathematics is "more meaningful when it is rooted in real life contexts and situations," language that might have been copied from one of Dewey's myriad publications. At the other extreme, Saxon Publisher's *Saxon Math*, with texts in print since 1980, states on its website that it relies on pedagogy which breaks "complex concepts into related increments, recognizing that smaller pieces of information are easier to teach and easier to learn," an approach of which Thorndike would have approved. And helping teachers understand how children think naturally and intuitively about numbers, as Magdalene Lampert, Deborah Ball, and others argue is also a current theme, an idea Hall would have supported.[42]

I am not taking sides in these wars over the teaching of arithmetic. As this brief history suggests, what goes on at the level of the uses of psychology in arithmetic texts and advice to teachers is messier than top-down views of the influence of psychology on education imply. What goes on in classrooms is messier still. As I sat observing a student teacher with a class of first graders in a school in Boston a few years ago, I thought about Hall's, Dewey's, and Thorndike's arithmetic methods. The children were using interlocking plastic cubes to try to find out how many combinations of numbers added up to eleven. This was not an easy problem for some of them. They lost track when they counted and did not understand that the two parts they were putting together should always make a row that was the same length. The student teacher showed the children how the blocks could come apart and then make wholes again. She tried to teach the problem step by step. She asked the children to challenge themselves, told them how much she loved arithmetic, and tried to come up with examples for how they could use the concepts they were learning. Meanwhile, some of the children had turned the cubes into swords and guns and were playing with them as toys.[43]

After the lesson the student teacher and I talked about how it had gone. She said it was hard to teach math because the children in her class were at such different levels. This was why she was not staying with the text. Some of the children were learning English and did not understand the directions and explanations that she was supposed to use. She was frustrated by some of the children's slow academic progress, worried about the tests that they would have to take, and exhausted by struggles with classroom discipline. We talked about whether the lesson was "developmentally appropriate," about "task analysis" and how she could break the content up into smaller units, and about how she could make up more "hands on" problems for the children to solve using "real life" objects rather than plastic cubes.

Here was a full array of psychologized teaching strategies, many of which Hall, Dewey, and Thorndike would have recognized, all mixed together, "psychologies in use," though the teacher may not have been thinking about them as she taught. Using this psychological language made the student teacher and I feel better, but I wondered how much it helped. Dewey might have recommended that she psychologize her arithmetic lesson based on the unique experiences of each child in the class. Thorndike might have wanted her to use more direct teaching and stick to the text, if it was organized as was one of his. Hall might have said to let the children keep playing with the cubes. But doing this, applying psychology to school subjects and making complex pedagogical decisions, in the heat of the moment in a busy classroom, is not as easy as Hall had promised. And doing it well depends on having well-educated teachers, who know the subject matter of mathematics, have strong teaching skills, have small enough classes, are working in well-run schools with good principals . . . and many of these are things about which, as William James warned, psychology cannot provide much help.

NOTES

1. William James, *Talks to Teachers* (New York: H. Holt, 1898), 22–24; G. Stanley Hall, "The New Psychology," *Andover Review* 3 (1885), 248, quoted in John M. O'Donnell, *The Origins of Behaviorism: American Psychology, 1870–1920* (New York: New York University Press, 1985), 128; Dorothy Ross, *G. Stanley Hall: The Psychologist as Prophet* (Chicago: University of Chicago Press, 1972), 113, 118.

2. Herbert M. Kliebard, *The Struggle for the American Curriculum* (New York: Routledge, 1986); Sheldon H. White, "Three Visions of a Psychology of Education," in *Culture, Schooling, and Psychological Development*, ed. Liliana Tolchinsky Landsman (Norwood, NJ: Ablex, 1990), 1–38; David Tyack, *The One Best System:*

A History of American Urban Education (Cambridge, MA: Harvard University Press, 1974); Thomas Popkewitz, *The Formation of School Subjects* (New York: Falmer, 1987); William J. Reese, "The Origins of Progressive Education," *History of Education Quarterly* 41 (2001): 1–24. On the relationship of psychology and education, see, among others, Barbara Beatty, "Rethinking the Historical Role of Psychology in Educational Reform," in *The Handbook of Education and Human Development*, ed. David R. Olson and Nancy Torrance (Cambridge, UK: Blackwell, 1996), 100–116; Kurt Danziger, *Constructing the Subject: The Historical Origins of Psychological Research* (Cambridge: Cambridge University Press, 1990); Ellen Condliffe Lagemann, *An Elusive Science: The Troubling History of Education Research* (Chicago: University of Chicago Press, 2000); and Jo Anne Brown, *The Definition of a Profession: The Authority of Metaphor in the History of Intelligence Testing, 1890–1930* (Princeton: Princeton University Press, 1992).

3. G. Stanley Hall, "The Contents of Children's Minds," *Princeton Review* 11 (May 1883): 249–72; John Dewey, *The Child and the Curriculum* [Chicago: University of Chicago Press, 1902], in *Dewey on Education*, ed. Martin S. Dworkin (New York: Teachers College Press, 1959), 104, 105; Edward L. Thorndike, *The Principles of Teaching, Based on Psychology* (Syracuse, NY: Mason, 1906).

4. Nicholas Pike, *A New and Complete System of Arithmetic: Composed for the Use of Citizens of the United States* (Newburyport, MA: J. Mycall, 1788).

5. Warren Colburn, *First Lessons in Arithmetic* (Boston: Cummings and Hilliard, 1821); Barbara Finkelstein, *Governing the Young: Teacher Behavior in Popular Primary Schools in 19th Century United States* (New York: Falmer, 1989), 72–78. See also Patricia Cline Cohen, *A Calculating People: The Spread of Numeracy in Early America* (Chicago: University of Chicago Press, 1982); Kim Tolley, *The Science Education of American Girls* (New York: Routledge Falmer, 2003), 75–94; and Walter Scott Monroe, *Development of Arithmetic as a School Subject*, Department of the Interior, Bureau of Education Bulletin, no. 10 (Washington, DC: GPO, 1917).

6. Hugo Munsterberg to James McKeen Catell, 25 February 1898, Hugo Munsterberg Papers, Boston Public Library, quoted in Brown, *The Definition of a Profession*, 65; O'Donnell, *Origins of Behaviorism*, 154.

7. On "colonization," see Barbara Beatty, "Comment on Labaree, *The Trouble with Ed Schools*," in *Brookings Papers on Education Policy 2004*, ed. Diane Ravitch (Washington, DC: Brookings Institution Press, 2004), and Joseph J. Schwab, "On the Corruption of Education by Psychology," *School Review*, Summer 1958, 169–84.

8. Ross, *G. Stanley Hall*; Alan Ryan, *John Dewey and the High Tide of American Liberalism* (New York: W. W. Norton, 1995); Geraldine Jonçich Clifford, *Edward L. Thorndike: The Sane Positivist* (Middletown: Wesleyan University Press, 1984).

9. Ross, *Hall*, 279–308; Clifford, *Thorndike*, 398–400; Kathleen Cruikshank, "In Dewey's Shadows: Julia Bulkley and the University of Chicago Department of Pedagogy, 1895–1900," *History of Education Quarterly* 38 (1998): 374–406.

10. G. Stanley Hall, *Educational Problems* (New York: D. Appleton, 1911); Hall, "Contents of Children's Minds"; Barbara Beatty, *Preschool Education in America: The Culture of Young Children from the Colonial Era to the Present* (New

Haven: Yale University Press, 1995), 75–76; Charles Strickland, "The Child and the Race: The Doctrines of Recapitulation and Culture Epochs in the Rise of the Child-Centered Ideal in American Educational Thought, 1875–1900" (PhD diss., University of Wisconsin, 1973).

11. Hall, *Educational Problems*, 341, 342, 344–45.

12. Hall, *Educational Problems*, 353, 351, 350, 351.

13. Hall, *Educational Problems*, 365.

14. Hall, *Educational Problems*, 375, 367.

15. Hall, *Educational Problems*, 392.

16. James Alexander McLellan and John Dewey, *The Psychology of Number* (New York: D. Appleton, 1895), 61.

17. McLellan and Dewey, *Psychology of Number*, xiii.

18. McLellan and Dewey, *Psychology of Number*, 42, 32, 59, 60, 61.

19. McLellan and Dewey, *Psychology of Number*, 83, 67, 150, 154–55.

20. McLellan and Dewey, *Psychology of Number*, 103, 216.

21. McLellan and Dewey, *Psychology of Number*, 144, 145–46, 146.

22. John Dewey, "The University School" (1896), in *John Dewey: The Early Works, 1882–1898*, ed. Jean A. Boydston, vol. 5, *Early Essays, 1895–1898* (Carbondale: Southern Illinois University Press, 1972), 440; Esther Camp Edwards and Anna Camp Edwards, *The Dewey School: The Laboratory School of the University of Chicago, 1896–1903* (New York: Appleton-Century, 1936), 385–86; Beatty, "Rethinking the Historical Role"; Laurel N. Tanner, *Dewey's Laboratory School* (New York: Teachers College Press, 1997).

23. Monroe, *Development of Arithmetic*, 131n.

24. Georgia Alexander and John Dewey, preface to *The Alexander-Dewey Arithmetic Elementary Book*, vol. 1 (New York: Longmans Green, 1921), iii; Commission on the Reorganization of Secondary Education, *Cardinal Principles of Secondary Education: A Report of the Commission on the Reorganization of Secondary Education* (Washington, DC: Department of the Interior, Bureau of Education, GPO, 1918).

25. Alexander and Dewey, "Preface," iii; Alexander and Dewey, *The Elementary Arithmetic Book*, vol. 1, 34; Georgia Alexander and John Dewey, *The Alexander-Dewey Intermediate Arithmetic Book* (New York: Longmans Green, 1921).

26. Clifford, *Thorndike*, 87.

27. E. L. Thorndike and R. S. Woodworth, "The Influence of Improvement in One Mental Function upon the Efficiency of Other Functions," *Psychological Review* 8 (May, July, November, 1901): 247–61, 384–95, 556–64; Clifford, *Thorndike*. See also Barbara Beatty, "From Laws of Learning to a Science of Values: Efficiency and Morality in Thorndike's Educational Psychology," *American Psychologist 53* (October 1998): 1145–52; and Lee S. Shulman and Kathleen M. Quinlan, "The Comparative Psychology of School Subjects," in *Handbook of Educational Psychology*, ed. David Berliner and Robert C. Calfee (New York: Macmillan, 1996), 399–423.

28. Edward L. Thorndike, *Educational Psychology* (New York: Teachers College Press, 1913–14), 418; Thorndike, *Principles of Teaching*, 9–10; Clifford, *Thorndike*, 235.

29. Beatty, "From Laws of Learning."

30. Edward L. Thorndike, *The Psychology of Arithmetic* (New York: Macmillan, 1922), 1, 23–24, 2–3, 6.

31. Thorndike, *Psychology of Arithmetic*, 6, 14.

32. Thorndike, *Psychology of Arithmetic*, 77, 81, 101, 83–95.

33. Thorndike, *Psychology of Arithmetic*, 52; Edward L. Thorndike, "Notes on Child Study," *Columbia University Contributions to Philosophy, Psychology, and Education* (New York: Macmillan) 8, nos. 3–4; Thorndike, *Psychology of Arithmetic*, 198, 201.

34. Thorndike, *Psychology of Arithmetic*, 147, 151.

35. Thorndike, *Psychology of Arithmetic*, 209, 212, 226.

36. Thorndike, *Principles of Teaching*, 113, 293; Beatty, "From Laws of Learning," 1147; James C. Albisetti, "Another 'Curious Incident of the Dog in the Night-Time'? Intelligence Testing and Coeducation," *History of Education Quarterly* 44 (Summer 2004): 183–201.

37. Edward L. Thorndike, preface to *The Thorndike Arithmetics* (Chicago: Rand-McNally, 1917), v; Beatty, "From Laws of Learning."

38. Clifford, *Thorndike*, 399, 400.

39. David B. Tyack and Larry Cuban, *Tinkering Toward Utopia: A Century of Public School Reform* (Cambridge, MA: Harvard University Press, 1995); Larry Cuban, *How Teachers Taught: Constancy and Change in American Classrooms, 1890–1990* (New York: Teachers College Press, 1993); David F. Labaree, "The Chronic Failure of School Reform," *Education Week* 18, no. 36 (1999): 36, 42–44.

40. Lagemann, *An Elusive Science*; David F. Labaree, *The Trouble with Ed Schools* (New Haven: Yale University Press, 2004).

41. U.S. Department of Education Institute of Education Sciences, What Works Clearinghouse, "Topic Report: Curriculum-Based Interventions for Increasing K–12 Math Achievement—Middle School," December 1, 2004; and National Research Council, M. Suzanne Donovan and John D. Bransford, eds., *How Students Learn Mathematics in the Classroom* (Washington, DC: National Academy Press, 2005). And see Jerome S. Bruner, *The Process of Education* (Cambridge, MA: Harvard University Press, 1961); Stanislas Debaene, *The Number Sense: How the Mind Creates Mathematics* (New York: Oxford University Press, 1997); and Jody Hall, "The 1960–64 Battle over Psychological Foundations of Learning: Cold War, Psychology, and Schooling," paper presented at the History of Education Society annual meeting, Philadelphia, 2002; Tom Loveless, ed., *The Great Curriculum Debate: How Should We Teach Reading and Math?* (Washington, DC: Brookings Institution Press, 2001); Jeremy Kilpatrick, Jane Swafford, and Bradford Findell, eds., *Adding It Up: Helping Children Learn Mathematics* (Washington, DC: National Academy Press, 2001); and Debra Viadero, "Math Programs Seen to Lack a Research Base," *Education Week* 24, no. 4 (2004): 1, 17.

42. "About Everyday Mathematics," http://everydaymath.uchicago.edu/about.shtml; "The Saxon Math Difference: Our Approach to Math Instruction," http://www.saxonpublishers.com/school/math/index.jsp; Deborah Ball, "Halves, Pieces, and Twoths: Constructing Representational Concepts in Teaching Fractions," in *Rational Numbers: An Integration of Research*, ed. Thomas P. Carpen-

ter, Elizabeth Fennema, and Thomas A. Romberg (Hillsdale, NJ: Erlbaum, 1993), 157–96; and Magdalene Lampert and Deborah Ball, *Mathematics, Teaching, and Multimedia: Investigations of Real Practice* (New York: Teachers College Press, 1998).

43. On teachers' informal use of psychology, see David R. Olson and Jerome S. Bruner, "Folk Psychology and Folk Pedagogy," in *Handbook of Education and Human Development*, ed. David R. Olson and Nancy Torrance (Cambridge, UK: Blackwell), 9–27.

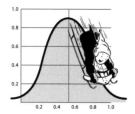

CHAPTER 3

The Rise of English-Only Pedagogy: Immigrant Children, Progressive Education, and Language Policy in the United States, 1900–1930

Carlos Kevin Blanton

IN THE FALL OF 1928 a new teacher came to Welhausen Elementary School in Cotulla, some seventy miles from the U.S.-Mexico border in southwest Texas. Completely segregated, Welhausen, referred to as the town's "Mexican" school, offered the only available education for children of Mexican American families who could afford to comply with the state of Texas's oft-ignored compulsory-attendance regulations. This teacher, a young man not yet graduated from a nearby teacher's college, often beat his students with homemade "switches" cut from the branches of a nearby tree. As mandated by state law, he punished his students both physically and psychologically for violating the school's cardinal rule against speaking Spanish, despite the fact that many of these children spoke Spanish only when they could not understand English or were on the playground among themselves. The gangly young man who taught at Welhausen during the 1928–29 academic year eventually went back to college to finish his coursework and moved on to other opportunities. While we now remember this as an era in which the education of Mexican American children was humiliating, these children as adults swore that this one teacher turned their lives around through his intense energy and compassion.[1]

The teacher's name was Lyndon Baines Johnson. In 1968, while president, Johnson signed the Bilingual Education Act, which federally censured the English-Only instructional system that he himself had used some forty years before.

Few subjects in United States history are as ultimately ironic or controversial as language policy in the nation's schools, and the tensions between bilingual education and English-Only education have been particularly acute. While the bilingual tradition in American history has generated a small but growing degree of academic interest from supporters and critics alike, the historical alternative of English Only instruction, the bilingual tradition's chief competitor, has been almost completely ignored. The absence of relevant scholarship and critique is unfortunate, since many opponents of modern-day bilingual education argue that English Only is the one, natural, obvious way of educating non-English-speaking children. Lost in this politically charged discourse is an awareness of historical alternatives. It is a fallacy to think that English-Only evolved as some mere "immersion" technique implemented by teachers unaware of viable alternatives. In fact, English-Only—which developed at the beginning of the twentieth century as a state-sponsored response to the growing linguistic heterogeneity of public-school children in the United States—has since its inception existed as an explicit pedagogical approach, one that was moreover initially sanctioned by progressive educators and progressive science.

HISTORY AND HISTORIOGRAPHY OF LANGUAGE POLICY

Throughout the nineteenth and early twentieth centuries, American educators traditionally offered bilingual instruction in both public and private schools. In the Southwest, bilingual schools served Spanish-speaking children. In the Midwest and the East, bilingual education served mostly German speakers, who wielded enough influence to demand varying degrees of bilingual instruction in the public schools of urban areas, including Baltimore, Cleveland, Cincinnati, Indianapolis, Milwaukee, and St. Louis. Teachers in private schools also provided bilingual instruction for German American children, as well as for students whose native languages were Czech, Polish, and Italian. Most of these schools taught children English while maintaining some degree of cultural and ethnic continuity through native-language instruction.[2]

The rate of English-Only's growth was astonishing. Blossoming from latent nationalist and nativist ideologies regarding language in American life, as late as the 1890s it was still only barely emergent. But by World War I, English-Only completely dominated the national discourse on educating non-English-speaking children. English-Only pedagogy was the result of a set of interrelated social attitudes pertaining to theories of language learning and ethnic assimilation. Although it only became truly relevant in the twentieth century, English-Only's roots stretch back to the early republic, as nationalist sentiments of the time focused on the creation of a thoroughly "American" English language. As historian Jill Lepore documented in *"A" is for American*, the founding generation sought to popularize and elevate American English through linguistic codification. Pedagogue and ardent Federalist Noah Webster, famous for his dictionary of American English, regarded "English dialects" as the equivalent of "political factions" or "local prejudice." To Webster, they constituted a poison. This nascent tradition of linguistic codification would later express itself in the battles over bilingual instruction for non-English-speaking immigrant children. Although Lepore further notes that Webster was relatively unconcerned about the prevalence of non-English languages in the nation, and in fact believed that English—the "natural" national language—would remain unthreatened, the precedent for English-Only had been set, long before the emergence of widespread public schooling.[3]

Some critics have dismissively equated the English-Only approach as little more than an expression of simple nativism. Although it was openly nativist, there was nothing simple about English-Only. One scholar recently alleged that English-Only pedagogy was equated with "the crusade for Anglo conformity" that emerged in the twentieth century, yet this writer failed to provide a reference to either its pedagogical theory or its relationship to the progressive education movement.[4] Most works examining English-Only's history do so in cursory fashion and focus on the politics of modern-day English-Only, bilingual education, or theories of language learning.[5] Similarly, histories of bilingual instruction generally ignore the role of English-Only pedagogy and focus instead on the more spectacular circumstantial factor of the nativism that arose during World War I as an explanation for the disappearance of bilingual education.[6] What were the origins of English-Only pedagogy? How was it practiced and where was it implemented? What were some of its consequences?

ORIGINS OF ENGLISH-ONLY PEDAGOGY

English-Only pedagogy in the United States was born of unique social conditions. The massive social, demographic, and political changes of the late nineteenth and early twentieth centuries transformed the way public education functioned. A 1909 study from the United States Immigration Commission indicated that 57.8 percent of the children attending classes in the nation's thirty-seven largest cities were foreign born; in New York, Chicago, and Boston the respective figures were at 71.5, 67.3, and 63.5 percent.[7]

Increasingly, these foreign-born children hailed from southern and eastern Europe, areas that had delivered only a trickle of émigrés to the United States prior to the Gilded Age. Non-Protestant, non-English-speaking, they were not regarded as "white," as previous immigrants had been. They were the "new" immigrants. As a result of the widespread passage of compulsory-attendance legislation, the schools were often the first public institutions to grapple with these new, non-English-speaking children.[8] For example, between 1899 and 1914, New York City experienced a 60 percent increase in student enrollment; scholars estimate that in 1905 between sixty thousand and seventy-five thousand potential students were turned away from the public schools for lack of space.[9]

These growing numbers and the increasing demographic diversity were frightening to many Americans. Members of the growing middle class, concerned business and political elites, and intellectuals sought to achieve a measure of order in their rapidly changing world.[10] Order came in many forms. Many progressive educators championed different forms of Americanization in response to perceptions that immigrant children were not sufficiently quick in their assimilation to American culture. With mixed motives, different states acted upon these fears and expanded the role of public schools by enacting compulsory-attendance laws in tandem with enforcing new restrictions on child labor. Progressive educators sought greater professional control of the schools. Through the use of IQ tests, which tracked students in the name of "efficiency," along with the implementation of a "socially relevant" curriculum of vocational education, civics and patriotism lessons, and education in health and hygiene, progressives also sought to facilitate the full Americanization of immigrant children. When it came to schooling, the seemingly separate groups of progressive educators and Americanizers worked toward the same ends. The synergy between the two movements was captured in a 1909 statement on progressive education by Stanford University professor Ellwood Cubberley: "Our task is to break up these groups or settlements, to assimilate and amalgamate these people as a part of our American race, and to implant in their children, so far as can be done, the Anglo-Saxon conception of righteousness, law and order, and popular government."[11]

Sentiments toward Americanization and notions of progressive education were not always synonymous. Nor were the views of progressive educators themselves uniform. Still, an Americanizing curriculum flowed naturally from the commitment to order and efficiency inherent in the ideology of many progressive school reformers.

The movements for progressive education and Americanization, though intimately linked, were not neatly defined homogenous entities. Progressive educators struggled to identify the best among several competing psychologies of learning and instruction. Using Herbert Kliebard's well-known typology, English-Only pedagogy represents the "social efficiency" wing of progressive education. Based on psychometric evaluations and other forms of testing, the scientifically defined social-efficiency curriculum was intended to train children according to their presumed future place in society.[12] Different notions of immigrant assimilation competed with one another prior to World War I; Americanization was not a settled course of action. Cultural pluralists such as John Dewey and settlement luminary Jane Addams argued for cultural diversity as a positive virtue in society and were critical of attempts to force conformity among different immigrant groups.[13] But their voices were those of a weak minority. Cubberley and his Stanford colleague Emory S. Bogardus represented the dominant perspective. For Cubberley, Bogardus, and other, like-minded scholars, Americanization was a state-sponsored form of social reconstruction that would eradicate the native cultures and languages of immigrants and impose a new set of English loyalties.[14]

THE GRAMMAR-TRANSLATION METHOD

The combined ideologies of progressive education and Americanization directly affected language pedagogy. Progressive educators of all stripes, even those representing contradictory schools of thought, sought to overturn the nineteenth-century, curriculum-centered philosophy of education. In the subfield of teaching non-English-speaking children, this entailed overturning the ancient "grammar-translation" method.

Since antiquity, scholars had spoken a national or regional vernacular but read and wrote in scholarly languages such as Hebrew, Greek, or Latin. Thus, it was quite natural for scholars to develop bilingual/biliteral techniques of teaching languages that consisted entirely of reading and translating academic languages into vernacular form.[15] During the nineteenth century the teaching of a second language to non-English-speakers in the United States traditionally involved the grammar-translation method—a method that involved learning the second language by breaking down sentences into component parts and then translating them into writing in the native tongue.

The oral recitation of the second or third language mattered much less than the ability to read, write, and understand that language. Therefore, learning a new language was an exercise primarily in written, not spoken, literacy. As one progressive linguist noted of the grammar-translation method, "[T]he foreign language is never spoken, and pronunciation is considered unimportant."[16] An advantage of this grammar-translation method was that "a child might learn more than one foreign tongue while learning to read, write, and correctly use his own."[17] In this method, language was language. English for English-speakers was taught in much the same way as English for non-English-speakers, or second languages to English-speakers.

By the end of the nineteenth century the widespread use of the grammar-translation method of instruction was increasingly contested. The unprecedented numbers of students who did not understand English hampered the ability of schools to employ the grammar-translation method effectively. Child-centered progressives critiqued its "tiring, grinding, mechanical drill" and rigid methods, which smacked of the old, nineteenth-century, curriculum-centered learning with its focus on mastery of dry, cold, lifeless content. Moreover, because it neglected the spoken word in favor of the written word, many thought that the grammar-translation method was inefficient and irrelevant. A critic stated that "the process of building sentences by declining pronouns or by conjugating verbs is equally futile in teaching a person to speak English."[18] Finally, many thought the grammar-translation method a primitive relic of ages past, a traditional, reflexive instructional approach that lacked proper scientific rationale. One language expert dismissed it because there was "no pedagogical theory back of it [sic], and it tends to laziness on the part of the teacher and the lack of interest in the student."[19] Another agreed that the grammar-translation method was "more or less discredited" and stated that its utility was limited to instruction in the classical languages only.[20]

THE DIRECT METHOD

The science of language and child psychology provided progressive intellectuals with new ideas about how children learned, how language was acquired, and how it could be more efficiently taught. Progressive education patriarch G. Stanley Hall wrote that children acquired languages at a very early age and that such instruction was "greatly reinforced by appeals to the eye, not in the form of the written or printed word, but through pictures."[21] Progressives such as Hall contributed to the formation of alternatives by synthesizing the ideas of French linguist François Gouin, who in the 1880s and 1890s revolutionized the way educators conceived of teaching foreign languages. In the late nineteenth century France implemented policies to foster national unity through the teaching of French in the remote, non-French-speaking countryside. This created the context for Gouin's new language theories.[22]

Scarred by his inability to learn sufficient German to further his graduate education at the desirable German universities, Gouin developed a technique for teaching second languages that bypassed the time-honored grammar-translation principles and substituted in their place what he regarded as a more "natural" method.[23] Drawn to Gouin's terminology and conclusions, American educators redefined his original theories of language pedagogy into "direct" and "indirect" methods. The direct method of teaching languages was essentially Gouin's "natural" system. It abstained from using any native-language referent in the teaching of a foreign language, thus banning any use of the native tongue. The indirect method involved translating a concept, idea, or word from the native language to the second language, and vice versa. Such bilingual translation was not an immediate and spoken association of word with form or meaning, thus rendering the method indirect.[24]

Gouin's advocacy of the direct method over the old, indirect method quickly became scientific orthodoxy in the United States. Under the direct method a second language was best learned as naturally as possible, that is, orally, as a child normally learned her or his own native language. Linguist Frank V. Thompson, one of Gouin's American supporters, warned that when the indirect method was put into practice it would "make use of the pupil's vernacular in teaching a second language." This would necessarily involve a complicated "triple association of idea, native expression, [and] English expression," which would act as "a retardant in the process of acquiring ability to use English as a means of communication and [result] in the hesitation so often noted in the speech of those who learn a language by the indirect method."[25] Thompson argued that the direct method used "the new language to be taught both as end and as means" and operated under the guiding principle that "teachers applying the direct method speak only English in teaching English to pupils."[26] As it turned out, Gouin's ideas were more influential in the United States than in Europe.[27]

With some modifications, Gouin's direct method offered an easy way to teach English to non-English-speaking children. The popular French scholar had limited his criticisms of the older grammar-translation method and had been careful not to imply its total inadequacy. Gouin had originally tailored his pedagogy of second-language learning to adult learners and presumed that adults learned in much the same way as children.

Progressive educators in the United States inverted Gouin's original formula. In the American adaptation of Gouin's direct method, the teacher did not need to know any language but English; conversely, five- and six-year-old children were assumed to be able to learn second languages as adults did. In retrospect, by reversing Gouin's theoretical arguments, by forcing children to learn in the same way as adults learned, American practitioners of English-Only made a series of erroneous assumptions about language learning that haunted the pedagogy's effectiveness for decades. The direct method also violated some progressives' commitment to a child-centered curriculum.

THE PRACTICE OF ENGLISH-ONLY PEDAGOGY

In their rigid application of the English-Only curriculum, mainstream progressive educators required a Herculean effort from pupil and teacher alike. Regarded as representing the most advanced scientific results of the time, the doctrine of English-Only was gospel; no deviance from this scientific orthodoxy was permitted. While many advocates of English-Only remarked upon the goodwill an instructor might accrue through some knowledge of students' foreign language, this was acceptable only as long as the foreign language was not used in the classroom or in any other meaningful manner.[28] Some schools advocated hiring teachers with bilingual capability in order to build a better rapport with immigrant students and parents, but were indifferent to those teachers' ability to practice bilingual education itself. Thus, members of a progressive organization praising Cleveland's initiation of English-Only in 1916 argued that knowledge of a few words of a group's language "might prove of inestimable value in establishing a sympathetic relationship between the teachers and the children, but more especially between the parents and the school."[29]

English-Only pedagogy brooked no competition. Unlike the old bilingual tradition, which was varied and ultimately dependent upon specific local demand, English-Only excluded any place for foreign languages. Henry Goldberger, a Columbia University specialist in teaching English to non-English-speakers and one of Gouin's chief advocates in the United States, insisted, in a federal publication, that "the teacher must refrain from *using* the foreign language in teaching." In spite of the sympathy it might create between student and teacher, Goldberger claimed that "every time the teacher resorts to translation in making clear a word or a sentence, she is making it easier for herself at the expense of the pupil's progress," since the more "English the pupil hears and uses the sooner will he be able to speak."[30]

In 1930 the state of Texas developed a "special" English-Only curriculum for Mexican Americans. As a Texas Department of Education document put it:

> The teacher must keep in mind that she is to make English function in every activity of the day. . . . Drill, drill, and *more drill* is an absolute essential here. . . . Teach the children English by the direct method and not by translation of their language into the English. Train them to *think* in English. This is absolutely essential if they are to acquire any facility in the use of English.[31]

In a draconian application of English-Only practice, a representative of a school designated for Mexican migrants from a labor camp in southern California boasted in 1921 that his school imparted English that was most practical in the day-to-day life at the camp. He drew special reference to language related to the picking, sorting, and handling of southern California fruits and vegetables, an extreme illustration of the social-efficiency approach.[32]

The direct method of teaching English required much from its pupils. The total absence of the native language, it was argued, stimulated a fluent acquisition of English. Ideally under the direct method, students would not just learn to speak in English, they would also learn to "think" in English. The student's growth in his or her native language would be halted like an unwanted weed.[33] One proponent of English-Only explained that "the pupils will need to make a special effort to understand—an exertion which will expedite the process of learning the English language."[34] An English-Only proponent who taught in Puerto Rico illustrated vividly the daunting nature of this work, using the example of what should happen when a teacher greeted the children in the morning:

> She should not be disturbed if at first the children do nothing but look at her. She should *not* tell them in Spanish what *Good Morning* means. She simply repeats "Good Morning" each morning until the children hear the expression so many times that they begin to respond more or less unconsciously.[35]

In practice, the direct method of English-Only demanded almost as much from the instructor as from the pupil. Instructors used pantomime to illustrate the sequence of actions associated with a sentence involving action. Not surprisingly, some observers occasionally referred to the direct method as the "dramatic" or "action" method. The official English-Only curriculum for Texas described such action teaching: "[I]n teaching the action words the teacher first performs the act several times herself, at the same time telling what she does."[36] Adding to recommendations to act out a simple sentence or a sequence of action words, other pedagogical experts echoed the early advice of G. Stanley Hall by advocating the use of pictures or visual representations to help establish cognitive links between words and meanings.[37]

While the techniques of the direct English-Only pedagogy were meant to be as socially and personally relevant to the intended audience as possible, practitioners often fell short of this aim. The everyday practice of English-Only was a far cry from the insistence of some progressives on a child-centered curriculum based upon the individual student's needs. English-Only pedagogy and its practitioners confused the study of foreign languages in later grades with the study of English by non-English-speakers in the lower grades. Many argued that if the equivalent of English-Only worked for American students in high schools spending an hour a day learning French, then it should thus work for five- and six-year-old, non-English-speaking children attempting to learn English in the first grade. Such commentators quietly overlooked the fact that very few high school foreign-language teachers with classes of English-speakers used the direct method, because it was so challenging. One American teaching in China wrote of the tremendous success he had had in teaching English as a second language through the direct method to university-level Chinese students. Based on this success he urged the United States to uniformly adopt the pedagogy for its immigrants.[38]

Not all supporters of English-Only were entirely confident of its effectiveness. Henry Goldberger, one of the most important champions of English-Only, indicated that though the direct method was supported by impressive theory, it nevertheless lacked concrete evidence of its efficacy. Goldberger went on to remark that the debate between the indirect and direct method was moot because "for most teachers there is no difficulty in deciding the question because they know no foreign languages."[39] Had American educators decided that the indirect method was best, they would have had to identify capable teachers, but teachers from foreign ethnic groups were viewed with suspicion. Many believed that ethnic teachers lacked professional training and conduct, were insufficiently Americanized, were afflicted with inferiority complexes, were caste ridden, were religiously bigoted, and would overuse their native language, thus retarding the absorption of English-Only.[40] And historical reliance upon ethnic teachers had helped to create the need for Americanization in the first place. Hiring ethnic teachers to teach in the indirect, bilingual method of the past would have served to empower linguistic minorities and hindered attempts at teaching them their place in the social order. English-Only served as the best available means for Americanizing immigrants by existing educational personnel, who were themselves limited in language facility and in their attitudes and assumptions.

GROWTH AND DISSEMINATION OF ENGLISH-ONLY PEDAGOGY

English-Only was officially instituted by the United States among conquered peoples and minority groups on the margins of national life, before it spread to the major urban areas of the East Coast by World War I. Its first use was under government sanction in the territorial possessions of Puerto Rico and the Philippines, wrested from Spain in the aftermath of the Spanish-American War. The public school system in Puerto Rico was perhaps the most important pedagogical laboratory for language learning. English was made the primary language of instruction for all subjects shortly after the American occupation in 1898. As was demonstrated by the territory's repudiation of English-Only in favor of officially administered Spanish-English bilingual education during the 1930s and 1940s, the policy ultimately failed. The public schools of the Philippines also instituted an official English-Only policy after

having been occupied also in 1898. At the same time, reform-minded officials in charge of the education of Native Americans had begun using vague
English-Only methods. On the reservation, the enforcement of "no Indian"
language policies was achieved through various means, including physical
beatings. In the 1910s American educators in Hawaii went so far as to attempt to close down private after-school language institutes organized by
Japanese laborers, arguing that the extra instruction in Japanese taxed and
confused the minds of the Japanese American children and hampered their
ability to master English in the public schools.[41]

How best to deliver specialized language instruction to a changing population proved problematic to educators. Immigrant arrivals of various ages
were often grouped together in ungraded classrooms located in "steamer"
or "soup" schools, to learn enough English to advance to more standard
classrooms. In the public education system of New York City, experiments
in English-Only classes occurred as early as the passage of compulsory-
education and child labor legislation in 1903.[42] Non-English-speaking students were divided into different gradations of age and expectation: the
"special" language class, *Grade C*, was reserved for young students who knew
no English upon entering school; *Grade D* referred to those students who
had not finished elementary-level work and, nearing the age of fourteen, were
expected to soon leave school; *Grade E* consisted of older students with academic promise and previous education in another language, but, having arrived at an advanced age, needed intensive English instruction to enter the
upper grades to which they were otherwise academically qualified.

By the 1904–5 academic year, there were approximately 250 such graded
schools for language-minority children in New York City.[43] The most common type of immigrant language school provided by city education officials
was the C grade. One longtime champion of English-Only pedagogy re-
counted, "[T]hen the so-called 'C class' was formed for the sole purpose of
enabling pupils to attain a knowledge of English sufficient to understand what
was said and to express themselves so as to be understood." This particular
school administrator concluded that "language is the main subject, and spoken language receives the greater part of the time."[44]

New York City was not alone in this pedagogical triage. By 1901 the
city of Cleveland had organized a series of "steamer classes" in its public
schools so that immigrant children could be "given an opportunity to learn
the language before they are placed in a class of 40 or more other children
and expected to carry on regular grade work." Cleveland authorities said
that they used "a special educational technique for teaching a new language
which is far different in its methods from that employed in teaching subject
matter to pupils in their own language." This technique, the school officials
maintained, had been "amply demonstrated in the special classes of several

of our cities, notably New York and Boston, and still more strikingly illustrated in the schools of Porto [*sic*] Rico and the Philippines."[45] The "special educational technique" was, of course, English-Only pedagogy.

LANGUAGE POLICY AND WORLD WAR I

The exponential growth of English-Only during the 1910s was in part the result of a new set of fears, engendered by, among other things, the paranoia and hysteria surrounding World War I. During the war, English was elevated to a mythic, sacrosanct status by school officials who sought to immunize immigrants against alleged disloyalty and subversiveness. It was important to succeed in teaching English because "the only sound basis for true Americanism rests upon a workable knowledge of English and a true understanding of our institutions."[46] The teaching of foreign languages—especially German—was critiqued as well. In pointing out the need for the schools to teach Spanish instead of the now-tainted German language, linguist Lawrence Wilkins argued that "the study of German, because of the cumbersome and awkward word order of the language, made for indirectness rather than directness in English expression." German "was fast becoming the second language of our nation," Wilkins feared, and he personally believed that it was taught "chiefly for the purposes of furthering propaganda originating in Berlin."[47]

The foreign-language-as-sedition rhetoric of the language pedagogues paled in comparison to that articulated by the federal government. President Woodrow Wilson actively sought to dissociate himself from American ethnic groups and their languages. In 1915, he discussed with his cabinet the possibility of using federal power to outlaw the teaching of German throughout the country. Wilson expressed his fear of ethnicity in a speech, saying that "any man who carries a hyphen about with him carries a dagger that he is ready to plunge into the vitals of this Republic."[48] In his role as national director of Americanization, Fred Clayton Butler linked concern with the potential for economic radicalism to alleged German-American complicity with the Kaiser's war effort.[49] One army psychologist furthered this paranoia by writing that "school and society had done little to prepare the minds of these ignorant and unintelligent laborers to withstand the pernicious doctrines that were being preached by the radical, the soap box orator, and the unscrupulous agitator." The officer then went on to identify such public enemies as the "I.W.W., the Anarchists and the Bolsheviki."[50]

Capitalizing upon the shrill public mood, the Wilson war effort indirectly succeeded in banning the teaching of German and other foreign languages in American public schools, particularly in the primary grades. Alleging potential subversiveness from America's immigrant children, the federal government worked hard to encourage individual states to outlaw any native language instruction for non-English-speakers and to replace it with the direct method of English-Only. Butler's official instruction manual directed that "state laws should be provided, if necessary, making English the primary language of the schools of the State, both public and private." Further, "All of the subjects of the school should be taught in English, and the school itself should be conducted in English in order that the future citizens of America may learn not only to talk but to think in the language of this land."[51]

Butler's appeal to state legislatures was remarkably effective. Between 1918 and 1919 twenty-four states either created or strengthened previously existing laws pertaining to the institutionalization of English-Only pedagogy and the criminalization of any form of bilingual instruction.[52] In Texas, for example, the state superintendent of public instruction during World War I, Annie Webb Blanton, published a fictional conversation with a non-English-speaking immigrant. "If you desire to be one with us, stay, and we welcome you; but if you wish to preserve, in our state, the language and customs of another land, you have no right to do this," Blanton said to the immigrant, advising this individual to "go back to the country which you prize so highly and rear your children there."[53]

In the war years as states rushed to heed the federal government's call to Americanize immigrants through English-Only instruction, some proponents pushed policy beyond the limits set by the Constitution. The state of Nebraska, for example, enacted an English-Only law that regulated classroom language in its public and private schools so stringently that the law was declared unconstitutional in 1924 by the United States Supreme Court. The Court, while clearly sympathizing with the state's desire to enforce assimilation in the public schools, nevertheless found the law too restrictive for private education. While the Court preserved bilingual education in the private educational sphere, it did not extend this protection to Nebraska's public schools.[54] English-Only instruction for non-English-speaking children in public schools across the nation persisted until the passage of the Bilingual Education Act in the late 1960s.

CONSEQUENCES OF ENGLISH-ONLY DOMINANCE

While English-Only pedagogy was the dominant instructional approach for teaching non-English-speaking children English between 1900 and 1930, it demonstrated an abysmal track record. Yet such failure was neither unexpected, nor deemed an argument for its dismissal or reform. Rather, the pedagogy's widespread failure lowered educational expectations for immigrant children and lent support to the notion that pedagogical segregation was a natural if not positive result of Americanization. Children in English-Only classrooms were simply not expected to thrive educationally. Educators made it plain that spoken English was the only objective; it took precedence over such other subjects as reading, mathematics, and science. Commenting on this limited curriculum, the language expert Goldberger perhaps best captured the prevailing ideology when he remarked that "since the problem with most foreign-born people in America is to train them to speak rather than to read or to write, the direct method is advocated."[55] To make matters worse for language-minority children and more efficient for progressives seeking to educate by the "natural" order, intelligence testing was widely used to further justify pedagogical segregation of linguistic minorities such as Mexican Americans.[56]

English-Only pedagogy institutionalized and rationalized academic failure. A New York City school principal estimated in 1903 that his Gouin-inspired English-Only method devoted the first two years of the child's total academic work to teaching five hundred to six hundred English vocabulary words. He estimated that native-English-speaking children arrived with an equivalent vocabulary upon entrance to first grade. In other words, it took immigrant schoolchildren two full years to get to the point at which they could cope with first-grade-level work in the English language.[57] One researcher noted that in Louisiana, English-Only instruction resulted in poor promotion rates, which helped support the researcher's assumption that all of the state's native-born French-speakers in the early grades automatically needed at least two years to complete the first grade.[58] A teacher wrote of her school's curricular practices regarding Mexican Americans in south Texas in 1934 and remarked that a quarter of the first-grade-age population usually obtained first-grade status after one year of "special" language instruction, and that half eventually reached the first grade in two years. The remaining quarter, she observed, were "nearly a total loss."[59]

ENGLISH-ONLY ENABLES SEGREGATION

The pedagogical approach used by the young Lyndon Johnson in Cotulla in 1928 was intimately bound up with the segregation of his students. English-Only justified pedagogical segregation for ethnic children, regardless of citizenship status, and on the sole basis of linguistic heritage. By 1930, the legal linchpin segregating Mexican Americans in the public schools of Texas revolved around the pedagogical need for special instruction, the kind provided by English-Only classrooms and taught by highly trained professionals using the latest techniques.[60]

The same legal rationale was used in California and other parts of the Southwest. Feeling that English-Only worked best in the strictly segregated primary school environment in a Southern California migrant camp, one specialist echoed Gouin's arguments that children best learned languages naturally and informally, in this case while in the schoolyard playing with other non-English-speaking children.[61] In reality, this was de facto racial segregation. The pedagogy of English-Only continued to serve as the key legal justification for pedagogical segregation in the public schools until it was successfully challenged in the federal courts during the 1940s and 1950s.[62]

Children of European immigrants were also segregated by pedagogy. In New York City, educators understood the connection between English-Only pedagogy and ethnic segregation as early as the 1900s. Segregation could last a few months for the very bright children who handled languages well. But it could last up to several years for children who were of more average linguistic abilities. The mandates for English-Only instruction in the urban Northeast varied in the degree and type of pedagogical segregation, but even without such mandates, large school systems could still effectively segregate white, immigrant children by means of standardized testing, tracking, and the creation of "special" curricula.

Sometimes the basis for such "special" instruction emerged from the Americanization curriculum without the English-Only component. Although segregation for European immigrants in the Northeast was less rigid or long lasting than that for Mexican Americans in the Southwest, English-Only instruction still played a significant role in the segregatory practices. In expecting failure from such a large percentage of its charges, and in believing that the purpose of education was to train children for their eventual place in society, many progressive educators betrayed their commitment to centering on the individual child and her or his own needs and abilities. For progressives, English-Only was the scientifically validated method, whether it worked or not.[63]

THE DECLINE OF ENGLISH-ONLY

After decades of English-Only instruction, it is ironic that it took the events of World War II to make the federal government and linguists realize that the nation's ineptitude with foreign languages was a serious wartime liability. This recognition prompted a movement to teach foreign languages in the elementary schools, and the federal government began supporting foreign-language study in cities such as Cleveland, New York, San Diego, Los Angeles, and El Paso. While in the previous world war educators eliminated training in foreign languages, by World War II bilingualism enjoyed a brief resurgence. But it was not until the 1960s that scientific advances in language-learning theory and child psychology demolished much of the old Gouin-inspired English-Only pedagogy, resulting in the rise of the modern bilingual-education movement. While the science of modern bilingual education is still subject to heated debate, historians and social commentators have ignored or forgotten the old English-Only pedagogy and its scientific rationale.[64]

As a system of instruction, English-Only pedagogy—despite its pervasiveness in the first half of the twentieth century—was never the one obvious method of choice for educating American immigrants and other non-English-speaking groups in the United States. Although linguistic unification has been a dream of nationalists since the days of the early republic, foreign languages were tolerated and even encouraged throughout the nineteenth and early twentieth centuries in schools in the United States. A Progressive Era invention, English-Only pedagogy was a conflation of legitimate if flawed language theory, political ideology, and desperation on the part of school experts.

Champions of the direct method of English-Only pedagogy advocated its implementation for seemingly contradictory purposes. They believed in the democratic ideal of a system of mass public education while simultaneously believing that most of the children in such a system were hardly educable. The modern bilingual-education movement of the late 1960s and 1970s is more rooted in the historical patterns of implicit multiculturalism, democratic tolerance, and local flexibility found in American education's nineteenth-century past than is the twentieth-century invention of English-Only pedagogy.

This does not mean that English-Only did not work for children with good, caring teachers. For example, according to interviews given by his former Cotulla students, Lyndon Johnson was a flexible practitioner of English-Only and made a positive difference in the lives of his students. As nativist, racist, and ultimately demeaning as English-Only pedagogy was for his students, *Johnson* was not so. It is equally important to understand, however, that most teachers were not Lyndon Johnson, and that the social attitudes embedded in the instructional approach were often reflected in the daily educational experience of non-English-speaking children.

In this chapter I make no attempt to evaluate current practices in bilingual education or the efficacy or degree of sophistication of any one of the many aspects of the American bilingual tradition. The history of bilingual education in United States history is a complicated phenomenon and does not lend itself to easy characterization. It raises as many questions as the answers it offers. English-Only instruction emerged out of the myth of the great American melting pot. Proponents of the myth held that English-Only was the scientifically correct method of instruction for non-English-speaking children. The pedagogy of English-Only is the point of rupture in an otherwise unbroken continuity of liberal, local, and inherently American traditions of bilingual schooling. When experts are called upon to comment on the recent wave of English-Only legislation, one might hope that they will be mindful of its troubled history.

NOTES

1. Carlos Kevin Blanton, *The Strange Career of Bilingual Education in Texas, 1836–1981* (College Station: Texas A&M University Press, 2004), 132–33; Robert Dallek, *Lone Star Rising: Lyndon Johnson and His Times, 1908–1960* (New York: Oxford University Press, 1991), 79; and Gene B. Preuss, "Cotulla Revisited: A Reassessment of Lyndon Johnson's Year as a Public School Teacher," *Journal of South Texas* 10 (1997): 28–29.

2. The most thorough and systematic attempt to historicize America's bilingual past remains Heinz Kloss, *The American Bilingual Tradition* (Rowley, MA: Newbury House Press, 1977). See also Steven L. Schlossman, "Is There an American Tradition of Bilingual Education? German in the Public Elementary Schools, 1840–1919," *American Journal of Education* 91 (February 1983): 139–86; and Shirley Brice Heath, "English in Our National Heritage," in *Language in the USA*, ed. Charles A. Ferguson and Shirley Brice Heath (New York: Cambridge University Press, 1981), 6–20.

3. Jill Lepore, *"A" is for American: Letters and Other Characters in the Newly United States* (New York: Alfred A. Knopf, 2002), 29.

4. Colman Brez Stein, Jr., *Sink or Swim: The Politics of Bilingual Education* (New York: Praeger, 1986), 2.

5. James Crawford, *Hold Your Tongue: Bilingualism and the Politics of "English-Only"* (Reading, MA: Addison-Wesley, 1992), chap. 2; Judith Lessow-Hurley, *The Foundations of Dual Language Instruction*, 2nd ed. (New York: Longman, 1996), 71–73.

6. Among recent works that have revived interest in English-Only, see Guadalupe San Miguel, Jr., *"Let All of Them Take Heed": Mexican Americans and the Campaign for Educational Equality in Texas, 1910–1981* (Austin: University of Texas Press, 1987); and Eileen Tamura, *Americanization, Acculturation, and Ethnic Identity: The Nisei Generation in Hawaii* (Urbana: University of Illinois Press, 1994).

7. Lawrence A. Cremin, *The Transformation of the School: Progressivism in American Education, 1876–1967* (New York: Knopf, 1961; reprint, New York: Vintage Books, 1964), 72.

8. Sol Cohen, *Progressives and Urban School Reform: The Public Education Association of New York City, 1895–1954* (New York: Bureau of Publications, Teachers College, Columbia University, 1964), 68.

9. David B. Tyack, *The One Best System: A History of American Urban Education* (Cambridge, MA: Harvard University Press, 1974), 230.

10. Robert Wiebe, *The Search for Order, 1877–1920* (New York: Hill & Wang, 1967).

11. Ellwood P. Cubberley, *Changing Conceptions of Education* (Boston: Houghton Mifflin, 1909), 15.

12. Herbert M. Kliebard, *The Struggle for the American Curriculum, 1893–1958* (New York: Routledge, 1986).

13. J. Christopher Eisele, "John Dewey and the Immigrants," *History of Education Quarterly* 15 (Spring 1975): 71–73; John Dewey, *Democracy and Education* (New York: Macmillan, 1916; New York: Free Press, 1966), 21–22; and Jane Addams, "The Public School and the Immigrant Child," in *National Education Association, Journal of Proceedings and Addresses of the Forty-fifth Annual Meeting Held in Cleveland, Ohio, June 29–July 3, 1908* (Winona: National Education Association, 1908): 99–102.

14. Cubberley, *Changing Conceptions of Education*, 15; Emory S. Bogardus, *Essentials of Americanization* (Los Angeles: University of Southern California Press, 1920), 13–14.

15. Frederick Eby and Charles Flinn Arrowood, *The History and Philosophy of Education Ancient and Medieval* (New York: Prentice-Hall, 1940), 832.

16. Charles Hart Handschin, *The Teaching of Modern Languages in the United States*, United States Department of the Interior, Bureau of Education Bulletin, 1913, no. 3 (Washington, DC: GPO, 1913), 94.

17. Mary R. Alling-Aber, *An Experiment in Education. Also the Ideas Which Inspired It and Were Inspired by It* (New York: Harper & Brothers, 1897), 159.

18. Henry H. Goldberger, *Teaching English to the Foreign Born*, United States Department of the Interior, Bureau of Education Bulletin, 1919, no. 80 (Washington, DC: GPO, 1920): 15.

19. Handschin, *Teaching of Modern Languages*, 95.

20. Bogardus, *Essentials of Americanization*, 283.

21. G. Stanley Hall, "The Ideal School as Based on Child Study," *The Forum* 32 (September 1901): 29–30.

22. Eugene Weber, *Peasants into Frenchmen: The Modernization of Rural France, 1870–1914* (Stanford: Stanford University Press, 1976), 67–72.

23. François Gouin, *The Art of Teaching and Studying Languages*, 9th ed., trans. Howard Swan and Victor Betis (New York: Longmans, Green, 1919), 10–34.

24. Handschin, *Teaching of Modern Languages*, 97–100.

25. Frank V. Thompson, "Schooling of the Immigrant," in *Americanization Studies: The Acculturation of Immigrant Groups into American Society*. Patterson Smith Reprint Series in Criminology, Law Enforcement, and Social Problems, vol. 1, ed. William S. Bernard (New York: Harper and Brothers, 1920; reprint, Montclair, NJ: Patterson Smith, 1971), 188, 189.

26. Thompson, "Schooling of the Immigrant," 188.

27. Steven G. Darian, *English as a Foreign Language: History, Development, and Methods of Teaching* (Norman: University of Oklahoma Press, 1972), 50–65.

28. Grace Abbott, *The Immigrant and the Community* (New York: Century, 1917), 230.

29. Herbert Adolphus Miller, *The School and the Immigrant. The Cleveland Educational Survey* (Cleveland: Survey Committee of the Cleveland Foundation, 1916), 57.

30. Goldberger, *Teaching English to the Foreign Born*, 14; emphasis in the original.

31. S. M. N. Marrs, Thomas J. Yoe, and M. Perrie Wygal, *A Course in English for Non-English-Speaking Pupils, Grades I–III*, Bulletin no. 268 (Austin: Texas State Department of Education, 1930), 19 and 33; emphases in the original.

32. George B. Hodgkin, "Americanization in a Labor Camp," *School and Society* 14 (26 November 1921): 492–94.

33. Thompson, "Schooling of the Immigrant," 205.

34. Bogardus, *Essentials of Americanization*, 283.

35. Maude Owens Walters, *The Teaching of English in the Primary Grades of Puerto Rico: A Course of Study and Teachers Manual*, University of Puerto Rico, College of Education Publications, no. 12, Bulletin no. 4 (Rio Piedras, Puerto Rico: University of Puerto Rico, Department of Elementary Education, 1935), 17; emphasis in the original.

36. Marrs, Yoe, and Wygal, *A Course in English*, 20.

37. John J. Mahoney, *Training Teachers for Americanization: A Course Study for Normal Schools and Teachers' Institutes*, United States Department of the Interior, Bureau of Education, Bulletin, 1920, no. 12 (Washington, DC: GPO, 1920), 46.

38. Henry Lee Hargrove, "An Experience in Teaching English in China by the Direct Method," *Peabody Journal of Education* 1 (July 1923): 56.

39. Goldberger, *Teaching English to the Foreign Born*, 14.

40. Pauline Young, "Social Problems in the Education of the Immigrant Child," *American Sociological Review* 1 (June 1936): 424; David Tyack, *The One Best System* (Cambridge: Harvard University Press, 1974), 104, 233–34.

41. Paul G. Miller, "Education in Porto [sic] Rico," *Education in the Territories and Dependencies*, Department of the Interior, Bureau of Education, Bulletin, 1919, no. 12 (Washington, DC: GPO, 1919), 8–9; Nancy Morris, *Puerto Rico: Culture, Politics, and Identity* (Westport, CT: Praeger, 1995), 29–30; and Melvin C. Resnick, "ESL and Language Planning in Puerto Rican Education," *TESOL Quarterly* 27 (Summer 1993): 262–63. Bonifacio P. Sibayan, "The Implementation of Language Policy," in *The Determination and Implementation of Language Policy*, ed. Maximo Ramos, Jose V. Aguilar, and Bonifacio P. Sibayan, Philippine Center for Language Study, no. 2 (Quezon City, Philippines: Oceana, 1967), 127. David Wallace Adams, *Education for Extinction: American Indians and the Boarding School Experience, 1875–1928* (Lawrence: University Press of Kansas, 1995), 140–41. Frank F. Bunker, *A Survey of Education in Hawaii*, Department of the Interior, Bureau of Education, Bulletin, 1920, no. 16 (Washington, DC: GPO, 1920), 127–33; and Eileen H. Tamura, "The English-Only Effort, the Anti-Japanese Campaign, and Language Acquisition in the Education of Japanese Americans in Hawaii, 1915–40," *History of Education Quarterly* 33 (Spring 1993): 37–58.

42. Julia Richman, "What Can Be Done in the Graded School for the Backward Child," *The Survey* 13 (September 1904): 129–30.

43. Francesco Cordasco, "The Children of Immigrants in the Schools: Historical Analogues of Educational Deprivation," *The Journal of Negro Education* 47 (Winter 1973): 50–51.

44. John H. Haaren, "Education of the Immigrant Child," in *Education of the Immigrant: Abstracts of Papers Read at a Public Conference Under the Auspices of the New York–New Jersey Committee of the North American Civic League for Immigrants*, ed. P. P. Claxton. United States Department of Interior, Bureau of Education, Bulletin, 1913, no. 51 (Washington, DC: GPO, 1913), 20, 21.

45. Miller, *The School and the Immigrant*, 72–73, 76.

46. Charles F. Towne, "The Organization of Lessons in English for Americanization Classes," *School and Society* 12 (September 11, 1920): 186.

47. Lawrence A. Wilkins, "Spanish as a Substitute for German for Training and Culture," *Hispania* 1 (December 1918): 206, 208; emphasis added.

48. Ernest R. May, *The World War and American Isolationism, 1914–1917* (Cambridge, MA: Harvard University Press, 1959), 345; and Sarah Deutsch, *No Separate Refuge: Culture, Class, and Gender on an Anglo-Hispanic Frontier in the American Southwest, 1880–1940* (New York: Oxford University Press, 1987), 111.

49. Fred Clayton Butler, *Community Americanization: A Handbook for Workers*, United States Department of the Interior, Bureau of Education, Bulletin, 1919, no. 76 (Washington, DC: GPO, 1920), 17.

50. Charles Scott Berry, "Some Problems of Americanization as Seen by an Army Psychologist," *School and Society* 13 (22 January, 1921): 101.

51. Fred Clayton Butler, *State Americanization: The Part of the State in the Education and Assimilation of the Immigrant*, United States Department of the Interior, Bureau of Education, Bulletin, 1919, no. 70 (Washington, DC: GPO, 1920), 24.

52. William R. Hood, *State Laws Relating to Education Enacted in 1918 and 1919*, United States Department of the Interior, Bureau of Education, Bulletin, 1920, no. 30 (Washington, DC: GPO, 1921), 149–51.

53. Annie Webb Blanton, *A Hand Book of Information as to Education in Texas, 1918–1922 Bulletin* 157 (Austin: Texas State Department of Education, 1923), 23.

54. "Robert T. Meyer, Plff. in Err. v. State of Nebraska," in *American Law Reports, Annotated*, vol. 29, ed. Burdett A. Rich and M. Blair Whailes (Rochester, IN: Lawyers Co-Operative, 1924), 1450–51. See also Paul Finkelman, "German Victims and American Oppressors: The Cultural Background and Legacy of *Meyer v. Nebraska*," in *Law and the Great Plains: Essays on the Legal History of the Heartland*, ed. John R. Wunder (Westport, CT: Greenwood Press, 1996), 33–56.

55. Goldberger, *Teaching English to the Foreign Born*, 14.

56. See Carlos Kevin Blanton, "From Intellectual Deficiency to Cultural Deficiency: Mexican Americans, Testing, and Public School Policy in the American Southwest, 1920–1940," *Pacific Historical Review* 72 (February 2003): 39–62.

57. Joseph H. Wade, "The Teaching of English to Foreigners in the First Two Years of Elementary Schools," *School Work* 2 (November 1903): 291–92.

58. John E. Coxe, "A Study of Grade Repetition in the Elementary Schools of Louisiana," *Peabody Journal of Education* 5 (July 1927): 42.

59. J. T. Taylor, "Americanization of Harlingen's Mexican School Population," *Texas Outlook* 18 (September 1934): 38.

60. *Inhabitants of Del Rio Independent School District v. Jesus Salvatierra*, 33 S.W. 2d Series 790 (Texas Civil Appeals, 1930), 790–96.

61. J. L. Merriam, "Play and the English Language for Foreign Children," *Journal of Educational Sociology* 4 (June 1931): 130.

62. San Miguel, *"Let All of Them Take Heed"*; and Blanton, *Strange Career of Bilingual Education*.

63. Leonard Covello, *The Heart is the Teacher* (Totowa, NJ: Littlefield, Adams, 1970), 22–27. See also Cordasco, "Children of Immigrants in the Schools," 44–53; Young, "Social Problems in the Education of the Immigrant Child," 423; Joseph L. Tropea, "Bureaucratic Order and Special Children: Urban Schools, 1890s-1940s," *History of Education Quarterly* 27 (Spring 1987): 29–53; Paul Davis Chapman, *Schools as Sorters: Lewis M. Terman, Applied Psychology, and the Intelligence Movement, 1890–1930* (New York: New York University Press, 1988); and Selma Berrol, "Immigrants at School: New York City, 1900–1910," *Urban Education* 4 (October 1969): 223.

64. See Theodore Andersson, *Foreign Languages in the Elementary School: A Struggle Against Mediocrity* (Austin: University of Texas Press, 1969); Blanton, *Strange Career of Bilingual Education*; and Elliot L. Judd, "Factors Affecting the Passage of the Bilingual Education Act of 1967" (PhD diss., New York University, 1977), 26–32.

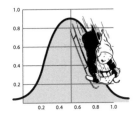

Raising "Precocious" Children: From Nineteenth-Century Pathology to Twentieth-Century Potential

Roblyn Rawlins

WINIFRED SACKVILLE STONER, JR., could both read and write by the time she was three. At the age of six, she published her first poetry and by age eight was conversant in five languages. Seeing her daughter's precocity as a personal triumph, in 1916 Mrs. Stoner wrote a guide explaining her child-rearing methods. Mrs. Stoner was ahead of her time; her book helped propel a shift in how parents and society viewed precocious children.[1]

In the United States, the scientific understanding and social meaning of early intellectual development in children changed from being a worrisome problem for nineteenth and early twentieth century parents to being an exciting challenge for parents after the 1930s. Late nineteenth- and early twentieth-century child-rearing experts warned parents against encouraging or allowing their children to undertake mental effort lest they suffer physical or psychological damage. Parents were advised to employ child-rearing and educational practices that would delay the precocious child's engagement in mental activities, such as regulating study hours and discouraging early reading. In contrast, mid- to late twentieth-century parents of children who exhibited early intellectual development were encouraged to vigorously pursue child-rearing and educational practices through which the gifted child could reach her or his full potential, including enrichment, acceleration, and other forms of enhanced learning opportunities. In the mid-nineteenth century, an advice-giver warned parents, "There is also a great mistake committed by hot-bed efforts to stimulate the minds of children to precocious maturity. . . . [T]heir bodily powers are soon exhausted; they become diseased and nervous; their brain is liable to inflammation, and a premature death often ensues!" But by the mid-twentieth century an expert warned, "By this refusal to recognize special gifts, we have wasted and dissipated, driven into apathy or schizophrenia, uncounted numbers of gifted children."[2] How and why was early intellectual development in children reconstructed from nineteenth-century views of precocity-as-pathology, to twentieth-century notions of giftedness-as-potential?

The scientific discourses constructing and reconstructing early intellectual development in children include those of adult genius, mental hygiene, developmental psychology, eugenics, giftedness, and intelligence. Late nineteenth- and early twentieth-century scientific conceptualizations of adult genius, childhood development, and mind-body relations, when combined with elements of American middle-class culture calling for protected childhood, constructed precocity as pathological. The transformation of early intellectual development in children from nineteenth-century pathology to twentieth-century potential hinged to a large extent on changing scientific accounts of intelligence and the measurement of children through the institutionalization of intelligence testing. Emerging experts on and advocates for the new social category of *gifted children* were able to use scientifically authenticated knowledge to successfully change public and parental opinion regarding early intellectual development in children.

CONSTRUCTING PRECOCITY-AS-PATHOLOGY

In colonial America, early intellectual development in children was not viewed as pathological or problematic. Fathers were encouraged to teach Scripture to infants and young children. In the 1820s, schools for infants as young as eighteen months were founded in Boston by social reformers. But public enthusiasm for early education soon waned; by the end of the 1830s, the Boston infant schools were closed.[3] Beginning in the mid-nineteenth century, newspapers, magazines, and the newly proliferating child-rearing advice literature devoted much space to the problems of precocious children. Child-rearing advice books often included a lengthy treatment of the problems and pathologies of the precocious child or infant. In child-rearing advice and the scientific literature, the precocious child was represented as vulnerable to a range of problems: self-consciousness with an accompanying loss of the simplicity and naturalness attributed to proper childhood; physical weakness, disease, and decline; overstimulation and depletion of mental and nervous energy, sometimes to the point of insanity; and finally, the specter of death as the result of the depletion of bodily and mental strength. Parents were urged to protect their children from these dangers through limiting the child's engagement in mental activities.

The bases of this construction of precocity as pathology included romantic and sentimental formulations of childhood and children in combination with concepts adopted from the scientific fields of genius, childhood development, and mind-body relations. Discourses of gender—specifically those of masculinity—that connected intelligence with feebleness and concerns with feminization of American boys also contributed to pathological precocity, as did social anxieties over racial degeneration.

SCIENTIFIC BASES OF PATHOLOGICAL PRECOCITY

Adult Genius

Scientific understandings of the nature of adult genius contributed to the construction of pathological precocity. Cesare Lombroso, whose theories about criminals were popular among American reformers in the late nineteenth and early twentieth centuries, argued that "genius was a true degenerative psychosis." Nineteenth-century alienists tended to view genius, insanity, and idiocy as equally abnormal and, often, as interchangeable. "Originality of thought and quickness or preponderance of the intellectual faculties are organically much the same thing as madness and idiocy" was the thesis of John Nisbet's *The Insanity of Genius*, which popularized Lombroso's theories in the U.S. Amariah Brigham's *Remarks on the Influence of Mental Cultivation and Mental Excitement upon Health*, originally published in Boston in 1833 and reprinted in the 1880s, greatly influenced American attitudes about precocity, insanity and pathology: Brigham stated that precocity was itself a disease.[4]

Prescriptive Developmentalism

American psychologist G. Stanley Hall's child study movement and German educator Friedrich Froebel's educational system (implemented as the kindergarten) were among the major scientific projects on children of the period. Hall's and Froebel's accounts of childhood, as well as Johann Heinrich Pestalozzi's earlier (and quite influential) educational scheme, gave scientific credence to concerns about pathologically precocious children. Hall and Froebel sought to discover natural laws of childhood development and urged that these developmental processes be allowed to proceed without adult intervention. Hall's theory of evolutionary recapitulation, which posited that the individual child developed through stages equivalent to those of the evolution of the race, meant that children must be protected from the demands of modern adult life while in their "premodern" stages. Froebel's gifts and songs (simple playthings presented in an age-graded fashion) were based upon the notion that children must learn and develop according to the rules of childhood, not those of adults. Hall in particular was explicit about hoping to "find true norms against the tendencies to precocity in home, school, church, and civilization generally."[5]

The prescriptive developmentalism of child study, child development, and progressive educational theories provided a scientific rationale for the age grading that increasingly shaped American children's lives in the late nineteenth and early twentieth centuries. Perceptions of intellectual precocity were related to changing practices regarding age grading in the schools. Prior to the 1870s, American students were likely to start school at different ages and to attend irregularly. As a result, the age of a child poorly predicted her or his level of academic skills or knowledge. By the 1870s, formally structured age-graded schools were established throughout most of the United States. According to Howard Chudacoff, the practice of formal age-grading in schools "eliminated incidences and tolerance of precocity," as the formal structure of such schools made it more difficult for children to enter elementary school, secondary school, or college before they had reached the institutionally stipulated ages.[6]

Model of Bodily Economy

Widely held ideas about the physical consequences of mental activity underpinned the view that precocity was dangerous for children. Medical authorities working in the field of mental hygiene warned of the dangers of overworked brains, American nervousness, and neurasthenia, synonymous disorders caused by overstimulation of the brain or nervous system at the expense of physical well-being. A model of bodily economy articulated in the discourse of mental hygiene provided a basis for the perceived dangers of early intellectual development. The bodily-economy model assumed that individuals possessed a finite amount of physical, mental, and emotional energy and that any expenditure of one type of energy necessitated a drawdown in the other two. A harmonious relationship between the intellect, the emotions, and the body was therefore imperative. This model was the predominant approach to early intellectual development in the writings of turn-of-the-century medical and psychological experts. As Newton Riddell put it, for example, "Precocious children exhaust the vital forces through the brain, with the result that the body fails to develop as it should." Precocity in these formulations implied a pathologically unbalanced development of intellectual, physical, and emotional capabilities. Bernard Hollander presented dozens of photographs demonstrating the unbalanced development of precocious children with relatively large heads and smaller bodies.[7]

Child-rearing experts drew upon physicians and, to a lesser extent, psychologists as they translated the concept of bodily economy into prescriptions for the care of children. Carrica LeFavre summarized the model in her advice manual by stating that "[t]he vital energies pertaining to the body, and generated in the organism, by which this growth and development are affected, are absolutely limited." As the "same forces" could not "be employed at the same time for two distinct ends," early intellectual development thus posed direct dangers to children's emotional and physical well-being.[8]

The eugenics-based discourse also played a role in developing the precocity-as-pathology theory. Focused in the United States primarily on the preservation of the race through the improvement of maternal and child health, eugenics contributed to the condemnation of intellectual precocity directly through fears of damaging children's reproductive capability and indirectly through fears of damaging their health. The bodily-economy model suggested that overstudy was particularly dangerous to reproductive capabilities for girls and for youths in puberty. Eugenicists sought to protect the race by protecting the fertility of white, middle-class children. For example, Mrs. E. G. Cook wrote that overstudy was particularly to be avoided between the ages of twelve to sixteen years.[9]

In light of turn-of-the-century concerns about the feminization of boys and degeneration of the race, potential enfeeblement of children's bodies provoked much concern among child-rearing experts. Parents were urged to strive for the equal development of their child's body and brain via exercise, fresh air, and avoidance of too much or too strenuous intellectual work. For ordinary, nonprecocious children, it was thought that physical problems related to overstudy were unlikely if the child took sufficient exercise. Some child-rearing experts went so far as to suggest that if children exhibited tendencies toward precociousness, parents should delay teaching them to read or otherwise retard their intellectual development in order to encourage their physical development. For example, Mrs. P. B. Sauer, a physician, advised, "It behooves a parent, if her son is precocious, to restrain him" by sending him to a quiet country place, delaying his entrance to school, and giving "directions to the teacher that he is not on any account to tax his intellect."[10]

CULTURAL AND SOCIAL BASES OF PATHOLOGICAL PRECOCITY

Sentimental Culture

Nineteenth- and early twentieth-century scientific accounts of precocity-as-pathology resonated with popular conceptions of children and childhood derived from sentimental culture. The concept of a natural childhood, first articulated in romantic accounts of childhood, was a key element in the development of a sentimental view of children and of childhood. Romantics viewed the child as not only distinct from adults but also in some ways superior: children were seen as messengers from the divine and as beings who were fresh, innocent, simple, and natural, qualities that seemed to some adults sorely missing in the contemporary adult world. In these sentimental formulations, childhood was constructed as a space in which qualities of nature could be preserved and protected from urbanization and industrialization. Romantic child-rearing prescriptions from Jean-Jacques Rousseau's didactic novel *Emile* onward posited that adult subversion of the ways of nature led to poor outcomes in child rearing and that children should be allowed to develop at their own pace in an environment suited to childhood.[11]

Protecting Children from Precocity

The urban, native-born, rising middle classes made up the audience for the prescriptive literature that depicted early intellectual development as pathological and urged parents to protect their children from the dangers of precocity. Child-rearing advice books were explicitly addressed to the middle classes and produced by middle-class experts carving out new areas of professional jurisdiction for themselves. Yet while condemnation of precocity was the dominant approach to early intellectual development in children, middle-class parents tended to valorize their children's accomplishments and strategies to consolidate or improve family class position, including encouraging the intellectual development of children, especially boys.[12]

   This seeming contradiction resulted from the ways in which intellectual precocity encoded other types of precocious sexual, economic, and social behavior. Late nineteenth- and early twentieth-century white middle-class families in America sought to assert their social distinction and moral superiority by protecting their children from the dangers posed by all forms of precocious behavior. Intellectual precocity, along with the more familiar troublesome nineteenth-century precocities (working children, masturbating children), became a boundary mark along which the newly emerging and consolidating middle classes created a category of distinction sufficient to separate "good" middle class from "bad" working-class/poor children and childhoods.

   As a dependent childhood became normative for the middle classes and scientific theories of child development became popular, children engaging in what were considered exclusively adult economic, sexual, or social behaviors came to be seen as precocious and abnormal. Social reformers sought to enforce this definition of childhood by legislating age-based rules for leaving school, working, and consenting to sexual relations, as well as by empowering juvenile courts to impose sanctions on premature independence. By the end of the Progressive Era, precocious children who failed to conform to the ideal of dependent childhood were considered deviant; pathological; and, sometimes, criminal. Intellectual precocity was condemned in these middle-class formulations because it was conflated with other types of precocity—economic, sexual, and social—that were the focus of late nineteenth-century and Progressive Era child-saving efforts.[13]

THE EMERGENCE OF THE GIFTED CHILD

As Leslie Margolin explains in his fine study of giftedness, the social category of *gifted children*, symbolizing virtue and health, emerged in the first few decades of the twentieth century together with the gifted-child expert.[14] The dominant image of the child who exhibits early intellectual development would henceforth be that of a child gifted with superior intellectual, physical, and emotional characteristics, one whose tremendous potential required thoughtful effort from parents and educators to ensure the realization of this potential. This transformation of pathological precocity to giftedness hinged to a large extent on the measurement of children through intelligence testing.

The first three decades of the twentieth century mark a point of transition in child-rearing advice regarding early intellectual development: experts began to articulate a "bright," "superior," or "gifted" child whose early intellectual development was to be encouraged and celebrated. The earliest use of the term *gifted child* appears to be in J. H. Van Sickle's "Provision for Gifted Children in Public Schools," published in *Elementary School Teacher* in 1910.[15] By 1946, the American Association for Gifted Children was formed to advocate for the special needs of gifted children and to offer informational resources and advice to families seeking to learn more about the child-rearing and educational practices they should adopt for their gifted child.

The topic of precocious and gifted children received much attention in the American print media of the twentieth century. As Michael V. O'Shea noted in 1914, "During the last three or four years, the newspapers and magazines of the country have given much space to the discussion of a group of so-called precocious children." Margolin confirms an increased incidence of stories about child prodigies in American media in the early twentieth century. An advice book published in 1958 contained a suggested reading list for parents that included fifty books on gifted children.[16]

Between the 1870s and the 1930s, as Viviana Zelizer has demonstrated, sentimental culture reconstructed middle-class children into "sacrilized" objects with no legitimate economic value but with immense sentimental value, thus rendering them both economically worthless and emotionally priceless. The metaphoric language of the market—as in the bodily-economy model—was applied to the priceless middle-class child and, increasingly in the first decades of the twentieth century, to all children as a result of the work of social reformers. Children should be "saved" and never "spent" or "wasted." In precocity-as-pathology, early intellectual development spent children and laid them to waste. In the new discourse of giftedness-as-potential, experts argued that gifted children were a valuable national resource that was in danger of wastage because of inadequate educational opportunities.[17]

In scientific and popular literature, the idea that gifted children were a resource not to be wasted gained prominence following the Russian launch of the Sputnik satellite in 1957. According to Margolin, research on giftedness quintupled following this perceived defeat of American science and technology. The first sentence of Willard Abraham's 1958 advice book begins, "As the page proofs for this book come through, Russia has already launched its first two round-the-world missiles. . . . And the gifted child is being 'discovered' by many." Florence Brumbaugh and Bernard Roshco also cited Sputnik, seeing it as "a major turning point in the American attitude toward the importance of educating the gifted to make the fullest use of their superior abilities," in their 1959 advice book for parents.[18]

The newly emerging experts on gifted children argued that gifted children were suffering from a lack of appropriate educational support. For example, as early as 1925 Alice Jones noted in her study of 120 "superior" children "a lamentable tendency upon the part of the schools to fail to provide adequate educational facilities for the maximum development of the potentialities displayed by members of this group." Abraham further argued that parents of the gifted and experts must work together to convince their communities to fund gifted education.[19]

INTELLIGENCE TESTING AND GIFTEDNESS

Beginning in the early twentieth century, the measurement of intelligence via the use of intelligence tests found rapid scientific and popular acceptance in the United States. Intelligence testing provided public school administrators of the 1920s and 1930s with a scientifically approved means of classifying students according to ability levels, thus enabling schools to rationalize the distribution of educational resources at a time when immigration and compulsory education and child labor laws swelled public school enrollment.[20]

The scientifically approved, socially accepted measurement of children's abilities through intelligence testing made the reconstruction of early intellectual development as giftedness possible. First, intelligence testing authenticated precocity by promising objective, scientific measurement of children's intelligence, and thus allayed parents' concerns with the authenticity of early intellectual development. Second, the new gifted-child experts used intelligence tests to classify children as gifted and then engaged in scientific studies meant to demonstrate that, far from suffering from the pathologies of the body and mind that nineteenth-century experts had associated with precocity, gifted children were in fact healthier and more emotionally stable than the nongifted. Third, since intelligence testing constructs early intellectual development as a capability or a potential—vastly different from the adult behaviors that economically, socially, or sexually precocious children engage in—measurement of children's intelligence through IQ testing helped decouple intellectual precocity from economic, social, or sexual precocity.

AUTHENTICATING EARLY INTELLECTUAL DEVELOPMENT

The adjudication of authentic precocity in children was necessary to allay nineteenth-century middle-class concerns about sincerity and authenticity. Such concerns arose in the context of increasing social and geographical mobility and the growing contact with strangers in the urban metropolis. Genteel Americans sought means whereby they could identify and safely associate with one another without the encroachment of "confidence men" or "strivers" who falsely represented themselves as members of respectable society. Etiquette advisers offered semiotic schemes promising to enable the middle-class reader to decode others' presentations and perceive their authentic social positions. In child-rearing manuals, sincerity, truthfulness, and lack of pretense were held up as virtues to be encouraged in children. According to one advice writer, "Parents are especially urged to resist the tendency of thinking all their geese are swans." But nineteenth-century American parents had no socially accepted and scientifically approved means of objectively measuring their children's intelligence and thus no reliable means of classifying their children as true intellectual swans versus inauthentic geese.[21]

Intelligence testing offered objective, scientific assessment as a way to confer authenticity on the notion of early intellectual development. Henceforth child-rearing experts would advise parents who suspected their child of possessing unusual intellectual abilities to obtain intelligence testing immediately and, if their child was indeed thus identified as gifted, to have recourse to gifted-child experts for child-rearing advice. In a chapter on the use of intelligence and other psychological tests in her 1924 advice book to mothers, Ruth Wilson explained that "where the mother needs most help from the psychologist is to learn how to distinguish between the precocious child who is a budding genius and the precocious child who is only 'a small, fatigued grown-up.'" Mid- to late twentieth-century advice books for parents of gifted children generally begin with a chapter on identification issues. For example, in her 1986 book *Enjoy Your Gifted Child*, Carol Addison Takacs poses the question, "What is it about the very young child which leads parents to suspect that their child is gifted and then to seek expert verification of their earliest discovering?"[22]

STUDYING GIFTED CHILDREN

Intelligence testing not only made it possible to scientifically adjudicate giftedness, but also was the means whereby precocious children were established by scientific authorities as objects amenable to classification, measurement, and scientific study. The educational psychologist John Edward Bentley noted this when he wrote in 1937, "It may be said that the intelligence test has discovered the child of superior ability." Psychologists quickly reported findings on the new social category of gifted children and established themselves as experts on early intellectual development in children. In the 1920s Lewis Terman and some of his former students, and Leta Hollingworth, a psychologist at Columbia, undertook a comprehensive program of study of "gifted children" identified by intelligence testing. By 1925 Terman was able to report the results of an initial study of 1,470 scientifically adjudicated gifted children, whom he defined as children whose IQs tested at 135 and over.[23]

From the start, the new gifted-child experts presented an image of the child who exhibits early intellectual development that was in opposition to the image of that child previously constructed by the discourse of precocity-as-pathology. Terman and Hollingworth in particular directly attacked the association of early intellectual development with emotional and physical problems and pathologies, through longitudinal studies of gifted children. Scholars of gifted children presented much scientific evidence demonstrating that children identified as gifted through intelligence testing were no longer considered especially vulnerable to physical or emotional problems; they were actually bigger, stronger, and emotionally more stable than other children.[24]

The new experts from the fields of psychology and education argued that gifted children had many virtues in addition to their early intellectual development: physical and emotional health, a strong sense of justice, vivid imaginations, a great sense of humor, leadership ability, superior psychological adjustment, popularity among their peers, artistic abilities, originality, generosity, and kindness. The long-term persistence of this idea is indicated by Ellen Winner's inclusion of the myth that "gifted children are better adjusted, more popular, and happier than average children" in her 1996 book *Gifted Children: Myths and Realities*.[25] According to the child-rearing experts, the challenges faced by families of gifted children no longer included protecting the child from the dangers posed by pathological precocity. Identification of gift-edness;, meeting the gifted child's special educational needs; and emotional and psychological issues related to the gifted child in the family, such as relation-ships with siblings, were now the focus of child-rearing advice.

CONSTRUCTING GIFTEDNESS-AS-POTENTIAL

Intellectual precocity in childhood had been condemned as part of the project of extending the period of dependency and constructing sheltered childhood. The precocious child, the child who grew up too soon, became a symbol of poor child-rearing in Progressive Era social reform efforts. How was the ten-sion between precocity and middle-class ideals of childhood resolved? Mea-surement of children's intelligence through IQ testing helped to decouple intellectual precocity from economic, social, or sexual precocity. Intelligence testing constructs early intellectual development as a capability or a poten-tial, a very different thing from the adult behaviors of working or having sex in which economically or sexually precocious children engage. All chil-dren possess the potential of adult behaviors: capabilities such as intelligence quotients do not transgress the boundary between adulthood and childhood integral to the maintenance of sheltered childhood in the same way that pre-cocious behavior does. After the institutionalization of intelligence testing, precocious children were defined as those engaging in activities considered appropriate for adults only. Consequently, children with high intelligence quotients were no longer included in this definition of precocity.

Finally, the reification of the intelligence quotient created a profound change in the way that most twentieth-century Americans viewed intellec-tual ability: as an entity forming a single dimension along which individuals could be classified as inferior subnormals, to normals, to superior supernormals. On this unilinear scale of intelligence, any individual might be ranked in accordance with the relative amount of a single substance—intelligence—that she or he has. Those who have the average amount of intelligence are classified as normals, while those who have lesser amounts are subnormal and those with greater amounts are supernormal. Intelligence testing simul-taneously reconstructs backward and precocious children and slow and ge-nius adults into the new categories of the "idiot," the "imbecile," the "moron" (H. H. Goddard's invention), and the gifted—and places those categories into relationships of inferiority and superiority.

Prior to the institutionalization of the intelligence test, scientific and popular conceptions of the backward child, the idiot, the precocious child, and the genius were not ordered into such relationships. Nineteenth-century scientific and popular conceptualizations viewed genius, insanity, and idiocy as equally abnormal and, often, as interchangeable. As late as 1916, Hollander displayed this understanding of precocity when he titled his book *Abnormal Children (Nervous, Mischievous, Precocious, and Backward)*. Intelligence testing was thus a mechanism for normalization. The creation of normally distributed scores reconstructed deviations from the mean (precocity as well as retardation), previously understood as equally abnormal and pathological, into relations of superiority and inferiority such that precocity became a positive good that was better than both normal and subnormal intelligence.[26]

RACE, CLASS, AND IDENTIFYING THE GIFTED

Intelligence testing of children in the 1920s established that highly intelligent children were most likely to come from white, middle-class homes. Terman emphatically argued that this resulted from biological superiority and not educational advantages: "The children of successful and cultured parents test higher than children from wretched and ignorant homes for the simple reason that their heredity is better." The fact that white middle-class students were most likely to be identified as having high innate intellectual ability allowed justification for their academic successes (such as in college admissions), cast the American educational system as a meritocracy, and helped middle-class parents feel comfortable with the idea of giftedness. While educational experts have since discredited the notion that poor heredity accounts for the lower likelihood that poor children will be identified as gifted, in practice such ideas may persist, with classroom teachers indicating lower expectations for poor students and students of color.[27]

Margolin argues that gifted-child experts articulated a model of the gifted child that incorporated the values and ideals of the white upper middle class, a child that embodied goodness in this particular cultural context. Furthermore, the typical gifted child—whether identified through intelligence tests, teacher recommendations, or other means—actually was (and is) white and upper middle class. The gifted-education programs in twentieth-century American schools thus put race and class distinction into practice by offering these children unique educational opportunities.[28]

PARENTS AND THE EXPERTS

In twentieth-century accounts of giftedness, the failure of gifted children to live up to their potential is attributed not to the pathologies of precocity, but rather to poor parenting and educational practices. This not only reinforces ideas about the special needs of gifted children, but also makes recourse to the educational and psychological experts increasingly important for socially approved parenting.

Expert knowledge regarding child rearing is one form of the specialized knowledge/language/power that arose in the nineteenth century and increasingly intruded into the realm of everyday life. Expert knowledge and experts themselves devalued local and traditional knowledge and deskilled its practitioners. As a consequence of the development of expert systems, practitioners of local or subjugated knowledge (such as parents or mothers in this case) experience "deskilling," but they also engage in "reskilling," often through the reappropriation of such expert knowledge. The buyers and readers of advice literature are as much participants in its construction as authors and institutions, such as expert systems, for which the authors may act as agents. Julia Grant, for example, argues that nineteenth-century American women as a consumer group demanded child-rearing advice even prior to the establishment of a child development profession and discusses several historical examples of mothers' critiques of and resistances to expert knowledge.[29]

ONE MOTHER'S RESPONSE:
MRS. STONER'S *NATURAL EDUCATION*

How do laypersons such as parents negotiate the tension between expert advice and what they themselves know experientially to be true? Winifred Sackville Stoner, Sr.'s, 1914 *Natural Education* and 1916 *Manual of Natural Education* exemplify a mother's resistance to the dominant scientific discourse, which considered her intellectually precocious child in the light of pathology only. Stoner's work illustrates how mothers can negotiate the tension between abstract expert knowledge as represented by child-rearing advice and their own experientially based local knowledge in the context of their interactions with their own children. Advice literature on child rearing is far from received wisdom universally applied. Stoner's work, in which she describes the process by which she trained her famously precocious daughter and lays out her own prescriptive educational scheme, illustrates this point. Her 1914 text contains one of the earliest accounts of nonpathological precocity.[30]

Born in 1902, Winifred Sackville Stoner, Jr.'s, precocious intellectual achievements were covered in the *New York Times* and other media outlets. Her mother attributed her daughter's precocious achievements to her own method of early training and education. Stoner Senior corresponded with Michael V. O'Shea, professor of education at the University of Wisconsin, author of an influential mental hygiene text, and editor of several child-rearing advice books, who encouraged her to publish her educational techniques. Her 1916 text, although written by a layperson and a mother, received scientific validation in the form of a foreword by Dr. O'Shea.

Stoner presented her daughter as her prime exemplar in her attempt to discredit the belief of "old-fashioned folk" that all precocious children must become physically debilitated or insane. She argued that the "so-called 'bright child'" was held back by American public schooling, which made no provision for their special needs, and prescribed instead her own educational system, which she termed "Natural Education." Stoner's use of the word *natural* seems calculated to address fears of the dangers of forced or so-called hothouse education of young children. Her educational scheme also circumvented the problems posed by the bodily-economy model by emphasizing the balanced development of a child's mental, spiritual, and physical capabilities. While acknowledging the "constant fear of parents that the child's mind was being overtaxed and he would find an early grave," and the popular belief that "there is a narrow line between the genius and the fool," Stoner argued that by following the principles of natural education, parents of precocious children could easily overcome the dangers of unbalanced development. A highly educated woman from a privileged class position, Stoner had a flair for publicity and possessed a photogenic and talented daughter. No doubt all these factors contributed to her ability to resist expert conceptualizations of precocity and the dangers of early training.[31]

CONTINUING CONCERNS ABOUT EARLY INTELLECTUAL DEVELOPMENT

Even after the establishment of giftedness as potential, the belief that parents could harm their children by unduly encouraging or forcing early intellectual development on them continued to be represented in the scientific and advice literature. In 1937, John Edward Bentley, professor of education and psychology, distinguished between "congenital precocity," or true giftedness, and other cases of precocity that resulted from early training and tutoring by parents or other family members. Bentley echoed the nineteenth-century idea that if children "are forced in their general information and studies, they will in all probability resemble hot-house plants that tend to wither when transplanted from the coddled environment." Norma Cutts and Nicholas Moseley included precocity in a section of their 1953 advice book on problems in mental hygiene particular to bright children. They argued that precocity could be caused either by parental pride, which would lead to the child "being exhibited in an emotionally unhealthy way," or by overstudy, usually in children pushed too hard because of unrealistic expectations on the part of their parents. Ruth Strang wrote in her 1960 advice book of "pseudo-giftedness" resulting from coaching or pushing by overambitious parents.[32]

Despite such warnings, twentieth-century American parents proved to have quite an appetite for consumer goods, such as books, toys, and videos, that promised to help them develop their children's intellectual abilities to their fullest extent at the earliest age possible. For example, Glenn Doman's 1963 book *How to Teach Your Baby to Read* outlined teaching methods that parents could use not only to teach infants to read but also to promote more rapid brain growth, beginning at age one with flash card lessons in reading and mathematics. Jean Piaget, whose stage theory of cognitive development has been very influential in twentieth-century American educational thought, criticized what he perceived as the American predilection for parental pushing of children's intellectual capabilities. When lecturing in the United States, he was so often asked by audience members for methods by which they could speed up their child's development that he came to refer to this as the "American question." Giftedness experts, such as David Elkind, president of the National Association for the Education of Young Children, nevertheless argued that, while contemporary research generally failed to demonstrate benefits of early training for ordinary children, gifted children were exceptional in this regard. By Elkind's reasoning, parents and educators should provide gifted children with accelerated learning opportunities at earlier ages than would be the case for other children so that gifted children might reach their full potential.[33]

At the level of academic discourse, psychology has been primarily responsible for constituting twentieth-century childhood as an object of the scientific gaze, although experts from the fields of education, social work, and child rearing have also claimed expertise in measuring, categorizing, and managing childhood and children. These fields of expert knowledge have shaped commonsense understandings of childhood as a natural state, so that we are all assumed to know what a child is and to be able to comment on what constitutes a proper childhood. For example, nowadays "everyone knows" that identification of giftedness in a child connotes potential, whereas in the nineteenth century "everyone knew" that the diagnosis of intellectual precocity in a child connoted pathology. Michel Foucault argues that the modern disciplines are primarily engaged in "making" people, that is, in assigning qualities and characteristics to individuals. Together with social and cultural changes, changing ideas generated by the twentieth-century scientific disciplines of psychology, education, and mental testing made over the child who exhibits early intellectual development from a precocious to a gifted child.[34]

While the dominant discourse of early intellectual development in contemporary American society is that of giftedness-as-potential, no discourse completely eclipses earlier related views. The discourse of pathological precocity lives on, generating images of brainy weaklings, obnoxious know-it-alls, and nerdy eggheads who fail at sports and social relations. Public concerns about the parental practice of coaching children, especially very young children, to perform intellectual feats seemingly beyond their years or about overly taxing educational standards and too much testing in the early grades still arise. While an imbalance in a child's intellectual, physical, and spiritual and moral development no longer poses the grave dangers warned of by earlier generations of scientists and experts and feared by earlier generations of parents, American culture favors a "well-rounded" individual, and parents and educational institutions seek to develop all of children's capabilities. Nevertheless, one of the most striking accomplishments of the twentieth-century scientific disciplines of psychology, education, and mental testing was the successful makeover of the child who exhibits early intellectual development from a pathologically precocious child requiring his parent's protection from his own mental abilities to a gifted child requiring her parent's careful nurturance of her great potential.

NOTES

    1. Winifred Sackville Stoner, Sr., *Manual of Natural Education* (Indianapolis: Bobbs-Merrill, 1916).

    2. Nicholas Murray Kirwan, *Happy Home* (New York: Harper and Brothers, 1858), 34; Sidney L. Pressey, "Concerning the Nature and Nurture of Genius," *Scientific Monthly* 81 (1955): 15.

    3. Barbara Beatty, *Preschool Education in America: The Culture of Young Children from the Colonial Era to the Present* (New Haven: Yale University Press, 1995); Dean L. May and Maris A. Vinovskis, "A Ray of Millennial Light: Early Education and Social Reform in the Infant School Movement in Massachusetts, 1826–1840," in *Family and Kin in Urban Communities, 1700–1930,* ed. Tamara K. Haraven (New York: Franklin Watts, 1977).

    4. Beatty, *Preschool Education in America;* May and Vinovskis, "A Ray of Millenial Light"; Anthony M. Platt, *The Child Savers: The Invention of Delinquency* (Chicago: University of Chicago Press, 1969); Cesare Lombroso, *The Man of Genius* (New York: C. Scribner's Sons, 1891), 333; John Nisbet, *The Insanity of Genius and the General Inequality of Human Faculty Physiologically Considered,* 6th ed. (New York: Charles Scribner, 1891), iv.

    5. Michael Steven Shapiro, *Child's Garden: The Kindergarten Movement from Froebel to Dewey* (University Park: Penn State University Press, 1983); Howard P. Chudacoff, *How Old Are You? Age Consciousness in American Culture* (Princeton: Princeton University Press, 1989); G. Stanley Hall, *Adolescence: Its Psychology and Its Relations to Physiology, Anthropology, Sociology, Sex, Crime, Religion, and Education* (New York: D. Appleton, 1904), viii.

6. Chudacoff, *How Old Are You?* 36.

7. Roblyn Rawlins, "'Long Rows of Short Graves': Sentimentality, Science, and Distinction in the 19th Century Construction of the Intellectually Precocious Child," in *Symbolic Childhood*, ed. Daniel Thomas Cook (New York: Peter Lang, 2002); S. Weir Mitchell, *Wear and Tear; or, Hints for the Overworked* (Philadelphia: J. B. Lippincott, 1874); George Beard, *American Nervousness, Its Causes and Consequences* (New York: G. P. Putnam, 1881); Bernard Hollander, *Abnormal Children (Nervous, Mischievous, Precocious, and Backward): A Book for Parents, Teachers, and Medical Officers of Schools* (London: Kegan Paul, Trench, Truebner, 1916), 28; Newton N. Riddell, *Child Culture* (Chicago: Child of Light, 1902), 95.

8. Carrica LeFavre, *Mother's Help and Child's Friend* (New York: Brentano's, 1890), 128.

9. Alisa Klaus, *Every Child a Lion: The Origins of Maternal and Infant Health Policy in the United States and France, 1890–1920* (Ithaca: Cornell University Press, 1993); Mrs. E. G. Cook, *Eutocia* (Chicago: Arcade, 1886).

10. Michael Kimmel, *Manhood in America: A Cultural History* (New York: Free Press, 1996); Thomas E. Jordan, *The Degeneracy Crisis and Victorian Youth* (Albany: State University of New York Press, 1993); Mrs. P. B. Sauer, *Maternity: A Book for Every Wife and Mother* (Chicago: L. P. Miller, 1891).

11. Roger Cox, *Shaping Childhood* (London: Routledge, 1996); Hugh Cunningham, *Children and Childhood in Western Society Since 1500* (New York: Longman, 1995); David Macleod, *The Age of the Child: Children in America, 1890–1920* (New York: Twayne, 1998); T. J. Jackson Lears, *No Place of Grace: Antimodernism and the Transformation of American Culture, 1880–1920* (New York: Pantheon, 1981); Jean-Jacques Rousseau, *Emile*, trans. Barbara Foxley (London: J. M. Dent, 1957 [1762]).

12. Andrew Abbott, *The System of Professions: An Essay on the Division of Expert Labor* (Chicago: University of Chicago Press, 1988); Stuart M. Blumin, "The Hypothesis of Middle-Class Formation in Nineteenth-Century America," *American Historical Review* 90 (1985): 299; Mary P. Ryan, *Cradle of the Middle Class: The Family in Oneida County, New York, 1790–1865* (New York: Cambridge University Press, 1981).

13. Rawlins, "'Long Rows of Short Graves'"; Stephen Mintz and Susan Kellogg, *Domestic Revolutions: A Social History of American Family Life* (New York: Free Press, 1988); Chudacoff, *How Old Are You?*; Joseph Kett, "Curing the Disease of Precocity," in *Turning Points: Historical and Sociological Essays on the Family*, ed. John Demos and Sarane Spence Boocok (Chicago: University of Chicago Press, 1978); Platt, *Child Savers*; Paul Boyer, *Urban Masses and Moral Order in America, 1820–1920* (Cambridge: Harvard University, 1978); Cunningham, *Children and Childhood*; Linda Gordon, *Heroes of Their Own Lives: The Politics and History of Family Violence* (New York: Penguin Books, 1988).

14. Leslie Margolin, *Goodness Personified: The Emergence of Gifted Children* (New York: Aldine D. Gruyter, 1994).

15. Margolin, *Goodness Personified*, 143.

16. Winifred Sackville Stoner, Sr., *Natural Education* (Indianapolis: Bobbs-Merrill, 1914), iii; Margolin, *Goodness Personified*; Willard Abraham, *Common Sense about Gifted Children* (New York: Harper & Brothers, 1958).

17. Viviana Zelizer, *Pricing the Priceless Child: The Changing Social Value of Children* (Princeton: Princeton University Press, 1985).

18. Margolin, *Goodness Personified*; Abraham, *Common Sense*, xi; Florence N. Brumaugh and Bernard Roscho, *Your Gifted Child: A Guide for Parents* (New York: Henry Holt, 1959).

19. Alice M. Jones, "An Analytical Study of One Hundred Twenty Superior Children" (Ph.D. diss., University of Pennsylvania, 1925), 67; Abraham, *Common Sense*.

20. See Paul Davis Chapman, *Schools as Sorters: Lewis M. Terman, Applied Psychology, and the Intelligence Testing Movement, 1890–1930* (New York: New York University Press, 1988); Lewis M. Terman, *Intelligence Tests and School Reorganization* (Stanford: Stanford University Press, 1922); Chudacoff, *How Old Are You?*

21. Karen Halttunen, *Confidence Men and Painted Women: A Study of Middle-Class Culture in America, 1830–1870* (New Haven: Yale University Press, 1982); John F. Kasson, *Rudeness and Civility: Manners in Nineteenth-Century Urban America* (New York: Hill and Wang, 1990); Robert Tomes, *The Bazaar Book of the Household* (New York: Harper and Brothers, 1875), 72.

22. Ruth Danenhower Wilson, *Giving Your Child the Best Chance* (Chicago: A. C. McClurg, 1924), 84; Carol Addison Takacs, *Enjoy Your Gifted Child* (Syracuse: Syracuse University Press, 1986), 3.

23. John Edward Bentley, *Superior Children: Their Physiological, Psychological, and Social Development* (New York: W. W. Norton, 1937), 105; Terman, *Intelligence Tests*; Lewis M. Terman, *Genetic Studies of Genius: Mental and Physical Traits of a Thousand Gifted Children* (Stanford: Stanford University Press, 1925); Leta Hollingworth, *Gifted Children: Their Nature and Nurture* (New York: Macmillan, 1926).

24. Terman, *Intelligence Tests*; Terman, *Genetic Studies of Genius*; Hollingworth, *Gifted Children*, 78; H. H. Goddard, *School Training of Gifted Children* (Chicago: World Book, 1928), 35.

25. Ellen Winner, *Gifted Children: Myths and Realities* (New York: Basic Books, 1996).

26. Hollander, *Abnormal Children*.

27. Margolin, *Goodness Personified*; Terman, *Genetic Studies of Genius*, 66.

28. Margolin, *Goodness Personified*; Daniel J. Kevles, *In the Name of Eugenics: Genetics and the Uses of Human Heredity* (New York: Knopf, 1985); E. Mensh and H. Mensh, *The IQ Mythology: Class, Race, Gender, and Inequality* (Carbondale: Southern Illinois University Press, 1991).

29. A. Giddens, *Modernity and Self-Identity* (Stanford: Stanford University Press, 1991); Julia Grant, *Raising Baby by the Book: The Education of American Mothers* (New Haven: Yale University Press, 1998).

30. Stoner, *Natural Education*; Stoner, *Manual of Natural Education*.

31. Stoner, *Natural Education*, 7; Stoner, *Manual of Natural Education*, 20.

32. Bentley, *Superior Children*, 87; Norma E. Cutts and Nicholas Moseley, *Bright Children: A Guide for Parents* (New York: G. P. Putnam's Sons, 1953), 28; Ruth Strang, *Helping Your Gifted Child* (New York: E. P. Dutton, 1960).

33. Glenn Doman, *How to Teach Your Baby to Read* (New York: Random House, 1963); David Cohen, *Piaget: Critique and Reassessment* (New York: St. Martin's Press, 1983); David Elkind, "Our President: Acceleration," *Young Children* 43 (1988): 4.

34. N. Rose, *Governing the Soul: The Shaping of the Private Self* (London: Routledge, 1989); Sue Scott, Stevi Jackson, and Kathryn Backett-Milburn, "Swings and Roundabouts: Risk Anxiety and the Everyday Worlds of Children," *Sociology* 32 (1998): 689–705; Michel Foucault, *The Birth of the Clinic* (New York: Pantheon, 1973).

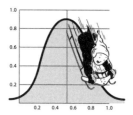

CHAPTER 5

When Physicians and Psychologists Parted Ways: Professional Turf Wars in Child Study and Special Education, 1910–1920

Stephen Woolworth

IN THE SUMMER OF 1916 Dr. Ira Brown, the crusading, assertive medical inspector of the Seattle public schools, sent a memo to the school board warning about the danger associated with the "constantly increasing number of mentally deficient children" in the schools. By calling the school board's attention to the issue of mental deficiency, Brown was doing more than just trying to raise awareness in Seattle about a topic of great concern to school leaders across the country. His communication was part of a broader strategy to construct a biomedical form of authority within the schools, an effort that began shortly after his appointment two years earlier when he instructed his staff of nurses to regard any child who was failing in school as a "medical subject." Brown had confidently proclaimed that the surgical removal of tonsils and adenoids, corrective procedures in student hearing and vision, and dental enhancements increased student learning by as much as 65 percent, and he even argued that problems with glandular secretions were to blame for children's falling behind in grade level. A few years later he went so far as to propose that grade promotions be determined by the results of a physical examination. In this particular case, though, Brown was laying the groundwork to expand the jurisdictional reach of his medical department. He was claiming control over the evaluation of mental status in "subnormal" children, a practice being steadily usurped by the diagnostic authority of Nellie Goodhue, a teacher with psychological training who served as the principal of the special schools and lead evaluator of mental deficiency in the Seattle schools' new child study laboratory.[1]

Goodhue was one of a cadre of teachers across the nation who had traveled to Henry H. Goddard's summer institute at the Vineland Training School for the Feebleminded in New Jersey to be trained in the administration of intelligence tests. Upon her return she advanced scientific ideas about clinical psychology by integrating the new technology of mental testing into the diagnostic regimen of the child study laboratory. But because established protocol required that low-achieving children receive a physiological as well as a psychological examination, Goodhue found herself in the position of having to negotiate responsibility for the evaluation of mental status with Dr. Brown, who she believed lacked understanding about both the psychological dimensions of mental retardation and the methods of diagnosis.[2] Not surprisingly, Brown and Goodhue clashed over the question of who possessed the scientific and professional authority to oversee the emergent diagnostic and pedagogical enterprise of special education in Seattle.

BIOMEDICAL AND PSYCHOLOGICAL DISCOURSES

The evaluation of mental status emerged as a contested practice in schools during the 1910s when two medicalized discourses on schooling—the biomedical and psychological—converged around the identification, classification, and regulation of low-achieving children. In the wake of compulsory-attendance laws that mandated a public education for all eligible school-aged children, concerns about students failing to progress through the graded curriculum intensified. Administrators struggled to develop and sustain institutional practices that, while upholding the common school ideal of inclusiveness, at the same time still adhered to the organizational goals of efficiency and order they pursued to attain that very ideal. One solution was the "ungraded" special classroom. Placing low-achieving children into specially designated classrooms empowered school administrators to both comply with the requirements of the attendance laws and prevent disruption in the regular classroom. Beginning in the 1870s, special schools and classrooms were incorporated within school systems as a way to accommodate and segregate children considered "backward" in their studies, truant and delinquent, or hindered by physical and mental impediments ranging from blindness and deafness to mental deficiency.[3]

Introducing the special classroom not only challenged administrators at the local level to legitimize a diagnostic program that sorted children according to mental, physical, and social criteria but also to mediate between competing sources of professional authority. The evaluation of mental status emerged as a jurisdictional arena marked by interprofessional conflict and competition between physicians like Brown, who were actively broadening their sphere of influence from preventing disease to preventing school failure, and the psychologists and special school teachers like Goodhue, who constructed their authority through the technology of intelligence testing in psychological clinics and child study laboratories.

Fueling the fire of these disputes were two separate but interrelated issues. The first involved the diagnostic authority of general medicine in relation to that of clinical psychology. The second concerned the regulation of public school enrollment through the determination of which children were believed to be inherently uneducable because of their innate mental deficiency. An explanation of how and why these disputes occurred, along with the dilemmas they presented for school leaders at the time, are a largely unrecognized yet central element of the larger story behind the organizational and ideological development of special education.[4]

PUBLIC HEALTH AND THE SCHOOLS

School psychological clinics and child health programs emerged at the beginning of the twentieth century as part of the larger cultural and scientific rise of medical authority in American life. Beginning in the mid-nineteenth century, physicians organized medical societies to promote health reform, formed boards of public health at the municipal and state level to institute and regulate public health practices, collected vital statistics, and applied public health practices within America's rapidly expanding cities. The establishment of the American Public Health Association, a national Marine Hospital Service, and a national system of quarantine regulations all symbolized the increased centralization of American public health policy by the end of the century. The most significant development behind the institutionalization of public health authority, however, was bacteriology, a laboratory science derived from the research of Robert Koch, Louis Pasteur, and others in Europe who demonstrated that germ microbes were the causative agents behind the spread of contagious disease.[5]

In their efforts to control and contain the spread of infectious disease, mid-nineteenth-century public health officials first targeted the schoolhouse and began sanitary inspections of school buildings. But the knowledge that such child killers as smallpox, tuberculosis, scarlet fever, and diphtheria were caused by the spread of microscopic pathogenic organisms, and not miasma or "bad air" as was previously believed, empowered public health boards to expand their practices in schools. Public health officials began changing their focus from negating environmental hazards through sanitary science and engineering, to the prevention of disease via the control and treatment of sick children. After an outbreak of diphtheria in 1894, for instance, health department physicians in Boston began entering the schools on a regular basis to examine students for either proof of vaccination or evidence of contagious disease. The following year, children were being lined up for inspections in the Chicago schools. Two years later, in 1897, an entire Division of Medical School Inspection was established in the health department of New York City, and by 1907 school medical inspections were under way in ninety cities, a figure that rose to nearly five hundred by 1913.[6]

Medical inspections were the first regulatory practice to position children as objects of examination in school settings. At first physicians, and then later school nurses, used their own disciplinary or biomedical lens to view children, their bodies, and their physical and intellectual functioning. Once physicians and nurses began examining children in schools they uncovered a host of untreated conditions and physical abnormalities in the general school population that led them to broaden their rationale for medical inspections from disease prevention to the correction of physical and mental defects. A resolution at the 1904 meeting of the Washington State Medical Association, for example, urged systematic and careful medical examinations in the public schools because "defects . . . upon the mental, moral and physical development" of children were "not fully appreciated by educators and the public at large."[7]

The publication of Leonard Ayres's *Laggards in Our Schools*, the influential and widely read 1909 study of retardation in city schools, legitimized the efforts of public health physicians to advance their scientific authority beyond disease prevention to the improvement of student learning. By calling attention to the problems of grade promotions in city school systems, Ayres's statistical survey effectively merged the concerns of the school-efficiency and school-health movements. "It is not surprising," wrote Ayres, "that the study of the school records . . . shows a high degree of correlation to exist between . . . marked physical defects and . . . school progress." Two years later, in 1911, the American Medical Association and the National Education Association formed the Joint Commission on School Health Problems to begin coordinating school health policies on a national level.[8]

PSYCHOLOGY AND THE SCHOOLS

As medical inspections were introduced in urban public school systems, psychology—as evidenced by the formation of the American Psychological

Association in 1892—was emerging as a professional discipline distinct from general medicine, philosophy, and biology. Rooted in Wilhelm Wundt's laboratory at the University of Leipzig in the 1870s, scholars such as James Cattell, William James, and James's student G. Stanley Hall all shaped the theoretical direction of the field in the United States. It was Lightner Witmer, however, a former student of both Wundt and Cattell, who first illustrated the practical applications of psychology to the study of low-achieving children in the schools when in the spring of 1896 a Philadelphia teacher convinced him to examine a "chronic bad speller" in his laboratory at the University of Pennsylvania.[9] If "psychology was worth anything to me or to others," Witmer would later write, "it should be able to assist the efforts of a teacher in a retarded case of this kind." After Witmer examined other children struggling to progress in the schools, he established the nation's first "psychological clinic" in connection with his university laboratory.[10]

Witmer envisioned the scientific field of inquiry he termed "clinical psychology" as playing a significant role in the public schools. In an address before the American Psychological Association, Witmer outlined a scope of work in psychology that included the application of clinical methods to the study of mental development in schoolchildren, the establishment of psychological clinics in conjunction with training schools to treat "children suffering from retardation or physical defects interfering with school progress," ongoing training for teachers and physicians in the field, and the formal preparation of students "for a new profession—that of the psychological expert, who should find his career in connection with the school system."[11] In addition to working in schools, psychologists established clinics in state training schools and juvenile courts. At such locales the normalizing tendencies of psychological discourse reoriented institutional practices around observation and diagnosis, measurement and classification, and treatment and prevention.[12]

EUGENICS AND INTELLIGENCE TESTING

Embedded within the professional ideology of clinical psychology, however, were long-standing beliefs about biological determinism that linked such social problems as crime, poverty, and moral degeneracy to the reproduction of inferior genetic stock—or innate feeblemindedness. Late eighteenth- and nineteenth-century assumptions about the relationship between intelligence and morality were revived and combined with meritocratic and scientific rationales for social stratification by Henry H. Goddard, the director of the research department of New Jersey's Vineland Training School for Feebleminded Children. Goddard translated Alfred Binet and Thomas Simon's 1908 intelligence test, administered it at the Vineland school, and upon assessing the results introduced a tripartite system of classification for mental deficiency, with categories of "morons," "idiots," and "imbeciles." Morons, whose mental age ranged between eight and twelve, were considered just below normal. Idiots were believed to have a mental age of less than two; in between were imbeciles, considered to have a mental age of between two and seven.[13]

Goddard was particularly concerned that morons, because they ranked just below the intellectual norm, could progress through the schools undetected and thus achieve a social position from which they could wreak considerable havoc upon an unsuspecting public. To prevent this from happening he set about using intelligence testing to determine the level of mental defectiveness in the general school population. It was Goddard's hope that, by identifying and segregating subnormal children, he would also increase the efficiency of school systems. After testing thousands of students in the New York City schools in 1911, Goddard came to believe that mental deficiency was so widespread that it warranted establishing a summer school at the Vineland Training School to train teachers in the administration of intelligence tests. Many teachers, in turn, used this experience as an opportunity to further their own professionalization efforts by developing a "specialized" identity within the field. Of course, taxonomic divisions had existed before Goddard's model. But with the rapid institutionalization of the Binet-Simon intelligence scale, Goddard's taxonomy of mental deficiency was soon encoded into the structure of public school systems as formal scientific knowledge.[14]

Further popularizing the use of intelligence tests was Stanford University's Lewis Terman, who revised Binet's intelligence scale, applied it throughout the California school systems, and then raised concerns about subnormal youth and their effect on school efficiency. But whereas Goddard urged testing for the purposes of segregating and controlling mental defectives, Terman had a broader social vision. He believed that universal intelligence testing had the power to order a more just and rational society in which individuals could be sorted into roles appropriate to their level of intelligence. The first step, Terman believed, was to identify, control, and eliminate the reproduction of mentally defective people who lacked the intellectual capacity to lead a moral life.[15] The dilemma for school officials, then, was not only to distinguish the subnormal from among the larger number of low-achieving children in the schools, but also to determine who was intellectually and morally unsuitable for enrollment in the public schools. Questions about who possessed the scientific and professional authority to make these determinations became a source of intense dispute, as events in Seattle illustrate.

SOURCES OF DIAGNOSTIC AUTHORITY
IN THE SEATTLE PUBLIC SCHOOLS

Public health interventions in the Seattle schools preceded provisions for low-achieving students as board of health physicians implemented school-sanitation and infectious-disease-control policies, such as vaccinations, beginning in the early 1890s.[16] Paralleling national trends, the health board then initiated a school medical inspection system in 1903. The new system accelerated the development of specialized classrooms to absorb the diverse range of children entering schools as a result of the compulsory school law passed that same year. It also helped the schools accommodate the swelling ranks of children who were being transferred from the overcrowded state residential institutions, thus pushing the responsibility for accommodating children considered defective in mental, moral, or physical capacity onto local school systems. Between 1907 and 1910 eighteen "ungraded" special school classrooms were organized for students identified as deaf, delinquent, stammerers, mentally deficient, or backward and for students who had fallen behind in their grades. Veteran school superintendent Frank Cooper immediately proclaimed the special classes "a legitimate part of the system."[17]

THE CHILD STUDY LABORATORY

The school psychological clinic originated as a clinic at the University of Washington run by a psychology professor and an education professor, who believed that neither physicians nor teachers had the expertise to deal with "backward and mentally defective children."[18] Diagnostic practices in the Seattle schools involved the examination of children by a health department medical inspector and then at the psychological clinic at the university.[19] After the opening of the university clinic, however, it soon became apparent that diagnostic services were needed at the Cascade School, where the majority of special school classrooms were located. The Cascade School's deficiency was addressed by the opening of a psychological laboratory there under the supervision of University of Washington psychologist Stevenson Smith.[20] Superintendent Cooper and the school board also enlisted four volunteer physicians (a pediatrician; an orthopedic specialist; an eye specialist; and a nose, ear, and throat specialist) to perform "additional" physical examinations. In the first year they examined 348 children, 125 of whom were recommended for placement in the special school classrooms. However, only half those recommended were actually enrolled, because of overcrowded conditions and parental resistance to placing children in the special schools. Nineteen children received "medical or surgical remedial measures" as a result of the examinations. Slight increases were reported for the following year as enrollment in the special schools tripled.[21]

When Smith left, Nellie Goodhue, who had been working in the special schools since their inception, became the new director of the psychological clinic at the Cascade School. In high school Goodhue had developed an interest in working with disabled children, an interest that had continued into college, where she studied psychology, at both the University of Minnesota and the University of Chicago. Goodhue also took courses in child psychology at the Universities of Washington and California and studied at Goddard's Vineland Training School for Feebleminded Children, where she learned to administer the Binet intelligence scale.[22] Goodhue would spend most of her time in the ensuing years traveling between schools administering tests, until the fall of 1914, when the psychological clinic was moved from the overcrowded Cascade School to the recently established medical clinic next door and renamed the Child Study Laboratory. With the relocation of the lab, Goodhue earned the title "principal of the special schools."

THE SCHOOL MEDICAL DEPARTMENT

During the same time that psychological discourse was gaining legitimacy within the schools, changes to the administration of school health practices were also under way. Frustrated with negotiating school health policies and practices with the city department of health, Superintendent Cooper and the school board elected to establish a medical department and a full service school health clinic. But unlike other school health clinics that functioned as diagnostic, prevention, and referral centers, the clinic in the Seattle schools was organized with the expressed purpose of providing medical treatment to children from the poorest families. Initially staffed by twenty-nine volunteer doctors and thirteen partially paid dentists, the clinic recorded more than eight thousand student visits in the first year alone, which resulted in 548 surgical operations (tonsillectomies, circumcisions, and hernia operations, among others). In the first two years, moreover, approximately five thousand dental treatments were administered, which suggests the extent to which medical interventions were conducted under the managerial authority of the schools.[23]

Appointed to lead the medical department was fifty-three-year-old Dr. Ira Brown, who had served for sixteen years in the United States Army Medical Department as a public health administrator.[24] Brown's years of administrative experience in the military guided the manner in which he ran the school medical department. He tirelessly strove to integrate the knowledge and practice of medical science with the principles of organizational efficiency through his supervision of the school nursing corps, the management of the school medical clinic, and the sanitary inspection of school buildings. Additionally, Brown quickly became the driving force behind the construction and exercise of medical authority in the schools.

DIAGNOSTIC PROTOCOL

With the medical clinic and child study laboratory now in the same location, the diagnostic protocol for evaluating the mental status of children was developed. Teachers reported students who had fallen behind in their classroom work to the principals, who then contacted Goodhue. She in turn arranged for the students to be tested and investigated at their school. Students who continued to fail in their schoolwork, tested low during the preliminary investigation, or were brought in by their parents then became candidates for a more thorough examination at the child study laboratory. Once at the lab a personal history of the child was taken from the parents. A school history from both the parents and the teacher was recorded; a report of the child's home environment from the teacher and the nurse was received; and a report on the child's physical health was produced at the medical clinic. The child would then be administered standard psychological tests and placed in the observation class. If testing determined that a child was too advanced for the special classes, she or he would be enrolled in the "Restoration Class" with the end goal of eventually returning to her or his home school. The other children, however, were sorted into one of the special school tracks—characterized by different vocational curriculums—where they were then continually tested each year. Children who showed no progress were either recommended for debarment from school or were sent to the Rainier School, where they were trained to work with their hands. Of those children, Superintendent Cooper once admitted bluntly, "[W]e are taking care of them because there is no place to send them."[25]

LOW-ACHIEVING CHILDREN AND THE POLITICS
OF PROFESSIONAL JURISDICTION

The issue of what to do with children regarded as too "defective" to benefit from school instruction, and thus abide by a code of moral conduct, troubled educational leaders across the nation, forcing them to grapple not only with issues of school efficiency but also with concerns about public safety. As the case of Seattle demonstrates, determining who these children were and implementing policies that debarred them from the schools exposed the epistemological tensions underlying the biomedical and psychological discourses informing the mental evaluation of low-achieving students. These tensions surfaced outright in Seattle after the school board turned decisions about debarment over to both Goodhue and Brown. In the jurisdictional conflicts that ensued, Superintendent Cooper was forced to intervene, mediate, and eventually choose sides.

These disputes started in the winter of 1917 when Goodhue wrote to Cooper asking for advice about students of the "imbecile type" who were able to be trained to some degree but basically were not, in her view, educable. Goodhue had previously notified Cooper of several adolescent students in the special schools who were no longer capable, in her view, of continued development. She wanted Cooper to help clarify whether these children should be kept out of the schools altogether. Cooper passed her concerns to the school board, noting that there were also many younger children in the low-grade special class at the Rainier School who met the same criteria. Several of them, he thought, belonged in the state institution at Medical Lake in eastern Washington.[26]

Although Cooper's belief that these children did not belong in the schools remained unchanged, he had become more hesitant to exclude them, knowing that there was no room for them at the overcrowded state institution. He told the board that as soon as children were debarred, the schools lost contact with them and they became "human driftwood." But when students were kept in school, Goodhue stayed in regular contact with the parents and eventually persuaded many of them to institutionalize their children. Out of the 128 children who had been removed from the schools in the child study laboratory's six years of operation, Cooper confessed to the board, he did not know what had become of many of them. "There are now at large in Seattle, [a total of] 170 low-grade imbeciles and idiots," he stated, and this "constitutes a considerable social menace." In a number of instances parents also threatened lawsuits if the schools refused admission to their children. As a result, school officials faced additional pressure to clarify and enforce their enrollment criteria.[27]

After Cooper's presentation, the school board directed Brown and Goodhue to confer about the most severely mentally disabled children and determine which students were "incapable of being educated."[28] Together, they recommended that four boys and two girls be debarred from the public schools. Beneath the surface their professional orientations were influencing the rationale for their decisions, which reflected the growing fissure between the work of the medical department and the child study laboratory. For instance, in one case Goodhue recommended one boy for debarment, while Brown suggested that the boy remain in school and be prescribed thyroid treatment. In another case, Brown recommended a student be dismissed, but

Goodhue countered that he be retained, since he had recently made progress in his work.[29]

After his conferences with Goodhue, Dr. Brown moved to gain greater authority over the operations of the child study laboratory. He began by forwarding a report to Cooper and the school board. Titled "A Basis for Debarring Mentally Defective Children from the Public Schools," Brown's report suggested the criteria for debarring students was "to be determined by the administrative and executive authorities of schools." It was evident that he included himself—but not the principal of the special schools—among that group. According to Brown, medical expertise was what was really needed in these decisions because even in the state institutions variation among the more marginal cases was common. The report suggested that three types of children be excluded from the public schools: those who had been classified as idiots and low-grade imbeciles; those who had been unable to profit from more schooling because they had reached the limit of their development or because their parents were unwilling to place them in state institutions; and those who had become a menace to the special classes because of mental defect.[30] Dr. Brown's report was accepted by Cooper and the school board as offering a sound rationale for district policy, suggesting that medical authority was key to establishing rules of public school exclusion.

SCHOOL FAILURE AS A MEDICAL PROBLEM

A year later, however, Brown authored yet another plan to reorganize the examination of children who were following behind in their grades. His plan positioned the medical department at the center of the evaluation process. It called for principals to provide the names and addresses of children who they thought needed an examination by a school nurse, who would then determine the extent to which environmental factors were influencing a child's performance in school. If the nurse thought the child should be sent to the clinic, then, Brown stated, she or he would be referred "for such corrective measures as may be done by medical men." The medical department, he concluded, was "the only one sufficiently well equipped to make these home investigations which have a great bearing upon many of these children's conditions."[31]

Dr. Brown's new plan allotted more time for the medical department to make a diagnosis. According to Brown, the current plan rushed children through the clinic, which led to unreliable diagnoses. Only after the clinic examinations were concluded, he proposed, should the principal send the students to the special schools for whatever training was deemed necessary by Goodhue. At the end of the school year, Brown suggested that the medical department collect from school principals the names of all students who had failed in their grades so that those children could be physically examined during the summer. Brown was confident that once physical defects were corrected, many children would be able to attend the regular classes, thus relieving the special classes of swelling enrollments.[32]

SCHOOL FAILURE AS AN EDUCATIONAL PROBLEM

For Goodhue, Brown's plan was the straw that broke the camel's back. She believed that his proposal to reorganize the examination of failing students was not only inefficient, but also incorrectly prioritized the physiological basis of mental retardation. "The question of retardation is primarily an educational question and not a medical one," she wrote to Cooper. "Hence the whole problem as to the causes, removal or remedying of the same, the proper placement of each child in the educational system and the best methods for the development of each should be under the direction of the educational department as represented by the Child Study Laboratory." In her letter to Cooper, Goodhue contested almost every detail of Brown's plan. For instance, she dismissed the medical inspector's assertion that the school nurses should be the ones to handle the initial interviews and investigations of students who were not performing well in school. Goodhue pointed out that this was "too delicate a matter to be entrusted to a school nurse" and should instead be turned over to the principal and teacher, both of whom "have an intimate understanding of the matter." Goodhue insisted that the principal and teacher were the only ones qualified to consult with parents about their children's school achievements. Whereas nurses were trained to recognize physical defects, Goodhue argued, their lack of sociological or psychological education rendered them susceptible to misdiagnoses. She furthermore contended that teachers who had received specialized training were better prepared than nurses to investigate the condition of children's homes.[33]

Goodhue also challenged Brown's assertion that the causation of student retardation was rooted in physiology. "This attitude is not unusual with medical men," Goodhue wrote to Cooper, because they are "unfamiliar with the psychological aspects of mental retardation" and are therefore "untrained in psychological methods of determining the same." Goodhue believed that the premise behind physical examinations was defeated if the emphasis was solely placed on physiological causes, because parents would then erroneously assume that their child's intellectual capacity would be normalized as soon as the proper medical procedures were performed. But in most of these cases, Goodhue observed, the medical exam obscured the real cause of the mental condition of these students and undermined the credibility of the teacher if students did not progress after their physical problems were remedied. "Experience has proven to us," Goodhue explained, "that physicians by virtue of their training are apt to make a diagnosis upon the physical condition only and parents as a rule are all too ready to accept this diagnosis" because they do not want to consider that the real cause of their child's difficulty is lack of mental development. While Goodhue agreed that physical causes were important to consider, she wanted Cooper to know that she would not agree to any plan that prioritized one cause over another before a final diagnosis was reached.[34]

Dr. Brown responded to Goodhue's critique with a vigorous defense of his new plan. While Brown conceded that the physicians on his staff had not reached every child, they were able to uncover the cause in every case they did examine, he said, and were therefore able to improve upon the attendance rates of those children. The medical examination of failing students "ought to be done along the line suggested by those who do it thus preserving current jurisdictional powers," Brown concluded. Cases of individual children demonstrate how these questions of expertise and jurisdiction persisted.[35]

DIAGNOSTIC TROUBLE: THE CASE OF VERA BROWN

In September 1919, Vera Brown's mother appeared before the Seattle School Board to ask the directors to review the decision to deny her daughter admission to the public schools. Goodhue had ruled that Vera suffered from extreme retardation, which prohibited her mother from enrolling her in school. Vera's mother then appealed to the school board, hoping she might get the decision reversed. After listening to her plea, the board referred the case to the authority of Dr. Brown, with instructions that if he did not think that Vera could be helped by the special classes, she should be permanently debarred from the public schools.[36]

After evaluating her, Dr. Brown recommended that Vera be admitted to one of the special schools that prioritized domestic-science work. But when Superintendent Cooper got word of Brown's decision, he told the school board that the girl could not be enrolled in the Rainier Special school. The Rainier School, Cooper reminded the board, was for children who could not benefit from instruction, yet Dr. Brown's recommendation clearly called for instruction in domestic-science work. Superintendent Cooper did not want to enroll Vera in the Ballard special school either, even though home economics was taught there, because it was specifically intended for "higher grade sub-normal children who can profit by instruction." At the Ballard special school academic work was a part of the curriculum along with the reading of receipts, the operation of gas stoves, and the use of sewing machines. These activities were, Cooper observed, beyond Vera Brown's ability.[37]

Because Goodhue and Brown had both reported that the girl had the mental capacity of a six-year-old, Cooper reasoned that Vera could not perform the tasks taught at the school. Furthermore, he declared, "teachers would hesitate about accepting the responsibility for [an] accident in such a case." Cooper also advised the board that if Vera Brown were admitted to the Ballard school, parents of the other children would complain about a child with low mentality. Parents were very sensitive, Cooper reminded the board, "and we have to protect the reputation of the Ballard Special and not have it become understood to be a school for imbecile children." There were probably a hundred children in Seattle with higher mentality than Vera Brown's, Cooper observed, but they were debarred from the schools against the wishes of their parents. A week later, after reading Cooper's position on the case, the members of the board unanimously voted to debar Vera Brown from the public schools, thereby overriding Dr. Brown's recommendation in favor of Goodhue's original evaluation.[38]

MORE DIAGNOSTIC TROUBLE: THE CASE OF BERTHA SCHRADER

Two weeks after the Vera Brown case had been resolved, the minister of the First Presbyterian Church, Mark Matthews, the most prominent and politically active minister in the Pacific Northwest, wrote a letter to the Seattle School Board questioning the diagnosis of mentally deficient children in the public schools. Matthews, who was behind the formation of the city's anti-tuberculosis society and closely allied with the county medical society, wrote to the board in support of the work of Dr. Brown. "I have had it brought to my attention," Matthews wrote to the school directors, "that perhaps one of your nurses or teachers has been trying to pass judgment on the mental condition of children." It appears, he added, "that Miss Goodhue has been usurping and exercising this authority (the authority of Dr. Brown) to the detriment of perhaps more than one case."[39]

In his letter to the school board, Matthews called attention to the case of Bertha Schrader to demonstrate that Goodhue was unqualified to assess the intelligence of children. Cooper described Bertha to the members of the board as

> one of those unfortunates belonging to the feeble minded class. She is fifteen years old, and the last test recorded in the Child Study Laboratory in January, 1918, shows that she was at that time four and one-half years retarded. She has done poorly in her school work, has been very hard to manage, showing a disposition to be violent at times. In a fit of temper, she cut off the hand of a younger brother, who is also feeble minded.

Bertha was initially brought to the juvenile court by one of the truant officers for poor school attendance as well as "vicious language and tendencies on the streets," including shoplifting. Court officials committed her to the state institution for the feebleminded, from where she was later released after the probation officer informed the superintendent that Bertha's mother was seriously ill and required her daughter's help.[40] Matthews charged that Goodhue had initiated the procedure that led to Bertha's unwarranted institutionalization, which showed how unqualified Goodhue was to be making such decisions.

Superintendent Cooper was quick to not only come to Goodhue's defense, but also to use this latest case as an opportunity to, once and for all, settle the issue of jurisdictional authority. He wrote a three-page report to the board that addressed Matthews's charges against Goodhue and the work of the child study laboratory. In his report Cooper stated that it was a mistake to hold Goodhue accountable for the institutional placement of Bertha Schrader and offered to show the members of the board both Goodhue's assessment of the girl and the court record as proof that her case had been handled correctly. In addition to citing Goodhue's experience and formal training working with the mentally deficient, Cooper included the opinions of national experts in the field of mental deficiency to both further support his defense of Goodhue and to align Seattle practices with scientific and professional trends. For instance, H. H. Goddard had referred to Goodhue as "one of the best" and noted that nonmedical people were diagnosing mental deficiency everywhere because "[i]t is not a medical problem." Cooper stated, "Physicians cannot diagnose mental abnormality unless also psychologists and especially trained." He also included a statement from Stevenson Smith, the University of Washington psychologist and cofounder of the child study laboratory, who regarded Goodhue as "superior in this kind of work."[41]

ALIGNING WITH NATIONAL TRENDS

Cooper then appended several sections from David Mitchell's text *Schools and Classes for Exceptional Children*, on the use of psychological testing in the Cleveland public schools, a report that Dr. Brown had used three years earlier to buttress his position. However, this time, Cooper shared sections that Brown had conveniently excluded from his memo, which highlighted the fact that there had also been some question in Cleveland "as to whether the mental tests should be conducted by the school physicians rather than by a trained psychologist." Mitchell had suggested in his 1916 report that the diagnosis of mentally deficient children clearly fell within the realm of the psychologist, and not the physician, who tended to regard "the problem of feeblemindedness . . . as purely a medical one." Because feeblemindedness was thought to be an issue of social fitness, Cooper explained to the school board, physicians were not the authorities on the diagnosis of mental status. As Mitchell's report on Cleveland had unequivocally stated: "Diagnosis of mental status should be made by a clinical psychologist. . . . He is the one upon whom the responsibility of the organization should rest. He should . . . take responsibility for . . . the segregation of a child."[42] Cooper concluded his report to the board by arguing that disputes pertaining to jurisdiction over the segregation of subnormal children needed to be settled within the public schools, so as not to cause embarrassment to the schools and the work they were trying to accomplish therein. Cooper requested that the board use its powers to render a decision about the responsibilities of the educational and medical departments in order "to prevent interference of the legitimate and proper work of one department with that of another."[43]

At the end of the month, Cooper wrote to Dr. Walter Vose Gulick, the former assistant superintendent at Washington's Western State Hospital and recent author of *Mental Diseases: A Handbook Dealing with Diagnosis and Classification*, to request that Gulick give his professional assessment of the work being done in the child study laboratory. Cooper wanted to know, Did Dr. Gulick believe that "the ordinary physician is a competent judge of the character and degree of abnormality?" Gulick responded that he was writing from the position of a physician, not a psychologist, but in his opinion the diagnostic work done at the laboratory was of a "careful manner, with competent results." It was his belief that "the training of the ordinary physician is not of a sort to acquaint him with the technical tests . . . or to qualify him with ability in judging deficiency from a school standpoint." Cooper then sent a copy of Gulick's letter to the school board and included along with it excerpted quotations from the likes of renowned psychologist Robert M. Yerkes and J. E. Wallin, president of the American Association of Clinical Psychologists and one of the leaders of the school psychology clinic movement. All the professional leaders Cooper quoted assigned authority in the determination of mental deficiency to psychologists and to those teachers, like Goodhue, who had extensive experience in teaching and testing the feebleminded.[44]

Despite Cooper's efforts to elevate Goodhue's authority in this arena, no formal ruling from the school board ever occurred on the issue of jurisdictional authority in the child study laboratory. The decisive factor in the dispute turned out to be a decision from the Washington State Supreme Court prohibiting the medical treatment of children in the school clinic. A group of parents, concerned about the expenditure of public funds supporting medical treatments in schools, had used the legal process to dismantle much of the infrastructure of the school medical department and therefore the diagnostic authority of Dr. Brown and his staff.[45] Intelligence testing, however, continued unabated. During the 1920–21 academic year, nearly six hundred Seattle-area public school students were enrolled at one time or another in the observation class at the child study laboratory, while some six thousand IQ tests were administered in the Seattle public schools. A dual organizational plan established special classes in the primary-grade buildings and special class industrial centers for older students. Seattle's special schools were thus further tied to the promise of vocational education as enrollment exceeded four hundred students.[46]

Following the passage of compulsory-attendance laws, school administrators nationally who were concerned about the institutional goals of order and efficiency invested in a differentiated structure of special school classrooms that separated students deemed "mentally deficient" from the "normal" school population. The diagnostic regimen assembled to make these distinctions was informed by the intersection of two medicalized discourses on schooling—the biomedical and the psychological. Respectively rooted in public health medicine and clinical psychology, these discourses converged when child health and child study practitioners competed behind the scenes to establish their respective authority over the diagnostic methods of special education. At stake in these disputes, as the case of Seattle demonstrates, were not only the boundaries of professional jurisdiction, but also the criteria governing public school enrollment, as decisions about admission and debarment ignited battles over who controlled this professional "turf."

By the 1920s, however, the dust from these turf wars had settled. The disciplinary authority of clinical psychology, exemplified by the institutionalization of intelligence testing, had surpassed the biomedical discourse on schooling. As a result, the work of physicians and school nurses in particular was relegated to disease-prevention practices. Meanwhile, special school teachers pursued opportunities for continued professional specialization within a special education arena governed by the scientific authority of clinical psychology.

NOTES

1. Ira Brown, Memorandum to Board of Directors, 13 July 1916, Seattle Public Schools Archives, Superintendent files, folder "Special Schools 1914–28." Dr. Brown's comments appeared in the *Seattle School Bulletin*, December 1914, vol. 2 (3); and theAnnual Report of the Seattle Public Schools, 1914, 76. See also Minutes of the Seattle School Board, 7 October 1918; Frank Cooper, Memorandum to Board of Directors, 12 October 1918, SPSA, Superintendent files, folder "Clinic 1913–21." On the history of views on mental deficiency see Steven A. Gelb, "Not Simply Bad and 'Incorrigible': Science, Morality, and Intellectual Deficiency," *History of Education Quarterly* 29 (Fall 1989): 359–79; Stephen Jay Gould, *The*

Mismeasure of Man (New York: W. W. Norton, 1981); Nicole Hahn Rafter, "Eugenics, Class, and the Professionalization of Social Control," in *Inequality, Crime, and Social Control*, ed. George S. Bridges and Martha A. Myers (Boulder, CO: Westview Press, 1994), 215–26; and Peter L. Tyor and Leland V. Bell, *Caring for the Retarded in America* (Westport, CT: Greenwood Press, 1984).

2. Nellie Goodhue, Memorandum to Frank Cooper #2, 9 May 1918, SPSA, Superintendent files, folder "Special Schools 1914–28."

3. Barry M. Franklin, *From "Backwardness" to "At-Risk": Childhood Learning Difficulties and the Contradictions of School Reform* (Albany: State University of New York Press, 1994); John G. Richardson, *Common, Delinquent, and Special: The Institutional Shape of Special Education* (New York: Falmer Press, 1999), 43; Joseph L. Tropea, "Bureaucratic Order and Special Children," *History of Education Quarterly* 27 (Spring 1987): 29–53, 32.

4. For more on professional jurisdiction, see Andrew Abbott, *The System of Professions: An Essay on the Division of Expert Labor* (Chicago: University of Chicago Press, 1988).

5. John Duffy, *The Sanitarians: A History of American Public Health* (Chicago: University of Illinois Press, 1990); Judith Walzer Leavitt, *The Healthiest City: Milwaukee and the Politics of Health Reform* (Madison: University of Wisconsin Press, 1982); William J. Novak, *The People's Welfare: Law and Regulation in Nineteenth-Century America* (Chapel Hill: University of North Carolina, 1996), 214; Roy Porter, *The Greatest Benefit to Mankind: A Medical History of Humanity* (New York: W. W. Norton, 1997); Nikolas Rose, "Medicine, History, and the Present," in *Reassessing Foucault: Power, Medicine, and the Body*, ed. Colin Jones and Roy Porter (London: Routledge, 1994), 48–72; Paul Starr, *The Social Transformation of American Medicine: The Rise of a Sovereign Profession and the Making of a Vast Industry* (New York: Basic Books, 1982), 197; Stephen Woolworth, "The Warring Boards: Sanitary Regulations and the Control of Infectious Disease in the Seattle Public Schools, 1892–1900," *Pacific Northwest Quarterly* 96 (Winter 2004/2005): 14–23.

6. John Duffy, "School Vaccination: The Precursor to School Medical Inspection," *Journal of the History of Medicine and Allied Sciences* 33 (July 1978): 344–55; Luther H. Gulick and Leonard P. Ayres, *Medical Inspection of Schools* (New York: Russell Sage, 1913); Ernest Bryant Hoag and Lewis M. Terman, *Health Work in the Schools* (Cambridge: Riverside Press, 1914). See also William J. Reese, *Power and the Promise of School Reform: Grassroots Movements During the Progressive Era* (Boston: Routledge & Kegan Paul, 1986); and Stephen Woolworth, "Conflict, Collaboration, and Concession: A Study of the Rise and Fall of Medical Authority in the Seattle Public Schools, 1892–1922" (EdD diss., University of Washington, 2002).

7. A. W. Hawley, "Defects of Eyes, Ears, Noses, and Throats in School Children," *Northwest Medicine* (Seattle: Washington Medical Library Association) 3 (February 1905): 53–58. See also Michel Foucault, *The Birth of the Clinic: An Archaeology of Medical Perception* (New York: Random House, 1973); and Theresa Richardson, *The Century of the Child: The Mental Hygiene Movement and Social Policy in the United States and Canada* (Albany: State University of New York Press, 1989).

8. Leonard Ayres, *Laggards in Our Schools: A Study of Retardation and Elimination in City School Systems* (New York: Russell Sage Foundation, 1909), 130; R. K. Means, *Historical Perspectives on School Health* (Thorofare, NJ: Charles B. Slack, 1975). On legitimization, see Steven L. Schlossman, JoAnne Brown, and Michael Sedlak, *The Public School in American Dentistry* (Santa Monica, CA: Rand Corporation, 1986), 8.

9. Donald S. Napoli, *Architects of Adjustment: The History of the Psychological Profession in the United States* (Port Washington, NY: National University, 1981), 12–15.

10. Lightner Witmer, "Clinical Psychology," *Psychological Clinic* 1 (March 1907): 1–9, 4–5.

11. Witmer, "Clinical Psychology," 5.

12. See Lilburn Merrill, "Diagnostic Methods as an Aid in Juvenile Court Administration," *Proceedings of the National Conference of Charities and Correction, Seattle, WA* (Fort Wayne, IN: Fort Wayne, 1913): 324–31; and John R. Sutton, *Stubborn Children: Controlling Delinquency in the United States, 1646–1981* (Berkeley: University of California Press, 1988).

13. Gelb, "Not Simply Bad and Incorrigible," 361, 375–77; Gould, *Mismeasure of Man*, 176–263; and Tyor and Bell, *Caring for the Retarded*, 105–22.

14. Gould, *Mismeasure of Man*, 176–263; Tyor and Bell, *Caring for the Retarded*, 105–22; Jeffrey Mirel, *The Rise and Fall of an Urban School System: Detroit, 1907–81* (Ann Arbor: University of Michigan Press), 8. See also Robert L. Osgood, "Becoming a Special Educator: Specialized Professional Training for Teachers of Children with Disabilities in Boston, 1870–1930," *Teachers College Record*, 101, no. 1 (1999): 82–105.

15. Gould, *Mismeasure of Man*, 204–13; Richardson, *Common, Delinquent, and Special*, 56–57.

16. Woolworth, "Conflict, Collaboration, and Concession."

17. The one exception was a parental school for wayward and incorrigible youth on Mercer Island that was started in 1901. Annual Report of the Seattle Public Schools, 1911, 24.

18. "University of Washington, Seattle, Psychological Clinic for Backward and Mentally Defective Children," document on file at SPSA, Superintendent files, box 4, misc., 1909–10.

19. Minutes of the Seattle School Board, 7 April and 16 September 1910; Annual Report of the Seattle Public Schools, 1910, 26–27.

20. Annual Report of the Seattle Public Schools, 1911, 23–24.

21. Annual Reports of the Seattle Public Schools, 1912, 29–30; 1913, 57–58. See also Napoli, *Architects of Adjustment*, 17.

22. Frank Cooper, Memorandum to Board of Directors, 24 October 1919, SPSA, Superintendent files, folder "Special School 1914–28."

23. Annual Reports of the Seattle Public Schools, 1914, 75; 1916, 161.

24. *Seattle School Bulletin*, 25 April 1914; *The Seattle Post-Intelligencer*, 28 March 1914, 28.

25. Nellie Goodhue, Memorandum to Frank Cooper, 15 September 1914, SPSA, Superintendent files, folder "Special Schools 1914–28"; Frank Cooper, Memo-

randum to Board of Directors, 28 July 1919, SPSA, Superintendent files, folder "Special Schools 1914–28."

26. Frank Cooper, Memorandum to Board of Directors, 16 January 1917, SPSA, Superintendent files, folder "Special Schools 1914–28."

27. Cooper, Memorandum to Board of Directors, 16 January 1917.

28. Minutes of the Seattle School Board, 16 January 1917.

29. Cooper, Memorandum to Board of Directors, 16 January 1917.

30. Ira Brown, "A Basis for Debarring Mentally Defective Children from the Public Schools," 12 February 1917, SPSA, Superintendent files, folder "Special Schools 1914–28."

31. Ira Brown, Memorandum to Frank Cooper, 27 April 1918, SPSA, Superintendent files, folder "Special School 1914–28."

32. Brown, 27 April 1918 Memorandum to Cooper.

33. Goodhue, Memorandum to Frank Cooper, no. 2, 9 May 1918.

34. Goodhue, Memorandum to Frank Cooper, no. 2, 9 May 1918.

35. Ira Brown, Memorandum to Frank Cooper, 16 May 1918, SPSA, Superintendent files, folder "Special Schools 1914–28."

36. Minutes of the Seattle School Board, 22 September 1919.

37. Frank Cooper, Memorandum to Board of Directors, 2 October 1919, SPSA, Superintendent files, folder "Special Schools 1914–28."

38. Minutes of the Seattle School Board, 7 October 1919.

39. Frank Cooper, Memorandum to Board of Directors, 24 October 1919, SPSA, Superintendent files, folder "Special Schools 1914–28." See also Dale Soden, "Mark Allison Matthews: Seattle's Minister Rediscovered," *Pacific Northwest Quarterly* 74 (April 1983): 50–58.

40. Cooper, Memorandum to Board of Directors, 24 October 1919.

41. Cooper, Memorandum to Board of Directors, 24 October 1919.

42. Cooper, Memorandum to Board of Directors, 24 October 1919. See also David Mitchell, *Schools and Classes for Exceptional Children* (Cleveland: Survey Committee of the Cleveland Foundation, 1916), 90–94.

43. Cooper, Memorandum to Board of Directors, 24 October 1919.

44. Memorandum between Frank Cooper and Dr. Gulick, October–November 1919, SPSA, Superintendent files, folder "Special Schools 1914–28"; Walter Vose Gulick, *Mental Diseases: A Handbook Dealing with Diagnosis and Classification* (Fort Steilacoom, WA: C. V. Mosby, 1918).

45. While the Red Cross took on some of the health work, the medical department was reduced to a fraction of its former size, which effectively marginalized Brown's authority in the schools. *McGilvra et al. v. Seattle School Dist. No. 1*, 113 Wash., January 1921, *The Pacific Reporter* 194 (St. Paul, MN: West, 1921), 817–20. See also Woolworth, "Conflict, Collaboration, and Concession," 257–71.

46. Quinquennial Report of the Seattle Public Schools, 1916–1921, 78, SPSA; *The Seattle School Bulletin* no. 3, 3 (June 1920).

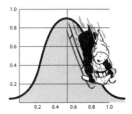

In the Voices of Delinquents: Social Science, the Chicago Area Project, and a Boys' Culture of Casual Crime and Violence in the 1930s

David Wolcott and Steven Schlossman

EPISODES OF POPULAR PANIC about juvenile crime and delinquency have punctuated twentieth-century American culture, reaching crescendos in the 1930s, 1950s, and 1990s. Especially in this last decade, highly publicized atrocities by high school, middle school, and even elementary school boys aroused considerable public anger and confusion. According to many observers, adolescent boys had become "worse," their values and lifestyles dictated more by peers, gangs, and graphic media violence than by family, religion, and school. Implicit in this discourse is a nostalgic yearning for an idealized, crime-free past, one that is inconsistent with current historical knowledge and that discourages empirical inquiry into the realities of American male childhood.

The recurring sense of crisis over juvenile crime has sometimes been accompanied by real changes in behavior; more often, however, it has not. The most recent panic reached its peak in the late 1990s, after a quantifiable increase in serious crimes by juveniles in the 1980s had already subsided.[1] Similarly, the 1950s panic over juvenile delinquency drew inspiration less from criminal acts per se than from more general changes in adolescent behavior and the emergence of newly autonomous youth cultures. Overall, these cultural concerns about juvenile delinquency revealed more about current perceptions of youth at a particular moment in time than about actual youth behaviors.[2]

Popular representations of juvenile crime present two special challenges for historians: first, to outline the contours of actual youth behavior; and second, to explain youth behavior in terms rooted in the youths' own self-understanding. These challenges exemplify a classic difficulty that has long haunted scholarship on the history of childhood. Sources for writing children's history remain problematic because children have rarely recorded their own experiences or participated in organizations that have collected detailed data about them. How, then, can we investigate the social and cultural contexts of male delinquency in ways that advance general methods of inquiry into the history of American childhood?

Studies of lower-class children's behavior that were conducted by social scientists and by practitioners of delinquency-prevention experiments provide one insufficiently used data source to expand our understanding of children's history. Happily for our project, the social lives of lower-class boys, particularly as manifested in the formation of playgroups and gangs, became a favorite subject of urban social workers and of academic sociologists in the early twentieth century. Members of the Chicago School of Sociology, in particular, conducted pathbreaking research on the nature of children's antisocial and criminal conduct in the city's teeming immigrant neighborhoods. Practitioners with the Chicago Area Project (CAP), an innovative, community-based social-action program that was strongly integrated with the research of the Chicago School, produced field reports and other ground-level accounts of children's everyday lives in several high-crime areas in the 1930s.[3] Together, these sources open a partial window into everyday life as experienced by second- and third-generation immigrant boys growing up in Chicago as well as in similar urban-industrial centers.

This chapter offers a distinctly unnostalgic perspective on urban male childhood in the early twentieth century. We emphasize, in particular, the conflict and violence that shaped family and social life for many of these boys, especially those drawn to the omnipresent neighborhood youth gangs—and that dismayed parents, indigenous community leaders, and middle-class reformers alike. We argue that a freewheeling antagonism to the society around them fundamentally conditioned the early adolescence of these Chicago boys.

THE CHICAGO AREA PROJECT, CLIFFORD SHAW, AND CHICAGO SOCIOLOGY

Begun as a local-level delinquency-prevention program in 1931 and incorporated in 1934, the CAP is best remembered today for the challenge it posed to the professional dominance of psychologists and social workers in addressing the problem of juvenile delinquency. It also pioneered the idea of "community based," "bottom up" social programming for children in poor neighborhoods, and invented the role of "detached worker" (or "fieldworker") in gang mediation.[4]

The CAP had intellectual roots in the urban research agenda of W. I. Thomas, Robert Park, and Ernest Burgess, of the sociology department of the University of Chicago. It was overseen by the research unit of the Illinois Institute for Juvenile Research, a state-sponsored child welfare agency that also had strong ties to the social sciences and to the university and was headed by sociologist and former University of Chicago graduate student Clifford R. Shaw. The foremost exponent of the "life history" or "own story" approach to understanding juvenile delinquency from the perspective of the child himself, Shaw conducted qualitative research that built creatively on W. I. Thomas's use of "personal documents" in his classic 1918 study (with Florian Znaiecki), *The Polish Peasant in Europe and America*. By conducting interviews with young offenders and encouraging them to write their life stories, Shaw sought to understand how urban youths defined their social existence.

The special attraction of own-story documents was the degree to which they captured children's point of view with vivid immediacy. They were an attempt to humanize the struggles of city children for recognition and survival by allowing them to situate themselves in the groups and neighborhoods that shaped the cultural contours of their daily lives. Whether or not their accounts were objectively "true" in every detail, the subjective own stories provided uniquely rich, ground-level documentation of both mundane and spectacular experiences. Own-story documents, Shaw believed, enabled children to reveal the social and emotional wellsprings of their day-to-day behaviors, to link their thought processes and actions to those of like-minded peers, and to lay bare the cultural assumptions that nurtured and sustained their daily conduct. The child's own story provided a distinctive data source that sociologists hoped to build upon to transform their discipline into an empirical science.[5]

In a more immediate way, Shaw used the findings from his research—especially the knowledge revealed from the life histories—to formulate the CAP in the 1930s. The CAP was an effort to apply Shaw's research findings to the job of remaking local communities at the neighborhood level. What truly distinguished the CAP in each neighborhood was that it was funded, staffed, and run largely by indigenous neighborhood organizations and local residents. Communal self-help was its guiding principle. The chief role and goal of each indigenous organization (e.g., the Russell Square Community Committee in South Chicago) was to build a new sense of potency among law-abiding residents with the aim of eliminating the conditions in their neighborhoods that facilitated juvenile delinquency.

CAP FIELD WORKERS

A better-known component of the CAP delinquency-prevention strategy, however, and one that generated far more controversy, was the use of field-workers to shadow and penetrate each community's principal juvenile gangs. The field-workers' goal was to gain the confidence of the boys and, having done so, to persuade them why it was both morally right and, ultimately, in their best interests to conform to the values and expectations of conventional society. The field-workers' concrete activities defy easy categorization; above all, they tried to spend as much time with boys as possible as they traversed the latter's neighborhoods in search of "action." Invariably—and consistent with the CAP's low-key, supportive, nonaccusatory style—the field-workers witnessed a considerable amount of crime and violence that they were power-less to prevent, much to the chagrin of cops on the beat. Many did little but stand idly by—or duck or run, depending on the situation—when boys com-mitted minor crimes and fought among themselves or with neighborhood youths.

Ideally, field-workers were young adults from the local community who shared ethnic backgrounds with the boys, and with whom, presumably, they could easily identify. These indigenous workers were supplemented, espe-cially at the beginning stages of community organization, by energetic, ide-alistic, educated young men from outside the neighborhood who were funded by the Institute for Juvenile Research (IJR) and who attempted to develop close rapport with groups of boys who regularly "hung out" and "got into trouble" together. The IJR field-workers' detailed reports—which either narrated or attempted to re-create dialogue between the children or between the field-worker and the children—built on the example of Shaw's life histo-ries and provide much of the historical evidence for our study.

FIELD REPORTS AS SOURCES

The field-workers encouraged the boys with whom they interacted daily in Chicago's immigrant neighborhoods to find their own voices, and they sought to capture and record these voices in their diaries and other written accounts. Consistent with the CAP's ecological philosophy, they emphasized getting to know children in their "natural" social groupings, secret haunts, and ter-ritorial enclaves, rather than in the artificial bureaucratic settings often used by professional social workers and psychologists during the interwar period. The field-workers encouraged children to talk freely about what they were thinking and feeling and—following Shaw's imprimatur—to make themselves understood in their own terms. In the CAP philosophy, talk and mutual comprehension were essential preconditions for effective social intervention. And in order to do effective strategic planning, Shaw needed to receive in-depth, honest, street-level information about delinquent children's daily lives and the meanings they assigned to events.

To date, the field-workers' reports have largely been neglected by scholars, and not without reason. To start, we know little about who the field-workers were (with the prominent exception of political activist Saul Alinsky); how well they knew Shaw personally; and how often Shaw met with them to plan, modify, and evaluate interventions. In addition, the field reports are quite varied, often incomplete, and discontinuous; they are consequently difficult to use systematically as representative historical data. Finally—from a modern scholarly vantage point, when the construction of historical memory has never seemed more problematic—the field reports contain more than a little obvious posturing and overt silliness by the children, besides which, the field-workers' ability to re-create street conversations verbatim strains credulity. No question, then: the field reports do have a downside as reliable data for historical analysis.

But these reports, we believe, also have considerable advantages in providing ground-level data on children's behaviors and, especially, in presenting their views of themselves and others in their own voices. The reports are particularly good for delineating the cultural parameters that shaped children's everyday expectations, experiences, and decision making. Chief among their virtues is their immediacy: their unselfconscious, "you are there" quality. This distinguishes them, for example, from Shaw's most famous life history, *The Jack-Roller*. Although the narrative is told in the first person, writing *The Jack-Roller* required its subject, Stanley, to recall his attitudes toward events that took place many years earlier. It also required Shaw to conduct systematic research to get Stanley's facts into line and to craft the story to produce a smooth narrative. Life histories such as *The Jack-Roller* were meticulously pieced together literary products that were forged by a lengthy process of construction, elaboration, extension, and reconstruction. This process becomes very clear when one examines numerous *unpublished* life histories in the IJR archives that include multiple drafts and rewrites.

Thus, the CAP field-workers' reports strike us as more "natural" documents than do Shaw's life histories. In our judgment, the children's dialogue captured in the field reports are at least as reliable data sources as the children's talk that gets recorded sporadically in the case files of charitable agencies, juvenile courts, and child guidance clinics. And the field reports are surely superior to formal case files for illuminating the more common forms of boys' antisocial behavior that never achieved official notice, intervention, or sanction by social-work or law-enforcement agencies.

Finally, the field reports have the additional advantage of introducing us to children who were younger, in less-serious family distress, and involved in less-serious crimes than the "average" individual documented in juvenile court and social agency records. All the young men about whom Shaw constructed formal life histories had committed crimes severe enough to warrant lengthy processing in juvenile and adult court and incarceration in correctional institutions; at least ten were involved in the infamous "42" gang studied by Chicago sociologist John Landesco.[6] By contrast, the children who appear in the CAP field reports, despite regular skirmishes with the police, generally committed less serious crimes (at comparable ages) than did those in the life histories. Furthermore, they generally penetrated much less far, if at all, into the juvenile justice system. The field reports that we use in this study deal only with younger boys between the ages of nine and sixteen. With a few exceptions, historical scholars have had little to say about the social characteristics of urban youths of this preteen and early-teen age group.[7]

In short, the reports produced by the CAP field-workers were legitimate offspring, once removed, of scholarly methods that made the study of juvenile delinquency central to academics' attempt to build sociology as an empirical discipline in the interwar period. They enable us to distill numerous detailed insights into how Chicago's immigrant children, in Thomas's terms, "defined" their "total situation" and explained their own behaviors.

ELEMENTS OF A BOYS' CULTURE IN CHICAGO'S IMMIGRANT NEIGHBORHOODS

A central theme of the Chicago School sociologists (as well as of the social workers who preceded them) was that immigrant parents were experiencing great difficulty in adapting their traditional child-rearing goals and methods to the demands of the new urban-industrial order. Many families were being torn apart emotionally by their inability to steer their children's lives in directions approved by religious and secular community leaders. Thus, it comes as little surprise that the CAP sponsored its initial delinquency-prevention programs in three neighborhoods noted for both heavy immigrant populations and high concentrations of delinquency. These neighborhoods were the Polish community surrounding Russell Square on the South Side of Chicago, the predominantly Polish and Italian district on the near Northwest Side, and the largely Italian near West Side.

Limited Parental Oversight

Whether or not these sociologists were fair in holding immigrant families accountable for delinquency, it was apparent in all three neighborhoods that many boys lived remarkably free of intrusive parental supervision. Families exercised minimal surveillance over the day-to-day lives of the prepubescent and early-adolescent sons who participated in the CAP program. Severe economic hardship during the Depression often removed fathers and mothers from the home for very long hours in order to earn a survival income, or created prolonged unemployment that could undermine paternal authority at home. Bars, which were ubiquitous in all three neighborhoods following the repeal of Prohibition in 1933, further tempted fathers to spend time away from family fraternizing in a male tavern culture. Apart from trying to get their children to attend school, many mothers and fathers seemed unable to provide significant sources of emotional support or guidance in their children's lives. When the children mentioned their parents in the CAP field-workers' reports, it was almost always to stress their erratic care, drinking habits, and sporadic but harsh discipline.[8]

Children who did engage in delinquency tended to come from disrupted families. Studies of children in juvenile court and in correctional institutions routinely found that only small minorities of young offenders came from homes with both parents. Moreover, boys in trouble typically held part-time jobs such as street peddling, performing errands, selling newspapers, shining shoes, collecting junk, and street entertaining. These jobs effectively removed them from parental oversight after school and on weekends and instead relocated them in commercial settings that facilitated their participation in a street culture of their own making. Boys with little parental supervision or economic support tended to create a structure for their lives with minimal adult participation and to count very little on their families for regular advice or sustenance.[9]

Boys' Group Culture

In place of families, these pre- and young-teen males oriented themselves mainly toward their peers; their own social groups; and, often, their gangs. Street culture was at least as important as family influence in organizing their time and directing their activities. The Chicago School sociologists emphasized that second-generation immigrant children tended to adapt to "disorganized" families and communities primarily through associations with one another. Frederic Thrasher, for example, maintained that, when large numbers of children are crowded together, "spontaneous play-groups are forming everywhere—gangs in embryo." Without supervision, these groups often found themselves in conflict "over the valued prerogatives of gangland—territory, loot, play spaces, patronage for illicit business, privileges to exploit, and so on."[10] Thus, from the perspective of Thrasher and many Chicago sociologists, the social primordial soup in which city children lived almost inevitably spawned gangs.

In practice, the CAP field-workers, unlike trained social workers, accepted the juveniles' group orientation as a reasonable adaptation to their environment and did not try to separate them from the group's influence. They argued that "delinquency in deteriorated areas may frequently be regarded as a very natural adjustment of the boy to the expectations, behavior patterns, and values of the group of which he is a part."[11] Peer groups could serve as home and family in place of absent, inadequate, or culturally alienated parents. The CAP dispatched field-workers to associate with each group, trying both to understand the group's internal dynamics and to modify its collective behavior. Although Shaw argued that energies should be directed toward work with the "natural leaders" of each group, with an expectation that the rest of the children would follow, this was rarely the case in practice. More often, the field-workers focused on the actions of the collectivity and rarely tried to distinguish any "natural leaders" among the gang members.[12]

Boys in these three Chicago neighborhoods organized themselves into their own groups by age, territory, and ethnicity. Age was critical in determining the boundaries of peer groups. In the 1930s, although economic opportunities were extraordinarily limited, youths older than their middle teens often left school and got jobs to support themselves or their families. In contrast, most boys ages sixteen and under remained obligated to attend school and were still subject to the legal authority of Cook County Juvenile Court. As a result, the life experiences and group associations of older teens were very different from those of younger teens. Logically, then, gangs differentiated themselves by age.

Juveniles of many ages adopted the associational form of the gang. Even very young groups such as the Cubs, whose members clustered between the ages of nine and twelve, organized themselves along the lines of a gang. In extreme cases, younger gang members learned from or looked up to older gang members. For example, one boy explained that "when you get in trouble, if you're a juvenile, you meet fellows older than you are and who are in for worse crimes. They teach you how to break locks and other crimes."[13] Equally often, though, gangs of different age levels ignored one another. For example, although two West Side Italian gangs in the late 1950s lived in the same housing project, the older Nobles, ages sixteen and upward, had little to do with the younger Dukes, ages fifteen and lower.[14]

Although age boundaries were vital in the organization of gangs, the boys in the three CAP neighborhoods tended to define their peer groups even more narrowly in terms of territory and ethnicity. The historian Eric Schneider has portrayed post–World War II youth gangs as primarily territorial, dividing their cities block by block and fighting over space and recreational assets such as playgrounds and swimming pools. In Depression-era Chicago, traveling in territories other than home potentially exposed boys to threats from other gangs. Attacks by "home" groups against strangers were generally anonymous, arbitrary, and swift. For example, a CAP field-worker reported an incident at a Polish dance in a Northwest Side park in the 1930s in which three "nice looking young Italian fellows" were beaten up by the crowd. "Many of the smaller boys never stray beyond their own neighborhood," according to Thrasher, in order to protect themselves. Even into the 1950s the younger boys in the Dukes "felt under a constant threat of being waylaid or of getting into a 'jam' [gang fight] with an enemy gang."[15]

Tensions Between Boys and Community Institutions

Bonded closely together by age, ethnicity, and territorial identity, boys in the three CAP neighborhoods exhibited striking alienation from and hostility toward mainstream authority figures and social institutions. These boys seemed forever angry at anyone outside their peer group, although they harbored antagonisms less toward family and more toward the central institutions in their communities, especially churches, teachers, and police officers. These antagonisms were not one sided, however; teachers and police officers expressed similar animosities toward the children and were not afraid to exercise coercive power over them. Their displays of authority often reinforced antagonisms on both sides.

Although the church was a key institution in most urban ethnic communities, pre- and early-teen boys in the three CAP neighborhoods generally expressed disinterest or animosity toward it. In the Polish South Side community of Russell Square, no institution aroused greater loyalty among adults than St. Michael's Church.[16] Boys from that area, however, were often reluctant to attend. For example, when encouraged to go to church, boys offered excuses that they were too tired or did not feel like attending, or that twice a year was often enough to go to confession. Moreover, when in confession, the boys were not motivated to tell the truth or to confess everything they had done. One said, "You tell the Priest what you think he wants to hear, and it's all right." Another announced that the priest "was full of bunk!" In addition, a group of older Polish and Italian boys on Chicago's near Northwest Side elicited the admiration of their younger contemporaries by robbing their church's donation boxes. Rather than an object of deference or a source of extraparental control over youth, the church often became a prime target for youths' hostility.[17]

These boys also experienced severe conflicts with schools. Nearly all the CAP's clientele were still in school (both public and Catholic), where they regularly struggled against both teachers and administrators. These conflicts manifested themselves through vandalism, truancy, and disruptions in class. The children's antagonism toward everyone and everything connected with school did not represent an organized rebellion against authority. Instead, it mainly expressed rejection of an institution in which most city children experienced numbing intellectual frustration, an institution that, in effect, provided society's imprimatur to their failure to conform to adult expectations.

School vandalism was often the work of boys in their early teens. Breaking windows and stealing from the schools were commonplace. For instance, members of a Russell Square gang, the Houston Herrings, stole tools from the machine shop at school. In addition, youth gangs were known to break into schools and damage furniture, desktops, walls, ceilings, and books. School kitchens also presented a favorite target, where the boys ruined food by throwing eggs and urinating in the milk. In one legendary case, boys broke into their school and defecated on the principal's desk and in the kitchen.[18]

Truancy represented a similar rejection of school authority. Rather than attacking the school itself, truants chose not to participate. This problem particularly affected children old enough to engage fully in the street culture yet young enough to fall under compulsory-attendance laws. For example, one field-worker described the large number of truants he saw casually walking the streets or entering stores during school hours on the near Northwest Side in 1938 and 1939. The CAP field-workers' descriptions of truants' attitudes also revealed the boys' animosity toward school authority. For example, one boy, Doc, commented about St. Michael's School: "Aw hell, they don't teach us nothin'. What the Hell! they don't know how to teach!" Another, Joe, asserted, "I never did like school. I wish it would burn down!"[19]

Antagonism between students and teachers was apparent in the classroom as well. While students rarely described the disruptions that they caused, they often commented on the physical force that teachers used in disciplining them. For example, Henry said that "all the Sisters in St. Michael's School believe in, is to pound lumps on a guy." On the other hand, the boys occasionally fought back. A field-worker reported that "the 'Sisters' in the Parochial Schools were not averse to the use of force in disciplining their pupils, and often the latter ones would strike back, so that occasionally attempts at discipline would degenerate into a hand-to-hand struggle between the Sister and the boy." According to the field-worker assigned to another Russell Square gang, the Red Wings, William "came over and said to me, that whenever a 'Sister' tried to clip him, he tells her that he's going to break her pointer, and then she doesn't do anything; William said that if his own sister wasn't in the same room, he would kick the fuckin' piss out of the Sister!"[20]

When not in school, many pre- and early-teen boys in the three CAP neighborhoods had regular encounters with the police. Along with teachers, police officers constituted a major source of coercive authority in their daily lives. In part because the police seemed to make life unnecessarily difficult, boys harbored deep resentments toward them. Young offenders described not only being hassled but also being beaten and even shot at by police. The recurrent conflicts between boys and the police carried significant symbolic, as well as quite real and dangerous, dimensions. A CAP field-worker who frequently observed interactions between cops and kids maintained that "the activities of the police with respect to these boys were marked on every occasion by arbitrariness and sometimes even by brutality. On many occasions the activities of the squads were quite obviously motivated either by a desire to show their authority or sometimes even by mere venal impulses."[21]

Police hassled kids particularly regarding their use of the public space of the streets. One Russell Square gang asserted that police regularly chased them out of their hangouts. Similarly, a group of young girls described an incident in which a police officer broke up a game of jacks that they were playing in public.[22] In these cases, police officers challenged the juveniles' right to use the streets, where their lives were centered. This sort of everyday conflict reinforced general hostility toward the police.

Hassling was one problem, but expressions of police animosity toward street children went much further. A long tradition in Chicago policing approved the beating of young children as the best deterrent to future misbehavior. For example, one boy from Russell Square claimed that, after being caught stealing fruit off a truck, "[d]em g[od damned] cops beat the s[hit] out of me, and J-C. did dey give it to me!" Other boys described being beaten or chased across town by police officers with guns for even the mildest misbehaviors.[23] On the Northwest Side, eleven-year-old Junior shrugged off incidents when the police shot at him for stealing coal from railroad company reserves: "We get coal here. I was caught once but Pete was caught five times, ain't it Pete? Day don't do nothin to ye. Da coppers shoot at your feet or in de air to scare ye. They don't shoot at ye."[24] The readiness of the police to beat up young delinquents and display their ability to unleash lethal force did little to build the children's readiness to respect and defer to adult authority.

In short, the boys whose lives and voices were captured by the CAP field-workers in the three neighborhoods appeared to construct a largely self-contained and self-directed way of life on the streets of Depression-era Chicago. They formulated their identities mainly in affiliations with other boys from similar backgrounds and circumstances. And the culture they developed was characterized by hostility to any authority figures that might rein them in, be they parents, teachers, agents of the churches, or police officers. Alienated as these boys were from mainstream institutions, their lives centered on exaggerated efforts to achieve status within the small worlds of their ethnic neighborhoods.

BOYS' DELINQUENCIES

No feature is more apparent in the CAP field-workers' reports than the ubiquity of low-level violence and petty crime in boys' daily lives. Of course, the whole reason that the CAP sent agents to intervene with these boys was to prevent delinquency, but casual physical confrontation and theft thoroughly pervades their accounts. In the Depression-era ethnic neighborhoods of Chicago, many boys both found entertainment and established status within their narrow communities by fighting with one another and by stealing from people around them.

Fighting

Low-level violence has frequently been a key element of early-adolescent boys' culture. As a number of scholars have shown, late nineteenth-century boys—when left to themselves in school, at play, at work, and in public—used violence to establish their fragile claims to honor and masculinity.[25] The peer culture of 1930s Chicago operated similarly. The boys with whom the CAP representatives worked spoke often about their fights, near fights, and threats to fight. While some of this talk can be disregarded as bragging, the field-workers witnessed enough scuffles to indicate that fights were common. Among pre- and young teens, violence less often involved weapons or the possibility of severe bodily harm than it did among grown men. Nonetheless, black eyes and bruises were commonplace badges of honor. In a Depression economy and in neighborhoods that offered few prospects for fulfilling the American dream of success, low-level violence appeared to provide considerable satisfaction. Fighting enabled these boys to demonstrate that they wielded power, at least in their limited social sphere.

Detailed attention to one group in particular demonstrates that casual violence in defense of a tenuous sense of honor could be an everyday occurrence for even young boys. No older than their early teens, members of Russell Square's Brandon Buddies fought against one another; other neighborhood juveniles; and their unsuccessful CAP field-worker, Joseph Ochwat. Ochwat's first report begins when he "found them fighting in the hall. Eddie R. pulled out a knife and said to the other boy, 'I'll stab you if you don't stop hitting me.'" Four days later, as Ochwat tried to teach them how to wrestle, he reports that Harry J. pulled a knife and "said look it if anybody jumps on me while I'm wrestling I'll cut 'em up. I took the knife away from him and told him that I'd give it back to him as soon as he finished wrestling."[26]

Casual, low-level violence was an accepted and expected element of the boys' group dynamic. Highly egotistical, they grew antagonistic if they did not get their own way. In the course of one month, Harry J. and Eddie R. fought because Harry hit Eddie in the face while playing tag; the boys were chased out of a crafts room for fighting; one boy started kicking another in the face after losing a boxing match; Eddie S. hit Stanley in the wrist with a stick; Frank broke a window in the game room while fighting with "some cocksucker who was fuckin around with me." These boys also admired violence by relatives and friends, especially if it improved their own standing in the group. For instance, Stanley described glowingly "the time my old man was battling with six coppers on the roof and he gave every flatfoot a beatin."[27]

Ochwat's relationship with the Brandon Buddies deteriorated in the course of his work with them. By September 1935, he wrote that when they went to the park together, "the boys all ran into the bushes and picked up lumps of dog dirt. 'Hey sour puss,' yelled S., 'I bet you can't get me,' he said. I knew that if I went after him they'd throw sand at me, so I didn't pay any attention to him. All of a sudden I was hit by dirt from all sides." The boys subsequently offered to cease tormenting Ochwat if he bought them candy or ice cream, but he did not because he had no money. As a result, one boy replied, "Fuck you then you dirty cocksucker we're going to try and get you fired." After the boys again threw dog dirt at him, Ochwat related that "I got mad and ran after S. till I caught him, and I slapped his face, but it didn't help any he did it all over again." Eventually, the boys simply refused to allow Ochwat to associate with them.[28]

The fighting mentality, combined with a strong peer orientation based on ethnicity and territoriality, might be presumed to have led inevitably to organized gang fights. We hesitate to draw this conclusion, however, especially for the younger boys. Based on descriptions by the CAP field-workers for the entire period between the 1930s and the 1950s, gang fights may be divided into two broad categories: first, staged "rumbles" between gangs and, second, fights initiated by gangs looking for an individual opponent who had offended them in some fashion. Organized fights of either sort seem to have been more common in the 1950s than in the 1930s, and to have more often involved older adolescents. Rumbles were surely less frequent than popular mythology (e.g., *West Side Story*) might suggest, and they were concentrated almost entirely in the post–World War II years. At least in Chicago, the Depression era saw growing awareness of juvenile gangs and commentary about their potential for fighting, but gang-based conflicts most often involved only a few individuals. Furthermore, homicide in the three CAP neighborhoods was almost never associated with pre- or early-teen boys, whether on their own initiative or as part of gang-sanctioned activity. A casual resort to low-level interpersonal violence was the more dominant characteristic of the boys' street culture.

Theft

Even more than fighting, many of these boys routinely engaged in petty thievery and shoplifting with an air of indifference to consequences or punishment. Almost every report by a CAP field-worker included the latest stealing escapades of his young charges. Most reports presented theft as if it were a natural, everyday phenomenon, a ritual undeterred by moral or legal misgivings and found to be widely acceptable within the children's culture.

Minor property crime was particularly common among boys on the near Northwest Side in 1938 and 1939. According to the field-worker, "[D]elinquencies varied with age, time, and location. . . . Stealing has almost as many forms as there are individuals and groups engaged in the practice. However, many forms of delinquencies are practiced so openly and so habitually that any one may observe them with very little effort."[29] For instance, the nine- to 16-year-olds whom this field-worker regularly observed stole coal from railroad yards without a second thought. He further explained, "To date I have seen Chink, Louie, Junior, Marion, and Bob steal coal from the neighboring coal yards. Conversation has divulged that practically every boy here has at one time or another stolen coal." In the course of one hour spent watching a coal yard, this field worker observed six groups of children and adults taking coal.[30]

Shoplifting was also a regular activity among these boys, especially at holiday times. The store detective for a Goldblatt Brothers Store estimated that he caught approximately one hundred shoplifters monthly, roughly 60 percent of whom were children.[31] The CAP staff confirmed that shoplifting was widespread. For example, in one trip to the Goldblatt Brothers Store on Chicago Avenue, a field-worker counted 321 children under age seventeen in the store at one time, without their parents. He saw only two buy anything, but he did see enough to suspect that this many children could only be up to no good. He observed a group of four boys between ages seven and nine milling around candy barrels, helping themselves to treats when the clerk was not looking. He also encountered several boys, ages roughly fourteen or fifteen, who asked him to drop a "surprise package" on the floor so they could grab it. On another trip to Goldblatt's, the field-worker ran into an eight-year-old boy who wanted the worker's advice on how to rob a peanut-vending machine.[32]

Younger teens also stole from passing trucks and local vendors, focusing on items of little value, such as fruit, because of their easy availability.

For instance, a CAP field-worker learned that one group in Russell Square regularly stole fruit off trucks when the boys offered him an ill-gotten bag of peaches. Even when the field-worker refused the fruit on principle, the boys offered him grapes they had also stolen, apparently thinking he just did not like peaches.[33] Likewise, one of the Brandon Buddies told his CAP worker that he had stolen apples from his father's store. Members of the Houston Herrings in 1938 reported taking cigarettes, pipes, oranges, apples, and tomatoes. During October 1935, another group, the Mackinaws, casually mentioned stealing grapes off a truck; tools from Woolworth's; and, in one instance, bicycles and automobiles. The field-worker finally asked a Mackinaw, "Hog," why he stole, and Hog responded, "Jesus! Joe, if I don't steal I ain't never got nothing so I steal things and sell them I buy candy and go to the show."[34]

The boys' attitude toward petty crime was not only casual but also playful, a vehicle by which children with few resources could invent games for individual and group amusement. Many of their activities seem best understood as recreational crimes, neither necessary nor remunerative. As one boy explained, "When we were stealing we always made a game of it. For example, we might gamble on who could steal the most caps in a day or who could steal in the presence of a detective and then get away. It was fun I wanted, not the hat."[35] The very inconsequentiality of these crimes to their young perpetrators reflected how routine and ubiquitous they were, and how central to the children's street culture.

Violent Crimes

Although petty crime was a regular occurrence in the three CAP neighborhoods, some boys less frequently, but just as nonchalantly, committed more serious crimes that involved premeditation and danger to the victim. Most prominent among these was purse-snatching, which required stealing from a moving, animate target. One field-worker's description of a member of the Houston Herrings' technique exemplified a more general pattern. This boy preferred to attack women who were alone and over age thirty, "as they were less agile and less capable of defending themselves." He would come up behind the woman, and just as he was about to pass her, he would grab at her pocketbook with his right hand and strike her in the abdomen with his left. According to the field-worker, this technique worked well; in ten months under observation, he was never caught.[36]

Other examples similarly involved both violence and coordination by the perpetrators. In the company of four other boys, twelve-year-old Chester would wait at corners, "jump on cars stopped for lights," and snatch purses from female occupants. His gang engaged in this early equivalent of carjacking for a month and earned the attention of two police squads before they were caught.[37] Although these robberies were more violent and less frequent than the property crimes that occurred routinely in the three CAP neighborhoods, they nonetheless arose from the same social context and appear to have been fully sanctioned by the children's culture.

Jack-rolling—the robbery and assault of vulnerable men—was the most violent crime by early-adolescent boys that was reported with any regularity. Although jack-rolling was significantly more serious than theft and involved more premeditated violence than most purse-snatchings, descriptions of jack-rolling suggest that its perpetrators regarded it in an equally casual manner. However, while very young children could shoplift or purse-snatch, children rarely began jack-rolling until they reached the ages of fourteen or fifteen, or a point of physical development at which they could either deceive or assault a grown man.

Stanley, the subject of Shaw's *The Jack-Roller*, exemplified the practice. Although he spent much of his youth among the boarding houses of the near West Side, Stanley was not a typical Chicago delinquent. His long history of arrests and incarcerations differentiated him from the casual shoplifters and gang members whose activities the CAP field-workers documented in such abundance. Nonetheless, Stanley described his early career in jack-rolling—which began at age fourteen, as he and a friend assaulted drunken men for their money—with a casualness much like that of other young offenders: "It was bloody work, but necessity demanded it—we had to live."

In spite of his nonchalance regarding violence, Stanley was not a large boy who could overwhelm his victims. At fourteen, he was only four feet two inches tall and weighed ninety-one pounds. Although he grew during his teens, at age eighteen he had still only become an average-sized man of five feet eight inches, 150 pounds. As a result, his jack-rolling often relied more on guile and assistance than on his own physical prowess. Most commonly, Stanley allowed homosexual men to approach him ("because I was so little and they like little fellows"), let them take him to a room, and then waited for an accomplice to break in and assault and rob the victim. Stanley rationalized the practice by thinking: "[W]as he not a low degenerate, and wouldn't he use the money only to harm himself further?"[38]

Stanley's particular crimes distinguished him from other pre- and early teens in our study, but his lack of concern for his acts and victims paralleled the attitudes that accompanied the regular practice of petty thievery by many boys in the three CAP neighborhoods. The parameters of the culture of casual minor crime and limited violence were broad enough to sanction more serious crimes as well.

CHILDREN'S VOICES AND THE "DELINQUENT AS A PERSON"

In this chapter we have described several configurations of antisocial and illegal behavior—a culture of petty crime and low-level violence—that were common among boys in three Depression-era Chicago neighborhoods. We have tried to portray these boys as willful actors who exercised considerable agency in shaping the contours of their day-to-day lives.

To construct this portrait, we have relied on rare documents that report the thoughts and behaviors of delinquent children, partially in their own words. To the CAP field-workers, understanding delinquents as children and learning to listen to them on their own terms were preconditions for trying to disrupt their "normal" entry into group-based antisocial behavior. We have placed special emphasis on the field reports that these workers filed, for it was the field-workers who bore the brunt of responsibility for reshaping the boys' values and behaviors. By coordinating data in the field reports with Shaw's more formal "life histories," it becomes possible to gain ground-level insight into the lives of delinquent children in Chicago's immigrant neighborhoods.

The use of "own story" documentation of children's lives reflected social scientists' heightened interest in and respect for "the delinquent as a person," their focus on individual rather than environmental or hereditary causes of delinquency. As the sociologist and former CAP staff member Solomon Kobrin put it, the Chicago studies "focused attention on the paradoxical fact that no matter how destructive or morally shocking, delinquency may often represent the efforts of the person to find and vindicate his status as a human being, rather than an abdication of his humanity or an intrinsic incapacity to experience human sentiment."[39]

At the same time, however, both the CAP field-workers' reports and Shaw's life histories can be read more pessimistically, and our interpretation of the evidence tilts in this direction. We have portrayed a vital and pervasive culture that nurtured antisocial values and behaviors in many children, evinced few signs of effective adult resistance, and was largely indifferent or hostile to appeals from "outsiders" for self-transformation. Even Shaw, eternal optimist that he was, ultimately granted that the only way to save *The Jack-Roller*'s Stanley from his criminal predilections was to remove him forever from the neighborhood that had so distorted his upbringing. Own-story methodology was profoundly humanizing and facilitated a welcome expansion of knowledge about how children were growing up in early twentieth-century ethnic neighborhoods. But the overall impression that we draw from this body of documentary evidence is that prospects for diverting these children's lives from pathways of crime, violence, and personal degradation—for achieving individual dignity and social approbation beyond the boundaries of neighborhood—were bleak indeed.

Inevitably, our analysis suggests some historical parallels between the experiences of potentially delinquent boys in the past and the present. Although the ethnic composition of modern-day cities is sharply different from that of cities in the 1930s, many common features that place today's male children at risk for criminal behaviors have clear counterparts in the Depression era. These include the prevalence of gangs, widespread truancy and indifference to school, confrontational relations with the police, a ready resort to fighting to display manly virtues, persistent petty stealing and vandalism, parents overwhelmed by poverty and cultural upheavals, and a nonchalant attitude toward committing or being victimized by personal violence. Nostalgia for an innocent time, when growing up was simple and safe, ignores many unpleasant realities in the history of working-class male childhood in American cities.

NOTES

1. Alfred Blumstein and Richard Rosenfeld, "Explaining Recent Trends in U.S. Homicide Rates," *Journal of Criminal Law and Criminology* 88 (Summer 1998): 1175–216.

2. James A. Gilbert, *A Cycle of Outrage: America's Reaction to the Juvenile Delinquent in the 1950s* (New York: Oxford University Press, 1986).

3. These field reports are stored in the Chicago Area Project Records, located at the Chicago Historical Society (hereafter cited as CAP Records), and in the personal papers of Stephen S. Bubacz, a CAP field-worker, located in Special Collections at the University of Illinois at Chicago Library (hereafter cited as Bubacz Papers). In *A History of Sociological Research Methods in America, 1920–1960* (Cambridge: Cambridge University Press, 1996), Jennifer Platt notes that it was common for Chicago sociologists to draw on field data that others had collected.

4. On the Chicago Area Project generally, see, among many others, Ernest W. Burgess, Joseph D. Lohman, and Clifford R. Shaw, "The Chicago Area Project," in *Coping with Crime: Yearbook of the National Probation Association*, ed. Marjorie Bell (New York: National Probation Association, 1937), 8–28; Solomon K. Kobrin, "The Chicago Area Project: A 25-Year Assessment," *Annals of the American Academy of Political and Social Sciences* 322 (March 1959): 19–29; Robert E. L. Faris, *Chicago Sociology, 1920–1932* (Chicago: University of Chicago Press, 1967); James Bennett, *Oral History and Delinquency: The Rhetoric of Criminology* (Chicago: University of Chicago Press, 1981); Steven L. Schlossman and Michael Sedlak, *The Chicago Area Project Revisited* (Santa Monica, CA: RAND Corporation, 1983 [republished, without footnotes, in *Crime and Delinquency* 26 (July 1983): 398–462]); Martin Bulmer, *The Chicago School of Sociology: Institutionalization, Diversity, and the Rise of Sociological Research* (Chicago: University of Chicago Press, 1984); and Platt, *A History of Sociological Research Methods in America*.

5. For examples of Shaw's own-story research, see his *The Jack-Roller: A Delinquent Boy's Own Story* (Chicago: University of Chicago Press, 1930); *The*

Natural History of a Delinquent Career (Westport, CT: Greenwood Press, 1931); and *Brothers in Crime* (Chicago: University of Chicago Press, 1938). More than one hundred "life histories"are collected at the Chicago Historical Society as the Institute for Juvenile Research Life Histories. See also James Bennett, *Oral History and Delinquency* (Chicago: University of Chicago Press, 1981).

6. John Landesco, "The Life History of a Member of the 42 Gang," *Journal of Criminal Law and Criminology* 23 (March 1933): 964–98.

7. These exceptions include David Nasaw, *Children of the City: At Work and at Play* (Garden City, NY: Anchor Press, 1985); Timothy J. Gilfoyle, "Street-Rats and Gutter-Snipes: Child Pickpockets and Street Culture in New York City, 1850– 1900," *Journal of Social History* 37 (Summer 2004): 853–82.

8. These reports only convey children's side of the story. One weakness of the Chicago School's focus on community disorganization was that it failed to establish any criteria to distinguish children who turned delinquent from those who did not; the sociologists implicitly suggested that nearly all kids from disrupted communities would become delinquents, when of course this was not the case.

9. See, as examples, Sophonisba P. Breckinridge and Edith Abbott, *The Delinquent Child and the Home* (1912; New York: Arno Press, 1970); Earl R. Moses, *The Negro Delinquent in Chicago* (Washington, DC, 1936); and Nasaw, *Children of the City.*

10. Frederic M. Thrasher, *The Gang: A Study of 1,313 Gangs in Chicago* (Chicago: University of Chicago Press, 1927).

11. Chicago Area Project, *Annual Report* (1939), 8, box 8, folder 2, Institute for Juvenile Research Papers, Chicago Historical Society.

12. Chicago Area Project, *Annual Report* (1939), 10, box 8, folder 2, IJR Papers; Schlossman and Sedlak, *Chicago Area Project Revisited,* 8–9.

13. "Cubs-Reports," January–July 1933, folder 74, Bubacz Papers; quote from Moses, *The Negro Delinquent,* 21.

14. "The Dukes," c. 1958; "The Nobles," c. 1958, box 102, folder 5, both located in CAP Records.

15. Eric C. Schneider, *Vampires, Dragons, and Egyptian Kings: Youth Gangs in Postwar New York* (Princeton: Princeton University Press, 1999); John L. Brown, "Diary of an Area Representative," 9 November 1938, 7, box 108, folder 12, CAP Records; quotes from Thrasher, *The Gang,* 174; "The Dukes," 4.

16. Schlossman and Sedlak, *Chicago Area Project Revisited,* 8.

17. "The Nature and Characteristics of Delinquents and Delinquency, in the South Chicago Area Project, as Revealed by Three Group Diaries," undated, chap. 1, 17–18, box 110, folder 1, CAP Records; Brown, "Diary of an Area Representative," 11 January 1939, 113–114.

18. [No first name given] MacMurray, "Introduction," c. 1935, 99, CAP Records, box 95, folder 12; Sue Reith, "West Side Community Committee," c. 1949, 14–17, box 103, folder 2, CAP Records; Schlossman and Sedlak, *Chicago Area Project Revisited,* 30–31.

19. John L. Brown, "Near Northwest Side," c. 1940, 27–28, box 91, folder 5, CAP Records; Faris, "A Study of Boys," 35; quotes from "Nature and Characteristics," chaps. 5, 2, 5.

20. "Nature and Characteristics," chap. 5, 5–6.

21. MacMurray, "Introduction," c. 1935, 28.

22. "Nature and Characteristics," chap. 5, 10; Alice Smith, untitled report on girl gangs, 1935, 6, folder 75, Bubacz Papers.

23. Joe Borbelly, "Extract from Leader's Report; Williams Club (Mackinaws)," 3 October 1935, folder 77, Bubacz Papers; Brown, "Diary of an Area Representative," 1939, 249.

24. Brown, "Diary of an Area Representative," 28 November 1938, 24.

25. E. Anthony Rotundo, *American Manhood: Transformations in Masculinity from the Revolution to the Modern Era* (New York: Basic Books, 1993); Joan Jacobs Brumberg, *Kansas Charley: The Story of a Nineteenth-Century Boy Murderer* (New York: Viking, 2003).

26. Joseph Ochwat, "Brandon Buddies [daily reports]," 8 February 1935, 12 February 1935, folder 70, Bubacz Papers.

27. Ochwat, "Brandon Buddies," February 1935.

28. Ochwat, "Brandon Buddies," September 1935.

29. Brown, "Near Northwest Side," 22.

30. Brown, "Diary of an Area Representative," 19 December 1938, 66.

31. "Interview with Goldblatt's Detective," 13 April 1934, folder 10, Mary E. McDowell Papers, Chicago Historical Society.

32. Brown, "Diary of an Area Representative," 13 December 1938, 57–58; 27 February 1939, 200–201.

33. "Extract from Leader's Report; Group—Burley Lions; Leader—J. L. Brown," October 1935, folder 73, Bubacz Papers.

34. Ochwat, "Brandon Buddies," 28 February 1935; untitled report on Houston Herrings gang, 18 November 1938, folder 76, Bubacz Papers; quotation from Borbelly, "Extract from Leader's Report," 22 October 1935.

35. Chicago Area Project, *Annual Report* (1939), 9, box 8, folder 2, IJR Papers.

36. MacMurray, "Introduction," 100–101.

37. Individual case file on "Chester," folder 49, Bubacz Papers.

38. Shaw, *Jack-Roller*, 85, 97, 86.

39. Kobrin, "Chicago Area Project," 21–22.

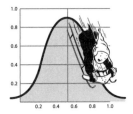

CHAPTER 7

The Whole Child: Social Science and Race at the White House Conference of 1930

Diana Selig

"SHALL WE DISMEMBER THE CHILD?" worried reformer Lillian Wald in *The Survey* shortly before the 1930 White House Conference on Child Health and Protection. Her answer was no. She advocated "a unified approach to the problems of childhood" that encompassed all aspects of child life. Such an approach would consider "the child as a whole and very human being, not merely as an actual or potential victim of malaria or hookworm, or of the many other adverse social conditions which can be considered *en masse.*" Workers in many fields should "pool our knowledge, love and efforts for all the children of America."[1]

To explain this "unified approach," Wald and other delegates at this conference marshaled the full weight of the new child sciences that had burgeoned over the previous decade. They drew on scientific advances to design and justify expanded programs for children. At the time of the conference, experts were redefining childhood as an extended, critical, and complicated stage of life, in which the early years were crucial to healthy development. New social science findings coalesced in the notion of the "whole child," a concept that included recognition of individual personality and cooperation among experts in the home, school, and community. Conference goers agreed that trained professionals, familiar with scientific methods of research and evaluation, should coordinate their work to benefit the nation's children.

Yet while the conference delegates drew on similar scientific trends, they disagreed about their ramifications. The incorporation of social science into social policy was not a smooth process. Wald's concern for the dismembered child hinted at the institutional and intellectual rifts that had come to characterize child advocacy by 1930. As activists struggled to translate the new findings into programs of action, they often were divided along professional lines. Wald's article was a defense of the federal Children's Bureau, threatened at the time by a proposal to transfer functions to the Public Health Service. At the same time, her appeal suggested a deeper split in approaches to child welfare. One school of thought reflected the well-established social welfare tradition of the Progressive Era, represented by the Children's Bureau network. Social workers and activists used statistical research studies and other social science tools to highlight the adverse environmental conditions that harmed children and to advocate expanded public aid for families.

A second school of thought, ascendant in the 1920s, emerged from the new psychological orientation in social science. Its proponents included psychiatrists, pediatricians, and child development researchers intent on establishing their new fields. Rather than addressing large-scale social ills, these experts focused on the pathology of the individual child: they promoted child guidance clinics and school psychologists as means to adjust personality and behavior. These two schools of thought were never entirely distinct, for psychologists sometimes acknowledged the environmental perspective and social workers incorporated psychology into their practice. Yet they generated conflicting impulses on reform. Despite the widespread faith in scientific expertise, child science offered no single path to social policy.

Tensions over how to interpret the new child sciences, though fractious at the time, could be dynamic and productive in the end. The heated debates at the conference produced fruitful results, most notably in how the delegates came to understand the impact of race on children. Racial discrepancies figured prominently in a number of research reports prepared for the conference, in part because of the presence on conference committees of black social scientists and reformers who were familiar with new thinking on race and culture. In the context of the early Depression, the reports argued that racial discrimination, along with unemployment and falling wages, harmed children from minority groups in the all-important first years of life. They wrought a compromise that brought together the two viewpoints prominent in the interwar period: experts from the social welfare tradition emphasized the social forces that limited the health care and education that African American and other minority children received, while experts in psychology explained the adverse effects on mental hygiene and individual adjustment. By combining the two approaches, conference participants created a powerful framework to document the devastating consequences of racism on child development.

Competing understandings of child science thus gave rise to compelling new ways to understand racial inequality in American life.

The work of the conference suggests that the psychological interpretation of child science was not entirely triumphant by the end of the 1920s, as some accounts have suggested.[2] Rather, the psychological perspective co-existed with the social welfare tradition, which remained vibrant and powerful at the time of the conference. Reports from the White House Conference also indicate that child welfare experts, whose post–World War II concerns with race have been well-documented, were alert to the impact of racial discrimination as early as 1930. The conference was an important vehicle for the development of their ideas. The conclusion they reached—that racial discrimination harmed the personality development of the minority child—would become the dominant framework for understanding the social and psychological effects of racism and would come to play a critical role on the national stage. This insight left a significant legacy for psychological research, public policy, and popular perception. It presaged further social science work, including the famous "doll studies" of psychologists Kenneth and Mamie Clark, and set the stage for the landmark ruling in the *Brown v. Board of Education* decision a quarter century later.[3]

THE WHITE HOUSE CONFERENCE OF 1930

The White House Conference on Child Health and Protection provides a remarkable map on which to trace the path between child science and child welfare. President Herbert Hoover convened the event, which occurred in Washington, DC, in November 1930. The conference draws an unusually clear connection between social science developments and public policy debates. It was an important outing for both science and child welfare, a highly publicized event that brought prominent experts from around the country to present their findings and recommend policy initiatives. Government officials attended alongside academics and social workers. Afterward, radio broadcasts and magazines publicized the findings, while follow-up conferences brought them to the state level.[4]

The 1930 conference built on the work of two earlier gatherings that had followed a social welfare approach in their focus on the needs of poor and disabled children. In 1909, the White House Conference on the Care of Dependent Children had brought attention to young people who, in the language of the day, were defective, dependent, or delinquent. Settlement house leaders Jane Addams and Lillian Wald helped organize that conference along with activists who were concerned with the plight of children in state custody and with members of the National Child Labor Committee who were worried about young people in the industrializing economy. Delegates came from social work, education, and medicine. Social welfare thinking dominated the meeting, whose thrust was toward local and state aid to support children in their own homes. Conferees discussed the needs of single and working mothers, recommended foster homes and adoption as alternatives to institutional orphanages, and affirmed government responsibility for child welfare. Their work resulted in the formation in 1912 of the federal Children's Bureau, charged with overseeing child welfare services, gathering statistics on infant and maternal health, and supporting programs to minimize child dependency.[5]

At the 1909 conference, Booker T. Washington, president of the Tuskegee Institute, gave a speech titled "Destitute Colored Children of the South." Washington echoed the conference focus on dependency, though not state aid, in an address that seemed intended to reassure white listeners that blacks would demand few resources. He avoided mention of the inequities of race, instead emphasizing the self-sufficiency of black communities in caring for dependent children without orphanages or government support. When a child was left without parents, Washington explained, neighbors took the child into their own families.[6]

Ten years later, the 1919 White House Conference on Standards of Child Welfare similarly emphasized "children in need of special protection." The gathering culminated in a Children's Bureau initiative to lower infant mortality rates during World War I. Julia Lathrop, the first head of the bureau, invited delegates from allied countries to discuss minimum standards for children. Like the first conference, the 1919 gathering reflected a social welfare focus. It reaffirmed state responsibility regarding child labor, the health of mothers and children, child welfare laws, and children in poverty. It led to the short-lived but influential Sheppard-Towner Maternity and Infancy Health Act of 1921, which awarded federal matching grants to the states.

The impact of racial injustice entered the 1919 proceedings in a talk by Howard University professor Kelly Miller, who bemoaned its damaging effects on youth. Unlike Washington, Miller highlighted unequal conditions brought by centuries of racism, detailing how slavery and partial freedom left parents little time or strength to care for their offspring. "The Negro child is born into an environment of economic and social depression," he lamented. "The stress of economic pressure falls heaviest upon the black race, and is felt most acutely by the black child." An impoverished child, Miller warned, would be stunted in physical, intellectual, and moral development. Following social welfare thought, he pleaded for the elimination of poverty, the extension of education, and the same levels of care for all children.[7] In response, the conference recognized "the abolition of racial discrimination" as fundamental to child welfare.[8]

A decade later, diverse groups of children received attention from psychological as well as social welfare perspectives. By 1930, the scope and size of the conference had broadened dramatically. While the first two gatherings had each drawn two hundred delegates, the third brought together three thousand delegates from around the country and from a proliferating variety of fields—psychologists and sociologists as well as social workers, educators, pediatricians, and government officials. As child specialists expanded their ranks to include new professions, they expanded their purview as well. New ideas about the development of personality and the nature of childhood encouraged conferees to look beyond the concerns of poor and disabled children. According to the conference chairman, Ray Lyman Wilbur, a physician who served as secretary of the interior, their aim was to consider "all children, in their total aspects, including those social and environmental factors which are influencing modern childhood."[9] They continued to examine the social welfare concerns that had dominated earlier conferences, but they also considered new psychologically oriented topics, such as child development, parent education, family life, mental hygiene, and sex education, for children who were immigrant and native born, black and white, "normal" and disabled, and urban and rural, from conception through adolescence—an "encyclopaedic platform," in the words of J. Prentice Murphy, who headed a children's agency in Philadelphia and served as a committee chairman.[10] While the 1909 conference had focused on "care of dependent children" and the 1919 on "standards of child welfare," the mandate in 1930 was "child health and protection" more generally. Rather than focusing on children with particular problems, participants now referred to "the problems of childhood" more broadly.

A scientific impulse motivated the work of the 1930 conference. Sixteen months before it took place, committees began research and study. Preliminary summaries of their work were distributed at the conference, and longer, complete versions of several dozen reports were published over the following six years. "The published reports will constitute a veritable mine to which those interested may go for years to come," noted one conference leader. "Each study is rich in significant facts and recommendations."[11] These committee reports have largely escaped the attention of historians, who have tended to examine only the summary volumes and proceedings. In fact, much of the work of the conference took place apart from the gathering itself as committees conducted research and published their findings. One physician termed the reports "a modern romance of science," products of the most advanced thinking of the time.[12] It was in these reports that experts articulated new ideas about the impact of racial discrimination on child development. The reports' findings were publicized in magazines and follow-up conferences and informed the views of committee members, many of whom went on to play influential roles in social science and social reform over the following decades.

THE NEW CHILD SCIENCES

The reports of the 1930 conference reflected the new sciences of the child that had come to prominence in the 1920s. This field differed in significant ways from the turn-of-the-century child study movement, which had gathered subjective data from mothers and teachers to transform parenting and educational practices. Child work in the post–World War I years moved steadily in the direction of developing more "objective" means of acquiring data on children to be used in child welfare. Volunteer child-savers gave way to professional social service providers who brought a new faith in science to their work. While Progressive reformers had been preoccupied with adolescent concerns, child sciences in the 1920s paid attention to the psychological growth of young children. And they claimed a new audience. While earlier reformers hoped to protect impoverished children from vice and degeneracy, these new professionals spoke of fostering the healthy adjustment of the "normal" child. The field now addressed millions of educated, middle-class parents who were convinced that scientific studies could help them raise their own children.[13]

Child sciences of the 1920s emphasized the importance of the early years to the personal development of every individual. Behaviorist psychology, which dominated social science and child-rearing literature at the time, posited that personality, like habits, was fixed at an early age and carried over to adulthood—a belief that was shared by psychoanalysts.[14] Behaviorism expanded the purview of child advocates through claims that *all* children—and their parents—needed the benefits of scientific expertise. Childhood appeared as a dangerous period, fraught with difficulties for even the most privileged. The "complex American child," even one who enjoyed good health and material advantages, was now assumed to need attention from trained experts familiar with scientific methods of research and evaluation. Parenting, personality, growth, and development became topics for expert study.

As they highlighted the dangers of childhood, professionals revealed their anxiety over the impact of modernity, an important concern of the interwar years. Conference goers made frequent reference to technological innovations, urbanization, shifts in family structure, and the new complexities of the social order. Delegates expressed ambivalence about these developments, which brought both opportunities and dangers for children. The next generation, which would greet this new world, became the focal point for their fears and plans. How could they protect children in the midst of these enormous changes? How could they prepare young people for the future? They found their solution in science. Greater knowledge would assist children growing up in the modern world, and expert guidance would steer them safely along the right path.

At the conference, the phase *the whole child* emerged as shorthand for the new child sciences. The whole-child idea honored the child as a distinct personality in her or his own right. Conferees invoked the American penchant for the sovereignty of the individual's deserving equal protection, as when Hoover asserted that in the interest of democracy, children's "varied personalities and abilities must be brought fully to bloom." Speaker after speaker emphasized the distinctiveness of each child. F. J. Kelly declared that "the most sacred thing to every child is his personality," while Mary E. Woolley cited "the principle of knowing the individual child."[15] To highlight individual nature, participants tended to use the singular rather than the plural, speaking of *the child* rather than *children*.

Cooperation among experts was also essential for the whole child. "Each child must be considered as a unit—mind, soul, and body," urged the committee on the schoolchild in a typical comment. The school, home, and community should function together to promote mental, spiritual, and physical health.[16] Delegates shared a sense that child life was moving from the family to the school and other agencies, for it was now beyond the capacity of parents to prepare their children for the intricate social and economic system in place. In this context, scientific coordination was more important than ever. Calls for integration were also a response to the specialization that accompanied the emergence of the new fields of pediatrics, child guidance, and parent education. Delegates favored these developments—indeed, many were trained and made their living in these new specialties—but they recognized that the division of services brought potential problems. J. Prentice Murphy worried that "many walls" separated the thinking of various professional groups; what was needed was "a vast amount of integration" and a "closer exchange of ideas."[17]

FROM SCIENCE TO POLICY

Conference delegates shared socially ameliorative impulses, eager for science to inform policy under the leadership of trained experts. But they disagreed on just what those policies, and who those experts, should be. Beneath their apparent consensus on the whole child lay important questions: What elements contributed to healthy personalities? Under whose tent would the conjoining of disciplines take place? Intellectual authority and professional security were at stake as conferees aimed to translate the findings into practical programs.

These tensions appeared in stark relief at the gathering when controversy erupted over the proposal to transfer the maternity and infancy health programs of the Children's Bureau to the U.S. Public Health Services. The debate played out in part in gendered terms as women active with the Children's Bureau resisted encroachment from the male medical establishment. Both sides drew on the new child sciences. Friends of the bureau emphasized its integrative approach, as in Lillian Wald's claim that it understood "the interrelated problems of childhood." Grace Abbott, chief of the bureau, affirmed "the unity of the child" and the value of bringing together various disciplines.[18] In contrast, the committee that recommended the transfer emphasized specialized expertise. It praised physicians as the professionals best prepared to implement new scientific findings. Only "a centralized authority, trained in the medical and biological sciences and with understanding of the fields of economics and sociology" could bring effective results.[19]

This institutional battle reflected the two understandings of childhood that competed for prominence in the interwar period. Some child welfare experts, including the Children's Bureau champions, understood the whole child largely as the product of social forces in an intellectual tradition that dated back to the Progressive Era. They drew on the casework theory of social work that placed each individual in an environmental context. Living and working conditions helped explain a client's personal difficulties, for external circumstances were at least partly responsible for internal problems. Social workers therefore needed to understand the neighborhoods in which their clients lived and to take an interest in community life, a concern that tied them to social reform movements. Arguing that the state should protect vulnerable citizens from danger, they advocated expanded public support for child welfare.[20]

In the 1920s, however, psychiatric theory and medical specialization began to challenge this sociological approach. Psychoanalytic explanations of behavior traced problems to personal maladjustment rather than external circumstance, while medical professionals focused on individual pathology and intervention. The child development experts, psychiatrists, and pediatricians who staffed the new child guidance and mental hygiene clinics began to analyze personality and mental process apart from social environment, urging personal reform for children and families who failed to meet new definitions for what was normal.[21] The tension between these two approaches was on view at the conference even as participants shared the familiar keywords of *personality*, *individuality*, and *collaboration*. Did the solution to "the problems of childhood" lie in environmental change or individual adjustment? Reports from the conference signaled the persistence of the sociological perspective, even as they hinted at the changing landscape of social science.

The psychological approach informed a conference report on mental hygiene authored by Harold H. Anderson of the Iowa Child Welfare Research Station. Anderson assumed that interior mental conflicts were the cause of childhood problems. He highlighted innate qualities: "The term 'the whole child' includes the original cells with all the hereditary characteristics they carry, plus the changes and development that the organism has undergone." Anderson saw the child as a self-contained unit of psychology and biology, made up of instincts and emotions, desires and urges. He recommended that school psychologists, visiting teachers, vocational guidance, and mental health clinics treat problems of behavior and personality.[22]

But even as psychology was reaching its heyday, the social welfare perspective remained influential. To a number of conference leaders, psychological insights enhanced but did not displace environmental considerations. They incorporated such concepts as personality and adjustment into their vocabulary, using new psychological insights to bolster traditional goals of social reform. The Family and Parent Education Committee, for instance, situated the new psychological analysis in a familiar social welfare context. Its chair, Louise Stanley, chief of the federal Bureau of Home Economics, emphasized the "interaction of personalities within the family" and urged knowledge of psychology, psychiatry, and mental hygiene. At the same time, her report put in the foreground the challenges that poverty posed for emotional satisfaction and mental health. Stanley brought psychology to bear on her call for state support: since economic stability would help to make the child a well-adjusted member of society, the state should promote a high standard of living and a basic income for every family.[23] In a conference address, Grace Abbott, a veteran of Progressive reform, also employed psychology for social welfare ends when she explained the burden children suffered in economic depression. Poverty made children vulnerable to disease, Abbott warned, "but it also does something to them that I shall leave to our friends, the psychiatrists, to explain." On both physical and psychological levels, children were harmed by the experience of economic crisis. For Abbott, this psychological harm reinforced her social reform agenda; to applause, she called for state aid to unemployed families.[24]

Although the early effects of the Depression were apparent by the time of the conference, few delegates other than Abbott mentioned them directly, perhaps because they had begun to prepare their reports sixteen months earlier, or because they were reluctant to criticize the Hoover administration, which had called the conference. By the end of 1930, social workers had noted a dramatic increase in demand for their services. Yet Hoover himself denied the impact of the economic crisis in his opening address when he declared that "the ill-nourished child is in our country not the product of poverty; it is largely the product of ill-instructed children and ignorant parents."[25] How Hoover could have made that assertion, remarked an outraged J. Prentice Murphy, "remains a mystery to many." Referring to several conference reports that did address poverty, Murphy responded that children were undernourished for purely economic reasons. He lamented that the final conference findings ignored the significant problems of unemployment, low wages, and the needs of children of "special racial groups."[26]

RACE AND THE CHILD

A decade earlier, in his speech to the 1919 conference, Kelly Miller had offered an impressionistic account of the suffering of black children. Now, experts made use of the new social science to illustrate the impact of racism on child development. Through extensive surveys, statistics, and graphs, committees documented the disparities that Miller had lamented, employing the new language of individual personality and psychological adjustment to give credence to their calls for social reform. In 1930, conference committees included in their research projects groups that were now seen to present "special problems"—African Americans most prominently, in addition to Indian, Mexican, migrant, and European immigrant children, and children in territories including the Philippine Islands, Alaska, Hawaii, and Puerto Rico. Three committee reports in particular—*The Young Child in the Home, The Adolescent in the Family,* and *Dependent and Neglected Children*—paid particular attention to the social environments of minority children and families. The racial disparities they detailed were worrisome in their extent and effect. To the experts, it appeared that discrimination could have disastrous consequences for the healthy growth and adjustment of the whole child. This version of damage imagery served to justify equal treatment and services for all children.[27]

The analysis of minority groups reflected the impact of new scientific understandings of race and culture. In the 1920s, social scientists had begun to discredit assumptions of scientific racism. Anthropologist Franz Boas, influential in this rethinking, argued that differences among races were the result of environmental rather than genetic factors and that no race was inherently superior to another. As black scholars increasingly entered the ranks of social scientists in the 1920s, they advanced these ideas, documenting racial inequalities in American life. By 1930, even as some scientists continued to champion older beliefs, the emerging consensus was that social factors explained racial discrepancies. Conference reports affirmed this new perspective as they denied hereditary failings and reviewed social and historical differences among groups.[28]

On the first morning of the conference, Secretary of Labor James H. Davis called attention to the impediments to the healthy development of

African American and American Indian children, obstacles that challenged democratic principles. Several other white delegates expressed similar concern, among them Will Alexander, a minister who headed an interracial organization in the South.[29] But for the most part it was black delegates who insisted that racial disparities receive adequate attention. Anna E. Murray of the National Association of Colored Women reiterated the economic needs of black families. "I trust that this part of the program will be given the fullest consideration and the fullest help," she concluded to applause. Educator Mary McLeod Bethune also received applause for her impassioned plea to strengthen black schools. A black delegate from Little Rock asked white colleagues to allow black children "an unfettered start and a fair chance in the race of life."[30]

African American individuals and organizations took active part in conference activities. Selena Butler, the president of the National Congress of Colored Parents and Teachers, invited the director of the conference to speak to her organization and encouraged her members to listen by radio to Hoover's address.[31] She joined two conference committees and reported in *The Crisis* that her service had "given national emphasis to the problem of health and protection for the children of our own people." Affiliation with the conference brought her inspiration: after a survey found that a majority of nursery-school kindergartens excluded black children, she began an effort to establish them in black communities.[32] The National Association of Colored Women participated as well by sending questionnaires to its constituents about the extent of parental and preparental education for African Americans.[33]

Committee reports revealed the influence of black members as they detailed injustices to African American children. The subcommittee on the Negro School Child, chaired by the director of the Division of Negro Education in North Carolina, offered a strong statement against the inadequacies of funding for black schools.[34] The Vocational Guidance Committee, which included a representative of the National Urban League, documented occupational limitations for black youth and urged that employers hire workers according to ability rather than racial bias.[35] Black committee members influenced the language of the reports as well; the editor of the published volumes agreed to capitalize the word *Negro* after consulting with Eugene Kinckle Jones, secretary of the National Urban League and chair of a conference subcommittee.[36]

The conjoining of the social welfare and the psychological approaches was evident in committee reports on racial discrimination. Committees achieved important compromises as they advanced, and to some extent reconciled, the two understandings of child science that were popular at the time. The point was not merely that minority groups suffered racial injustices, although committee members did feel the need to spell out those inequities in detail; it was that those inequities had adverse effects on personality development. Racial discrimination—and the economic exclusion that resulted—caused "maladjustment" in children. This finding, prominent in the committee reports but not the conference proceedings, represents one of the most far-reaching achievements of the conference. Experts used the new formulation to articulate a program of racial equality, taking their committee work as an occasion to design forceful arguments for why all children deserved equal protection and services.

THE YOUNG CHILD IN THE HOME

The impact of racial discrimination on psychological health emerged as a central theme of *The Young Child in the Home*, the report of the Committee on the Infant and Preschool Child. The committee chair was John E. Anderson, a psychologist who directed the Institute of Child Welfare at the University of Minnesota. Other members included child development experts from institutes at Berkeley, Iowa, and Columbia, along with child psychiatrists and pediatricians, figures from social work and reform such as Lillian Wald, and representatives of public health organizations, parent-education programs, and public welfare departments. Butler, of the National Congress of Colored Parents and Teachers, served as well. The committee determined to produce a scientific, comprehensive, up-to-date survey of the home life of young children. Eight hundred field-workers interviewed three thousand mothers, including black interviewers who spoke with two hundred African American families. The committee made an effort to secure a cross section of the population, representative of the country as a whole. The resulting study, not published until 1936, found wide variations in material conditions. Families of high socioeconomic status lived in homes that were far better equipped than those of others. "The evidence for the existence of differential environments so far as the child is concerned is overwhelming," the committee reported. Differences began at birth and affected every aspect of life as a child developed, suggesting "a society composed of a series of cultures."[37]

These disparities appeared as particularly sharp when Anderson and his team compared the findings on white and black children. Compared to the average white home, the black home "is more crowded, is in poorer condition, and is less completely equipped with modern equipment and appliances," the authors explained. Black homes had fewer toys, smaller yards, and less access to public playgrounds. Black families were less likely to own their own homes or to have telephones, electric lights, indoor toilets, radios, and automobiles. The authors emphasized that these differences were caused by environmental factors beyond the control of black parents themselves, who were largely excluded from the upper classes. The result was that black and white children grew up in distinct physical surroundings.[38]

These differences appeared to be of critical importance, for material conditions helped explain psychological growth. In a nod to the two approaches represented on the committee, the report affirmed the centrality of both individual development and the "environmental opportunities" needed to make that development possible. Alongside parents, home environments helped to develop character and personality. The authors acknowledged that their survey did not measure the actual effects of the environment on the child—it did not, for instance, demonstrate that children from poorly equipped homes were more likely to be maladjusted. But the implication was clear: the child in a home that lacked particular items was at a disadvantage in growth and adjustment, while the child from a more affluent home "develops in a more stimulating environment," one conducive to healthy adjustment.[39]

The report's conclusions incorporated psychological insights into a social welfare framework. When black children were less likely than white to enjoy proper provisions, "[a]re we then justified in assuming that the children of the United States have equal opportunities?" asked the report. A child who grew up with few books or toys, who lived in a crowded home in a poor neighborhood, was disadvantaged from the start, deprived of opportunities available to more fortunate children. Since the early years were so critical to healthy adjustment, these deficiencies could have enormous significance for the entire life span. Greater equality in housing conditions and material comforts would contribute to the well-being of every child.[40]

THE ADOLESCENT IN THE FAMILY

The Subcommittee on Home Activities in the Education of the Child similarly cited personality adjustment to explain the adverse effects of economic deprivation and racial inequality. E. W. Burgess, sociologist at the University of Chicago, chaired the subcommittee, while his research assistant, Ruth Shonle Cavan, drafted the report. Among the subcommittee members were prominent names in child development, pediatrics, and education, including R. R. Moton, head of the Tuskegee Institute. The subcommittee designed an ambitious project: a survey of thirteen thousand public-school children in grades eight through ten, including children of immigrant, African American, and white native-born parents. In addition, college students wrote autobiographical accounts of their family experiences. The project was only partly completed by the time of the conference gathering; the final report, a lengthy volume titled *The Adolescent in the Family: A*

Study of Personality Development in the Home Environment, was published four years later.[41]

The report offered two broad findings. First, most significant for personality development were the intangible aspects of family life, such as affection and confidence between parents and children. While this finding differed somewhat from that of *The Young Child in the Home*, it too traced personality to economic security, for affectionate relationships were most possible when there was little financial strain. Second, urban children scored higher than rural children in personality adjustment, even though they spent less time with their families and were more likely to have parents who were separated or divorced. This finding surprised the researchers and tempered alarm over broken homes and urbanization. While family patterns among Germans and Russian Jews were similar to those of native-born whites, Italians and Mexicans suffered overcrowding, ill-equipped homes, and less unity between parents and children. These economic and cultural limitations harmed emotional development. Crowded homes failed to foster independent personalities. Mexican children faced additional challenges, including discrimination because of their dark skin.[42]

The chapter "The Negro Child" further illustrated how economic exclusion led to cultural disadvantage. The survey described in the report included two hundred black children in rural Alabama (where Moton was located) and twelve hundred black children from southern and northern cities. These children tended to be from lower socioeconomic classes than were their white counterparts, even when the fathers had similar educational attainments, and were more likely to come from broken families. The report firmly embraced an environmentalist perspective to explain these differences. The low economic standing of black families was not the fault of the families themselves, for blacks faced exclusion from better-paid occupations. The report cited recent studies by prominent black social scientists E. Franklin Frazier and Carter Woodson, who looked to the history of blacks in America to reject the idea that broken families resulted from moral failings or innate irresponsibility. White attitudes were largely to blame for social ills: "[t]he problem of the Negro child is rooted in the prejudices of the white community quite as much as in the low state of cultural and educational development of the Negro community."[43]

These adverse social conditions injured the development of black children, whose personality adjustment averaged lower than that of white children. Racial inequities brought psychological harm to black youth, who were "subject to more emotional conflicts and unsatisfied longings than [was] any other group." The report's lead authors, trained in sociology, brought psychology into the realm of social welfare, integrating new concepts into an environmental perspective. "Vocational training, better provision for Negroes in the economic system, and training of parents and of young people into higher ideals of family life" were all needed. They recommended such psychologically oriented solutions as family research institutes, consultation centers, and guidance clinics, along with such social welfare measures as the extension of mothers' pensions and day nurseries.[44] It appeared that the injuries of racism could be countered by both social and psychological reforms.

DEPENDENT AND NEGLECTED CHILDREN

To explain the needs of minority groups, the report *Dependent and Neglected Children* placed psychological adjustment in the context of racial discrimination. This report emerged from the Committee on Socially Handicapped, headed by Homer Folks, a prominent social worker from the State Charities Aid Association, and J. Prentice Murphy, the children's-agency chief from Philadelphia; both men were vehement critics of racial discrimination at the conference.[45]

Folks appointed a series of subcommittees, headed by prominent reformers, to investigate how race, nationality, and mass migration affected child dependency. The group on "the Negro in the United States" included southerners and northerners, black and white, with Ira DeA. Reid from the National Urban League writing the report. To explain why black children represented a disproportionate share of the dependent population, Reid drew on social science work by W. E. B. Du Bois, E. Franklin Frazier, and Charles S. Johnson that detailed the economic and social injustices of racial discrimination. Following an environmental approach, he made clear that social forces rather than inherent weakness caused high rates of poverty. Recent migration to northern cities exacerbated social problems and led to racial prejudice, race riots, and hostility from white neighbors.[46]

"All of this has its effect upon the Negro child," Reid asserted. Racial prejudice placed strains on children in particular through parental absence, poor health care, high infant and maternal mortality, ill-equipped schools, and inadequate provisions for social welfare. He traced the idea of black inferiority back to two centuries of slavery, to a "leering gargoyle of race" whose handicap "becomes the heritage of the Negro child," who was both innocent and vulnerable. The solution was not easy, for prejudice limited the amelioration of these ills. Reid appealed for the elimination of discriminatory practices in child welfare, insisting on full resources to promote the physical, spiritual, and mental development of black children.[47]

Homer Folks drew on this work in his summary report. Like other social welfare leaders at the conference, he incorporated new scientific perspectives into his analysis to detail unemployment's "devastating effects on children." Children who grew up in poverty were at a psychological disadvantage, prone to "inefficiency, ill-health, and personality and behavior problems," he explained. To place this damage in sociological context, Folks included a strong defense of the black family: the dependency rate, though high, was lower than might be expected for other groups in similar circumstances. The report applauded the independence of the black family and the tradition of help among relatives and neighbors, while lamenting social and economic limitations and inadequate resources for social welfare work. Mothers' aid to black families was limited, facilities for relief and child care were meager, and many agencies were willing to care only for white children.[48]

Although these committee reports were intended to promote equal conditions for all children, their attention to psychological indicators brought its own complications. The reports' authors ran the danger of stigmatizing certain groups of children as they implied that personality development would be impaired for those who grew up without proper material provisions. When physical surroundings, family income, and material items were held out as predictors of child development, certain groups were doomed to fail. The researchers who directed these reports were motivated by genuine desire to correct injustices and equalize conditions for all American children. But in their efforts to bring together social welfare and social science, they implied that certain groups of children—particularly those from black families— would face inevitable deficiencies in personality development. The link between racial discrimination and personal adjustment could become a means to marginalize particular groups of children, even as it justified more equitable distribution of material benefits.

A CONFERENCE LEGACY

The reports on racial disparities challenged the optimistic vision that President Hoover put forth. "I am convinced that we have a right to assume that we have a larger proportion of happy, normal children than any other country in the world," Hoover had proclaimed in his opening address.[49] In objection, J. Prentice Murphy pointed out that American child welfare legislation lagged far behind that of European countries and was limited by discrimination. In an article in *The Survey* shortly after the conference, Murphy lamented the oversight in Hoover's boast. "When our childhood population includes millions of poor-Negro and poor-white children, thousands of Indian and tens of thousands of Mexican and Porto Rican children, not mentioning those in the Philippines," formidable challenges to child welfare remained. Murphy noted a discrepancy between the committee work and the conclusions of the conference as a whole. He was pleased that the problems of racial minorities

"for the first time entered the arena of a White House Conference" but re-
gretted that the final recommendations omitted these findings.[50] Hoover's
celebration of America's "happy, normal children" suggested the shift that
had occurred in child sciences by 1930. Child study had increasingly come
to focus on the health and development of the "average" child, as researchers
in psychology and medicine tracked the process of growth and individual
adjustment. Murphy's response signaled the persistence of the social welfare
outlook, along with a new awareness of racial discrimination's impact on
child well-being. Studies would continue to balance these perspectives on the
whole child, linking social ills to individual personality.

The Children's Charter encapsulated the results of the tension over the
new child science that characterized the 1930 White House Conference. The
charter was a nineteen-point document approved at the end of the conference and widely distributed to schools and child-care groups. Like the conference as a whole, while it presented competing claims over how to bring
scientific insights into the realm of public policy it simultaneously endorsed
"the rights of the child as the first right of citizenship" and set forth ideals in
health and housing, education and recreation, home and community life. The
charter urged for every child "the guarding of his personality as his most
precious right," suggesting a program of psychological care and child guidance. At the same time, it enshrined "the right to grow up in a family with
an adequate standard of living and the security of a stable income as the surest
safeguard against social handicaps," a plea for expanded social welfare programs. The charter closed with a call "for every child these rights, regardless
of race, or color, or situation, wherever he may live under the protection of
the American flag."[51] As the conference reports made clear, this equality had
not yet been achieved. Racial discrepancies highlighted the distance still to
travel. Not every American child enjoyed an adequate standard of living or
the promise of equal opportunity.[52]

In the weeks after the conference, critics complained that it had not
accomplished enough to solve the problems of child protection. Secretary
Davis himself had warned on the first day that the recommendations "will
be of interest to social historians but will not improve the lot of children"
unless fully implemented.[53] Several weeks later, *The Survey* reported complaints that in the end the conference had merely "brought forth a mouse."
The Nation editorialized that the year of intensive expert study had resulted
in "little tangible achievement." It dismissed the Children's Charter as bland
and uncontroversial, commenting that "it is a pity that a gathering of the
leading experts in child welfare could not have been allowed to give the public
a more inspiring platform than this string of platitudes."[54]

But through the work of its committees, the conference advanced a new
way of thinking about racial inequities in American life. The intellectual ten-

sions that characterized the conference revealed underlying conflicts over how scientific findings should shape public policy decisions. In the course of these debates, and over the following few years, conference goers developed an important new understanding of the impact of race on child well-being. This work left a legacy for subsequent conferences. The 1940 White House Conference on Children in a Democracy—whose leaders included Homer Folks, Louise Stanley, Charles Johnson, and Grace Abbott—cataloged not only the material deprivations suffered by minority children, but also the psychological costs: "the more subtle, but no less searing deprivation that comes from the consciousness of being excluded, despised, unwanted, unacceptable; of belonging to parents who are not granted the status of equals among equals in the public esteem." In segregated schools, minority children were made to feel inferior.[55] At the Midcentury White House Conference on Children and Youth, held in 1950, Mamie Clark and Kenneth Clark contributed studies that described feelings of inferiority, humiliation, and low self-esteem among minority-group children. It now appeared that dominant-group children suffered a cost as well, for "prejudice has harmful psychological effects upon those who are prejudiced."[56]

The insight that racial discrimination harmed personality development prefigured later social science developments. This idea, articulated by committees of the 1930 conference, would gain increased visibility and influence in subsequent years as psychologists and sociologists—some of whom had been involved in that conference—made it the center of important investigations. It shaped the studies of the American Youth Commission in the late 1930s; Gunnar Myrdal's *An American Dilemma*, published in 1944; and the famous "doll studies" of Kenneth and Mamie Clark, which were prominently cited in the *Brown v. Board of Education* decision of 1954. This viewpoint would influence intellectual and popular belief throughout the second half of the twentieth century. Its origins date back a quarter century before *Brown*, to debates that shaped the deployment of new scientific findings at the 1930 White House Conference on Child Health and Protection.

NOTES

1. Lillian D. Wald, "Shall We Dismember the Child?" *Survey* 63 (15 January 1930): 458.

2. For a recent work that emphasizes the influence of psychology, see Ann Hulbert, *Raising America: Experts, Parents, and a Century of Advice about Children* (New York: Alfred A. Knopf, 2003).

3. On the evolution of damage imagery, see Daryl Michael Scott, *Contempt and Pity: Social Policy and the Image of the Damaged Black Psyche, 1880–1996* (Chapel Hill: University of North Carolina Press, 1997).

    4. The Medical Section met in February 1931. On follow-up activities, see "The White House Conference Carries On," *School Life* 17, no. 2 (1931): 23–24.
    5. On the 1909 conference, see Kriste Lindenmeyer, *"A Right to Childhood": The U.S. Children's Bureau and Child Welfare, 1912–46* (Urbana: University of Illinois Press, 1997), 18–22. On the conferences as a series, see Rochelle Beck, "The White House Conferences on Children: An Historical Perspective," *Harvard Educational Review* 43, no. 4 (1973): 653–58.
    6. *Proceedings of the Conference on the Care of Dependent Children* (Washington, DC: GPO, 1909), 113–17.
    7. Kelly Miller, "Racial Factors," *Standards of Child Welfare*, Children's Bureau Publication no. 60 (Washington, DC: GPO, 1919), 66–70.
    8. *Minimum Standards for Child Welfare*, Children's Bureau Publication no. 62 (Washington, DC: GPO, 1920), 3.
    9. *White House Conference 1930: Addresses and Abstracts of Committee Reports* (New York: Century, 1931), v–viii. For an overview, see "Memorandum Number 1: White House Conference on Child Health and Protection," White House Conference Records, Accession folder/Preliminary Index, Hoover Institution Archives, Stanford, California (hereafter WHC).
    10. "Official Proceedings of the White House Conference on Child Health and Protection," supplement to the *United States Daily* (Washington, DC), 5, no. 228 (1930): 46.
    11. "Official Proceedings," 53.
    12. Haven Emerson, "The Child Takes the Lead," *Survey* 65 (15 March 1931): 649.
    13. On child sciences, see Julia Grant, *Raising Baby by the Book: The Education of American Mothers* (New Haven: Yale University Press, 1998); Hulbert, *Raising America*; Hamilton Cravens, *Before Head Start: The Iowa Station and America's Children* (Chapel Hill: University of North Carolina Press, 1993); and Steven L. Schlossman, "Philanthropy and the Gospel of Child Development," *History of Education Quarterly* 21, no. 3 (1981): 275–99.
    14. John B. Watson, *Behaviorism* (New York: Norton, 1924).
    15. "Official Proceedings," 4, 22, 23.
    16. *White House Conference 1930*, 167.
    17. J. Prentice Murphy, "When Doctors Disagreed," *Survey* 65 (15 December 1930): 311–15, 348–51.
    18. Wald, "Shall We Dismember the Child?" 458; Abbott, "Minority Report," 19 November 1930, Abbott Papers, box 52, folder 70, Joseph Regenstein Library, University of Chicago. For accounts of the controversy, see Lela B. Costin, "Women and Physicians: The 1930 White House Conference on Children," *Social Work* 28, no. 2 (1983): 108–14; Lindenmeyer, *"A Right to Childhood,"* 164–70; and Robyn Muncy, *Creating a Female Dominion in American Reform, 1890–1935* (New York: Oxford University Press, 1991), chap. 5.
    19. White House Conference on Child Health and Protection, *Preliminary Committee Reports* (New York: Century, 1930), 72.
    20. Roy Lubove, *The Professional Altruist: The Emergence of Social Work as a Career* (Cambridge: Harvard University Press, 1965), 47; Regina Kunzel, *Fallen*

Women, Problem Girls: Unmarried Mothers and the Professionalization of Social Work (New Haven: Yale University Press, 1993), 126.

21. Lubove, *Professional Altruist*, chap. 3, and Daniel J. Walkowitz, "The Making of a Feminine Professional Identity: Social Workers in the 1920s," *American Historical Review* 95, no. 4 (1990): 1051–75.

22. Harold H. Anderson, "School Relations with the Home in the Interests of Mental Hygiene," box 45, folder "Section IIIC: The School Child," WHC.

23. *Preliminary Committee Reports*, 135, 147; *White House Conference 1930*, 133–50.

24. "Official Proceedings," 18–19.

25. "Official Proceedings," 3.

26. Murphy, "When Doctors Disagreed," 313, 351.

27. On damage imagery, see Scott, *Contempt and Pity*.

28. John P. Jackson, Jr., *Social Scientists for Social Justice* (New York: New York University Press, 2001), chap. 2.

29. "Official Proceedings," 4, 38–39.

30. "Official Proceedings," 36, 37–38, 44. Bethune is incorrectly identified as "Mrs. Mary McCleod" of Bethune, Florida.

31. Mrs. H. R. Butler to Dr. H. E. Barnard, 9 June 1930; Butler to Barnard, 7 July 1930; Barnard to Butler, 11 August 1930; Butler to State President and National Chairman, 19 August 1930, box 43, folder "Sec. IIB, John E. Anderson," WHC.

32. Mrs. H. R. Butler, "Forward with the White House Conference," *The Crisis* 37, no. 10 (1930): 374–75; White House Conference on Child Health and Protection, *Nursery Education* (New York: Century, 1931), 93–94.

33. Louise Stanley to H. E. Barnard, 26 October 1929, 13 February 1930, and 22 October 1930, box 42, folder "Section IIIA, The Family and Parent Education," WHC; "Official Proceedings," 44.

34. White House Conference on Child Health and Protection, *Report of Sub-Committee on the Negro School Child* (Washington, DC, 1933); White House Conference on Child Health and Protection, *The School Health Program* (New York: Century, 1932), 306–15.

35. White House Conference on Child Health and Protection, *Vocational Guidance* (New York: Century, 1932), 260–67.

36. Katherine Glover to Eugene Kinckle Jones, 23 December 1930; Jones to Glover, 26 December 1930; Glover to Jones, 27 December 1930, box 54, folder "Sec. IVC, Dependency and Neglect," WHC.

37. White House Conference on Child Health and Protection, *The Young Child in the Home* (New York: D. Appleton-Century, 1936), xi–xii, 5, 23, 401.

38. *Young Child in the Home*, 269.

39. *Young Child in the Home*, 6, 9, 44.

40. *Young Child in the Home*, 23.

41. White House Conference on Child Health and Protection, *The Adolescent in the Family: A Study of Personality Development in the Home Environment* (New York: D. Appleton-Century, 1934), xi–xiv.

42. *Adolescent in the Family*, 7, 69, 72.

43. *Adolescent in the Family*, 45–63, 90.

44. *Adolescent in the Family*, 56, 310.

45. White House Conference on Child Health and Protection, *Dependent and Neglected Children* (New York: D. Appleton-Century, 1933).

46. *Dependent and Neglected Children*, 279–312.

47. *Dependent and Neglected Children*, 279–312.

48. *Preliminary Committee Reports*, 512–14; *White House Conference 1930*, 323–26, 335.

49. "Official Proceedings," 3.

50. Murphy, "When Doctors Disagreed," 314, 351.

51. *White House Conference 1930*, 45–48.

52. *The Young Child in the Home*, 5.

53. "Official Proceedings," 4.

54. *The Nation*, 3 December 1930, 595; *Survey* 65 (15 December 1930): 307; Murphy, "When Doctors Disagreed," 311.

55. White House Conference on Children in a Democracy, *Final Report*, Children's Bureau Publication no. 272 (Washington, DC: GPO, 1942), 51, 57.

56. Midcentury White House Conference on Children and Youth, *A Healthy Personality for Every Child* ([Raleigh, NC]: Health Publications Institute, 1951), ii, vii, 48–49.

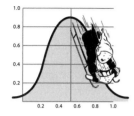

CHAPTER 8

White Teachers and the "Black Psyche": Interculturalism and the Psychology of Race in the New York City High Schools, 1940–1950

Jonna Perrillo

ON A JUNE MORNING in 1943, teacher Rose Nurnberg brought thirteen of her best students from James Madison High School in Brooklyn to PS 113 in Harlem. Nurnberg reported that her students wrote and delivered speeches on "various aspects of Negro life," including art, education, poetry, jazz, and civil rights, and that "each speech, so carefully prepared to avoid being offensive or condescending, ended on as hopeful a note as possible." Afterward, Nurnberg knew that her group had reached the audience as she heard the warm applause. In addition, a number of black students responded with statements of their own. Nurnberg described one such student: "Little Ann Owens, nine years old, looking like any pretty white child, with blue eyes and brown curls, spoke with great poise. 'My people, the Negro people, are all working together in war as well as in peace for a better world.'" Thomas Bunn, an eleven-year-old, also made a comment: "'We are not doing so good now, but when the world goes better, we will do better too.'" The PS 113 students then sang several spirituals for their guests. When it was over, Nurnberg found the experience to be a "thrilling and exciting adventure." In the day's events, she wrote, "[w]e had made contact with real life."[1]

The intercultural movement to which Nurnberg belonged was begun by New York City educators and focused on celebrating the nation's ethnic and religious diversity. [2] By the 1940s, interculturalism had been adopted by several school districts nationally, though with a new focus. Although the movement retained the same name, interculturalism during and after World War II centered on the more pressing "test of democracy in America . . . the test of color."[3] In response to events abroad, American race advocates argued that the elimination of prejudice was vital to the national health. Creating a "national cultural unity," interculturalists argued, required a careful balance between fostering an appreciation for racial difference and avoiding an "exaggerated [sense] of cultural diversity." Most important for intercultural experts such as Rachel Davis DuBois, director of the Intercultural Education Workshop, unity began not with political mechanisms but with the transformation of individuals' attitudes towards racial difference. If interculturalists of the 1920s worked for a greater appreciation of the cultural contributions of diverse ethnic groups, they now more fervently argued that "prejudice is a psychological disease" and that "the price of psychological illiteracy is disaster." Schools were to help children overcome their psychological deficiencies by enabling students across races to experience events with "a common emotional core."[4] Within this psychological context, appreciating diversity would be learned not just through "doing what [good] citizens do" but by becoming tolerant and feeling a genuine acceptance for others.[5]

PSYCHOLOGIZING PREJUDICE

The growing intercultural fascination with the psychology of prejudice was just one manifestation of a national therapeutic culture that gained ground during and after World War II. Many Americans felt that the world was shifting in profound ways that the average citizen was little able to control. Within this atmosphere, psychologists came to influence many of the most important issues of the day, from war policy to parenting techniques. Wartime psychologists focused especially on morale. In contrast to the "authoritarian personality" that had created havoc abroad, a democratic morale was defined by optimism, reasonableness, and tolerance. Happiness, which psychologists defined as the goal of psychotherapy, depended first on feelings of security, self-awareness, and reduced tension.[6]

Influenced by the work of social scientists such as W. E. B. Du Bois and Gunnar Myrdal, both of whom argued that black Americans faced systematic social, political, and economic duress, 1940s psychologists expanded theories about the psychology of individuals to explain the psychology of communities. In a wartime culture in which all Americans were feeling stressed, they claimed, some were more stressed than others. "Community disorders," they contended, heightened the psychological disorders of the people within them. This was especially the case for black Americans, whom white psychologists and social scientists depicted as suffering from damaged egos and psychological repression caused by racist oppression. All together, these problems called for "first aid [for] the wounded [black] personality."[7]

Interculturalism aimed to heal the damaged black psyche while improving the psychological health of white America. American psychologists and educators claimed that children were especially important objects of study, for childhood was when many of the most important psychological patterns were set. They aimed to do more than train children to become democratic citizens. They sought to create in them democratic personalities: outgoing, tolerant, and optimistic. To enable these personal transformations in children's psyches, there needed to be several changes in public education. The influence of psychology in framing race relations came to alter curricula both in public schools and in teacher-education programs, especially in New York City. When Rachel Davis DuBois attended Teachers College in the early 1930s, she took classes in educational sociology and child psychology. By the end of the decade, she was teaching her own courses in interculturalism at New York University. New teachers entered the schools in the 1940s versed in techniques for "changing race attitudes," developing "intergroup relations," and planning activities that would provide students with a "common emotional core."[8] Their more experienced colleagues received similar training by participating in the many in-service workshops offered to teachers.

With its focus on initiating tolerance rather than empowering black students more directly, interculturalism was endorsed by many black leaders (including W. E. B. Du Bois and A. Philip Randolph) but operated independently of black civil rights organizations.[9] Instead, interculturalism was a movement largely administered and practiced by white experts. These experts depended on the cooperation of New York City teachers, also mostly white, to adapt their work, incorporate intercultural ideas in their classrooms, and perform as social reformers. In preparation for this role, experts hoped that teachers would transform a potential fear of the racial other into a dynamic locus of psychological study. Throughout the war period, DuBois claimed that "no outside help can fight our own battles," that if educators overcame their own intolerance they would become "new persons" and "better teachers."[10]

DuBois's repeated declarations worked as a call to service and a promise of personal and professional growth. This call extended to teachers such as Rose Nurnberg whose students were not black. All teachers stood something to gain by becoming less defensive, more tolerant individuals. By the end of the 1940s, the connection between white teachers' psyches and those of their black students was well in place. Unfortunately, while these connections served to address old problems they also created new ones.

"NO RACISM HERE": WHITE TEACHERS AS REFORMERS

Nurnberg's class trip to Harlem was typical of intercultural activities in several ways, beginning with its staged series of events and conversations between students of differing races. Interculturalists such as Nurnberg transferred a mainstream view of prejudice—one that stressed psychological over political reform—to their vision of education. In so doing, they focused on classroom as vehicles for communicating values and beliefs rather than on the societal and organizational structures that produced inequalities in the schools—such as segregated districting and the tracking of black and white students into vocational and academic programs. They used plays and assemblies, cross-cultural visits to private homes and to schools, educational films, extracurricular activities such as involvement in UNESCO and the Junior Red Cross, and clubs that stressed the importance of international and interracial relations as the main modes for the transmission of new cultural values. In the classroom, educators diversified their curricula to include literary and musical works, scientific achievements, and historical accomplishments of black Americans.

Also representative was Nurnberg's anxiety that she and her students, though "convinced that . . . prejudice sprang from selfishness and ignorance," could easily offend black students and teachers and therefore needed to "carefully prepare." Nurnberg's fear that her students could easily insult their "hypersensitive" black counterparts was one product of the damaged-black-psyche theory. Implicitly connected to the damaged black psyche was the healthy white self-image, the maintenance of which was frequently as much at the center of intercultural discourse as was black improvement. Many interculturalists, including Nurnberg, feared charges of racism directed at themselves or their white students. As a result, a reliance on upbeat and inspirational black student testimonies, such as those of Ann Owens and Thomas Bunn, were especially important. They confirmed teachers' convictions that a physical confrontation with racial difference, even under the most carefully orchestrated circumstances, allowed racially and socially privileged students to come closer to "real life" than they could within their more homogenous classrooms and neighborhoods or through media reports. Nine years old and "looking like any pretty white child," Ann Owens, along with her schoolmates, offered a nonthreatening but still "real" encounter with blackness, a means by which Nurnberg and her students could confront racial otherness without having to confront the poverty and discrimination that children like those of PS 113 experienced outside the classroom.

But as interculturalists such as Nurnberg set out to record their experiences for their colleagues in the city and across the nation, they found that the enactment of psychological transformation—both for whites and for blacks—was easier to show than to assess. Thus, even as interculturalists emphasized psychological change, many of their recorded experiences centered around the performance of tolerance, a phenomenon that was easier to capture. When teachers like Nurnberg brought white students to black schools, they wanted them to see socially "mistreated" children like Ann Owens and Thomas Bunn who were attentive, optimistic, and courteous. These ideal black students modeled the kinds of tolerance that interculturalists wanted white students to feel and enact as well. When Nurnberg wrote about the experience for other teachers, she wanted to reproduce this image as well as another: that of her white students with "outstretched hands [warmly] received."[11] The two groups of children in Nurnberg's tale of intercultural awakening constituted a democratic portrait of "good" students in wartime America: cooperative, tolerant, and psychologically secure.

DIAGNOSING THE "BLACK PSYCHE"

Yet intercultural reports often revealed as much about the psychological dilemmas of the teachers who wrote them as it illuminated about the students they portrayed. Side by side with accounts like Nurnberg's in education journals were reports of hypersensitive black students. White teachers across the political spectrum agreed that black students often possessed a "chip on the shoulder" attitude. For many, ascribing hypersensitivity to black students became a way to explain problems teachers were witnessing in the schools and, at the same time, to deflect charges of racism in the classroom. Categorizing black students as hypersensitive reinforced the view that disagreements between black and white students were manifestations of psychological problems, as opposed to issues that could only be resolved by radical transformations in the society at large. This much is clear in teacher Henry Hillson's account of the founding of a Negro History and Culture Club at Eastern District High School. "When the club was first organized," Hillson reported, "members frequently brought up grievances which they felt existed in the school. The discussion that followed was freely participated in by both members and a faculty advisor. It was found in practically every instance that the grievances were more imaginary than real."[12]

Both Nurnberg's and Hillson's reports reflect the strain between intercultural educators' conflicting desires. On the one hand, they yearned to create a greater sense of democracy through the fostering of tolerance and other democratic values. On the other hand, they (perhaps subconsciously) naively assumed that their classrooms already operated as democratic models and needed little, if any, intervention. Whether performing democratic encounters or disregarding black students' complaints, both teachers indicated a desire to prevent any potential exchanges that might have tested the self-image of white students and teachers. Believing that the black psyche was not only "wounded" but also fragile encouraged teachers to become psychologists in the classroom and to see that black students "deliberately avoid social contacts which would expose them to criticism." The behavior that could result from the tendency to "magnif[y] the slightest incident all out of proportion to the reality," one teacher explained, "takes the appearance of surliness and antisocial behavior."[13] Once they had made a diagnosis, teachers could then shape their curriculum to provide students with "a feeling of confidence in meeting situations" both in and outside of school.[14]

All together, white teachers' representations of the black psyche revealed a certain amount of anxiety about the new import of race relations on the practice of teaching. This was true even for teachers who were enthusiastic about the opportunity to participate in social reform and to work outside the confines of their own classroom. In intercultural reports, black students often became a trope by which white teachers could demonstrate their own psychological well-being. In her description of an intercultural concert, for example, Mary Riley described "a tall well-built Negro" student who "stood beside an equally blond girl." Even more "outstanding" was the black tympani player. "Every fiber of his being," Riley wrote, "his delicate wrists, graceful hands, and his entire body accentuated the rhythm and brought perfection to the performance." Her account of the concert and of the key performer, she concluded, pointed to one fact: "no racism here."[15] Anxious for her concert to be seen as a successful performance of interracial unity, Riley eagerly depicted both black students as harmonious as the concert itself, true "equals" of their blond band mate. The emotive black drummer with his slender, rhythmic body was unique from other students and, at the same time, an integral part of a larger whole. Typical of interculturalists, Riley wanted to pay attention to her black students and, simultaneously, to advertise for the merits of interculturalism and efforts of its practitioners.

The portraits of students in accounts such as Riley's became an easy target of critics of the movement, including other liberal teachers. In 1944, the same year as Riley's concert, former New York City high school teacher Marie Syrkin wrote about the psychological depictions of black students found in intercultural accounts. Although Syrkin always considered herself a liberal teacher, she had come to realize that her thinking in the past was often misinformed and unintentionally detrimental to her students. "Had I been asked to generalize about my Negro pupils ten or fifteen years ago, I probably would have answered 'they are gay,'" she wrote, charting her own naïveté. Her basis for this belief was what she called her "first impression" of her black students: "an infectious light-heartedness, a dazzling smile which came into ready to answer one's own smile." In hindsight, she conceded, "I am well aware to mention these characteristics irritates a great many intellectual Negroes." Syrkin referred to protests against the Amos-and-Andy portrayal of the black American as naturally optimistic, beneficent, and non-threatening. Such romanticization, black leaders in the 1930s and 1940s argued, echoed hereditarian theories of personality and served as justification for the continued exploitation of black Americans. Syrkin believed that her previous "facile characterization" of her students reflected "the typical white tendency to portray the Negro as a kind of clown." "Nevertheless," she concluded, "my impression was a common one."[16] In their depictions of black students and their psyches, white teachers more accurately represented many of the problematics of race in America.

THE MANY FORMS OF WHITE ANXIETY

Nurnberg's account of her class trip and Riley's report of the concert reflect both teachers' struggles with suppressing their own stereotypes, struggles that existed simultaneously with their visions of achieving national unity and racial harmony through intercultural teaching methods. More specifically, both teachers' challenges in representing black students exemplified their effort to devise a "color-blind" approach to race. Interculturalists' calls for their colleagues to become color-blind was part of a larger, liberal reform platform. But it was also an attempt to assuage the fears of white conservatives who were fearful about the growing numbers of black students in the schools. When the racial composition of a Brooklyn high school changed to include 250 black students, for example, Henry Hillson reported that although the "students constituted only eight percent of the student body, their presence was felt out of proportion to their number."[17] Anti-integrationists found evidence for their anxieties in studies that reported that black juveniles were five times more likely than whites to be delinquent.[18] Such statistics only heightened a sense that black students, much like the problems those students created, rarely existed alone. Teachers such as Nurnberg and Riley wanted to counter negative images of black students as uncontrollable and dangerous by creating positive new images of them, both for themselves and for their white students. Thus, the "real life" black Americans in whom interculturalists were interested were those whom they found most useful for quelling the white anxiety experienced by both conservatives and liberals.

This problem was compounded by a still larger issue, for even as interculturalists worked to integrate their curricula, they still did not confront the more systematic and volatile racial problems in the city public schools. In 1948, an article exposing the inequities of city schools claimed, "Most teachers resented appointment to Harlem, [and] hated their Negro, Spanish, and Italian pupils."[19] Housing discrimination and, after the war, the concurrent suburbanization and ghettoization of large urban areas only heightened disparities in urban public schools.[20] Teacher shortages and lack of resources in black schools led to racial tensions and social protest. In 1945, a violent confrontation—one that took two days to quell—broke out between black and white students at a Harlem high school. At the same time, black parents organized in Brooklyn to protest segregated districting in their neighborhood public schools. By 1950, several public schools in central Harlem were reduced to three-hour school days because of overcrowding; community politicians worried that students with working parents were left locked in their apartments or to wander the streets.[21] But white educators and school officials largely ignored the protests of black civic leaders and community members in the 1940s.[22] In fact, much of the interculturalist ideology belied the state of race and ethnic relations not just outside of the classroom but also within it.

"WHAT CAN I DO?": THE LIMITATIONS
OF PSYCHOLOGICAL REFORM

Many of the problems faced by black schools in New York City were created by the fact that white teachers like Rose Nurnberg may have been interested in visiting Harlem for a day but rarely were excited to teach there full time. White teachers' reluctance to teach in black schools went beyond the schools' lack of resources or even fear of black students' hypersensitivity. To be certain, for teachers who spent little if any time in black communities otherwise, being appointed to schools with a significant black student population forced them to confront their own feelings about race, a potentially challenging and uncomfortable prospect. Eugene Maleska described the moment of being assigned to teach in a junior high school in Harlem as such a confrontation. In the beginning, he described, "I confess I was afraid. My previous contacts with the Negro race were few. I had nothing to guide me but word-of-mouth knowledge and stories from the newspapers. . . . [B]oth sources made me feel like a Daniel stepping into the lion's den." Interculturalists aimed for white students to overcome their fear of black children whom they did not know, but Maleska revealed that teachers also often shared those fears. Seven years after he began teaching in Harlem, he understood his appointment as a critical opportunity for expanding his own social and political views. After a "first year of adjustment," he had found that he "liked just as many Negroes as whites among the faculty."[23] Only with an extended encounter, Maleska argued, was he able to build more authentic and meaningful relationships with his black students and colleagues.

In an effort to enact greater political change, Maleska hoped to convince teachers that black students and schools could be more than a field-trip destination. But in reality the brief intercultural encounters such as those described by Numberg remained the norm. This created a number of ideological and pragmatic limitations, the most obvious being an oversimplification of "real life" that came with a mere one-hour view. Under pressure to enact social reform in a single class period, interculturalists worked to make interactions between groups as friendly and productive as possible. More than staging interracial encounters, interculturalists saw themselves as staging democracy. To successfully model democratic encounters, however, interculturalists depended on the expression of democratic personalities. All students were expected to be interested and enthusiastic participants in school assemblies, extracurricular clubs, and interschool visits. More specifically, the success of interculturalism required whites to be tolerant and cooperative and blacks to be understanding of white naïveté and immune to inadvertent insult. In other words, overcoming racism demanded as much from the black psyche as it did from the white.

A CRISIS OF EXPERTISE

Black students' "hypersensitivity" may have been most visible to white educators, but theirs were not the only grievances in the schools. In 1950, Rachel Davis DuBois described a meeting held at a city school to allow teachers to air their complaints. Many teachers' complaints revolved around not black children but black adults, including "extreme inferiority feelings on the part of some Negro parents and extreme bitterness on the part of others," the absence of black mothers from PTA meetings, and "the problem of the Negro teacher in the Negro districts who feels that if she understands Negro children that is all that can be asked of her."[24] DuBois referred to the meeting not to challenge the veracity of the teachers' claims but to argue for a theory of "personal relations," in which white teachers could be leaders of intergroup discussions rather than feeling marginalized. But white teachers' concerns with black teachers and their characterization of them as anti-intellectual was more complicated than feeling ostracized. Rather, the teachers in this meeting experienced a crisis of expertise: they did not understand the behavior of their black students, the black parents, or their black colleagues.

While DuBois wanted to explain this lack of understanding as stemming from a lack of communication, the teachers implied that it might be something more. The characterization of the "Negro teacher" who "understands Negro children" suggests that white teachers realized their black colleagues and students were approaching the classroom with a different kind of knowledge from their own. This knowledge was experiential and instructive—unique from the child psychology and educational sociology training white teachers held and, at the same time, unavailable to them. Throughout the war and postwar eras, white teachers struggled with the dilemma of how to credit a certain kind of knowledge to black students and teachers without diminishing their own expertise in race relations. Often, teachers were advised by experts and their colleagues to "[lean] backwards to refrain from any action that might be wrongly construed" in order to make up for their own lack of knowledge about their students' experiences.[25] DuBois attempted to aid white teachers by assembling scripts and other materials for them to use in their classrooms as though offering a book of etiquette. In a list of "dos and don'ts," for example, DuBois warned against using terms such as "your people" but to instead say "those of us of Negro background." Such a simple shift prevented "a patronizing air [that] can so easily slip into a phrase or the bearing of a white leader."[26] As reflected in the design of assemblies and school visits, DuBois believed discrete intergroup moments could enact larger change because during those moments "our common American culture is richer . . . [and] the problem of race and culture conflict is solved."[27]

But as white educators were being asked to reconsider themselves as professionals, to investigate and overcome their feelings, many also sensed that what they were supposed to feel, as in DuBois's dos and don'ts, was scripted. Keeping black students "grievance free" was hardly a position of agency for teachers not used to having their authority challenged by their most marginalized students. In response, teachers complained that "the intercultural movement comes from the top and not from the great mass of teachers. . . . The movement must become universally professional rather than merely missionary."[28] Unlike intercultural experts, many teachers did not see interculturalism as sacred but rather as more of the same in a long pattern of administrative didactics. Teachers who registered complaints against interculturalism often did so less on the basis of its ultimate goals than on its failure to speak to what many teachers were most concerned about, including classroom management and the academic subject matter they were required to teach. Many saw the time-consuming faculty meetings designed to train them in intercultural beliefs and techniques as indicative of leaders' disregard for the everyday demands of the profession. Education experts warned their colleagues that some new teachers resented the intercultural training that had become part of certification programs in New York City, training that was "geared toward the mediocre mind" and was "neither very demanding nor very rewarding." Castigating the "missionary" zeal and "weird dogma" of the movement, critics conflated interculturalism with anti-intellectualism and claimed that both were taking over the schools.[29]

Increasingly, many educators sensed, adopting interculturalism was no longer a freely chosen political position but an indicator of one's professional ability. In 1944, teacher Charles Slatkin posed his unease with interculturalism as a tension between the old and the new. "I'm a bit worried [that] the young people coming out of college into the teaching profession . . . will regard me as a fogey before I have even reached the doddering forties," Slatkin confessed. "I have a feeling they will want to know how my classes study literature. What do they study. . . . Have we a course on intercultural understanding? Do we have a Hall of All Nations? Posters on Interracial Unity?"[30] Slatkin feared that the new teachers entering the profession would evaluate him based on the degree to which the physical space of his classroom exhibited a commitment to interculturalism; interracial posters and other displays of tolerance (such as the Hall of All Nations) had become a quick way to assess a teacher's talents and beliefs. Overt displays of devotion to interculturalism, it seemed, were becoming status symbols among the ranks of white educators.

Slatkin's fears were representative of those of many teachers who felt themselves at the center of a change not only in thinking about race but also in thinking about the practice of teaching. Most teachers in New York professed to want racial equity when asked; more troublesome to them were the methods and rhetoric of the movement itself. Interculturalism's message of psychological rebirth, in all its abstractions, spoke to what some teachers feared about the movement more largely: its proclivity to reduce enormous and complex social problems to clichés. Teachers complained of tolerance being "forced down the throats of the recalcitrant young . . . like castor oil" and of "love-your-neighbor pills to be swallowed three times a week for credit."[31] Others were more earnest in their reservations. "Among the many misgivings this writer has had concerning the efficacy of our efforts in intercultural education," teacher Michael Glassman wrote in 1949, "has been the feeling that we were merely 'playing' with beautiful generalities and high sounding platitudes like 'Love your neighbor' and 'All men are brothers,' and only occasionally coming to grips with realities in our social relations." Rather than teach students to view the world through rose-colored glasses, Glassman urged, "[o]ur constant problem has been to devise approaches to which will answer the question 'What can I do?'"[32]

VISIONS OF REFORM

In reality, it was difficult for educators to know how to change the world around them and what to do for students whose life experiences challenged the very platitudes on which intercultural rhetoric depended. In fact, for some, doing the best for their students in the here and now provoked moral quandaries for the future. "Sometimes I wonder when sending so many untrained colored girls to this [clerical] firm if I am helping them or hurting them," questioned vocational guidance counselor Estella Unna. "In the past, the only jobs open to them were light housework and factory work. . . . They are simply thrilled when I offer them clerical jobs and thereafter nothing else will do." She questioned whether she was doing her students a favor by setting their sights higher, since their choices might later be foreclosed. She wondered, "[I]f they are going to be unhappy because only factory jobs are open to them in the future, perhaps I have done the wrong thing in giving them a taste of heaven."[33] In her comments, Unna implicitly acknowledged the failure of interculturalism to acknowledge systematic discrimination in employment, housing, and education. At the same time she reflected on how negotiating between her desire to "give [students] a permanent lift"— economically and emotionally—and knowing that she was making them vulnerable to disappointment led to her own self-doubt and sense that she may have "done the wrong thing." Embedded in Unna's doubts were the difficulties of characterizing race progress in psychological terms. The rhetoric of psychological improvement gave her stronger means for sympathizing with her students than it did the tools for advocating for them.

Educators such as Glassman and Unna aspired to a type of social reform that valued action as much as feeling, in which their desire to help students might not be compromised by the prospects of psychological harm. But intercultural experts' reliance on psychology deflected them from a more substantial reform project. Intercultural leaders saw an emphasis on action as less intellectual than an attention to feeling and, even more, as addressing the problem of racism in a backward fashion. Throughout the 1940s, Rachel Davis DuBois repeated that for social relations to be different they first had to feel different, and she saw most teachers as "conscious enough of the problems of prejudice" but largely unpracticed in "thinking about the cultural richness which could evolve from our heterogeneity." As a result, she charged most teachers with "not [being] 'gripped by a goal'" and instead interested "only in the immediate object of preventing street riots."[34] The concern that teachers were focused on day-to-day conflicts at the expense of long-term goals was one that administrators had expressed before in other contexts. Teachers recognized this familiar argument and, at the same time, stood by their claims that interculturalism failed to address what actually happened in the classroom.

Overall, the spectrum of teachers' criticisms of interculturalism reflected many of their own inconsistencies as a professional body in addressing race. In response to DuBois's claims, many teachers contended that interculturalism gave them a stronger vision of an ideal classroom but few skills with which to negotiate race relations both inside and beyond the confines of their own four walls. At the same time, many educators were highly invested in believing that racism was not a serious factor in the daily interactions within their schools. Some of this resulted from a belief in the damaged black psyche, the "chip on the shoulder" attitude that caused black students to misread innocuous situations. And white liberal educators did not always know how to reconcile racist occurrences with a rhetoric of good intentions. It was just this sort of contention that teachers had criticized the movement for failing to address during the war. Innuendo and courtesy, they argued, would never be strong enough to combat the kinds of social tasks that public schools were now charged with or the challenges they faced. Feeling well and doing good, many teachers suggested, were two different skills entirely.

REAL-LIFE REFORM: THE LEGACIES OF INTERCULTURALISM

By the 1950s, courtesy was no longer an option for many teachers in New York City public schools. As some teachers had anticipated, a race tolerance movement that focused on the psychology of prejudice—at the expense of investigating social and political relationships—did not provide the ideological apparatus for attending to the changing "actual" events in the schools. Even more, educators such as Glassman and Unna argued, it did little to change events outside school. From her study of relationships between black and white students in schools, interculturalist Sandra Holbrook agreed, writing, "Real comradeship between Negro and white children is rare . . . [though] there is little outward discrimination." The greater challenge, Holbrook argued, was one of performance outside school, for as one student explained to her about another, "Bella (a colored girl) is awfully well-liked in history class—everyone admires her brains. She's pretty too. But as soon as we get out of the door, we forget Bella."[35] Holbrook's story reflects the influence of political structures outside schools—notably, the segregation of black and white neighborhoods—as one of the greatest obstacles to intercultural success within it. Because students often did not live in diverse communities, there frequently existed a split between what they were taught to feel and how they actually had to be.

In 1954, *Brown v. Board of Education* codified both the premises and the problems of interculturalism into law. Built on the same psychological theory that interculturalists operated from—that of the damaged black psyche—the *Brown* decision argued that segregation caused powerful feelings of inferiority in black students.[36] In this respect, schools across the nation in the 1950s and 1960s were positioned to be on a trajectory established by wartime New York City schools. Only one fact was inconsistent with the apparent mainstreaming of interculturalism during World War II: rather than gaining momentum, the movement had disappeared.

Historians have offered multiple explanations for why interculturalism dissolved at a time when public schools in both the North and South were diversifying all the more. In 1953, Rachel Davis DuBois was subpoenaed before the McCarthy hearings. Although she was eventually exempted from all charges, the conflation of interculturalism with communism led to a decrease in funding in the 1950s. The interest in interculturalism similarly diminished as the immediate pressure for tolerance in postwar America subsided and the civil rights movement gained ground. It is likely that the "real life" encounters that interculturalism advocated lost relevance in the face of more substantial interracial encounters that were legally mandated by *Brown* and events thereafter. Interculturalism had sought to change students' hearts and minds, but civil rights advocates after World War II more ambitiously strove to change students' lives. The burgeoning demands for racial justice from the black community made it more challenging for white teachers to repeat a generic rhetoric of good feeling as the 1940s transitioned into the 1950s. A call for tolerance that felt like a liberal gesture to many during World War II sounded like an apology for inequity a decade later.

If the gains black students gained from interculturalism were unclear at the end of the 1940s, however, so too were the advances that it offered to teachers. Even as the movement positioned teachers in the middle of a national project to improve race relations, it firmly reentrenched them in a world of feeling and sentiment—a dynamic that, far from radical, was actually quite familiar. Even if the new psychological theories changed the rhetoric and terms upon which teachers performed in the classroom, the belief that they were the emotional caretakers of children dated to the feminization of teaching and was connected to the justification of lower salaries and unequal treatment between men and women teachers in school regulations. In addition, the movement had fewer ideological resources with which to revise the political relationships that often compromised teachers just as much. In the end, interculturalism did little to forge relationships between teachers of different classroom environments. Teachers such as Rose Nurnberg and Michael Glassman appear to have worked as autonomous agents in their classrooms, much as teachers had done in the past. For others, such as Charles Slatkin, the possibility of other teachers evaluating what occurred in their classrooms created a great deal of anxiety. In the writings of Rachel Davis DuBois there are numerous stories of teachers banding together against various phenomena—whether they were white teachers complaining about their black colleagues or teachers mutually resisting the time demands imposed by intercultural faculty workshops. Yet most teachers seem to have worked autonomously rather than collaboratively. In this sense, teachers served as instruments, rather than as partners in social reform, more valuable for what they might individually disseminate than for what they might collectively design.

But if it is difficult to measure the concrete benefits of the programs and policies of interculturalism to students and teachers in the 1940s, the ethical and ideological legacies of the movement are more solid. The *Brown* decision—as well as the widespread development of multiculturalism in public education—speaks to the changes that the movement introduced to school life. Most important of these was a vision of intergroup relations that could be institutionalized, even if not always with complete success. If psychology was a difficult staging ground for reform, many of the changes interculturalists introduced were more tangible and easily measured. Specifically, interculturalists claimed that the curriculum could no longer act as a cultural monolith but needed to represent the individual histories and psychic needs of the students to whom it was taught. Extracurricular activities that during World War I had been seen as useful for developing the student as a whole person were now seen as a critical part of a student's education; learning came in an increasing number of forms and none were mutually exclusive. Most important, both interculturalism and *Brown* made race a topic in public school discourse that could never be taken off the table again.

In modern multicultural programs, we also may see some of the challenges of the earlier movement. Many within the "culture wars" continue to argue for something closer to "national cultural unity" on their own terms rather than for true compromise or for open debate.[37] For this reason, understanding interculturalism is important for more than appreciating a particular race movement; in fact, it provides a historical context for examining and historicizing contemporary debates about multiculturalism in education.

But in this respect, interculturalism can offer one final reminder: social reform projects might be enacted through institutions (such as public schools or the Bureau of Intercultural Education), but institutional objectives—especially those aimed at transforming the psychological makeup of individual students—will always be accepted or rejected at the level of their participants. The writings of wartime teachers reveals how they did both; modern educators can perhaps learn from them about the difficulties of teaching racial tolerance and engaging in social movements. The most resonant memoirs from the intercultural era are those that neither bought intercultural idealism wholesale nor cast it off as merely missionary dogma, but instead questioned the movement's vision in an effort to improve it. In the end, this kind of questioning allowed World War II interculturalist teachers to take powerful political positions. In doing so, they anticipated a new decade in which the struggles were often more fierce and feelings all the more difficult to capture on page.

NOTES

1. Rose Nurnberg, "Children of Freedom," *High Points in the Work of the High Schools of New York City* 25 (September 1943): 15–18.

2. For accounts of interculturalism before World War II, see Nicholas V. Montalto, *A History of the Intercultural Movement, 1924–1941* (New York Garland, 1982) and Diana Selig, "Cultural Gifts: American Liberals, Childhood, and the Origins of Multiculturalism, 1924–1939" (Ph.D. diss., University of California, Berkeley, 2001). Though interculturalism was largely concentrated in New York City, Selig shows that by 1935, published accounts of pluralist activities in the schools were reported by educators from cities as geographically diverse as Los Angeles; Santa Fe; Atlanta; and Kirksville, Missouri. See Selig, 18.

3. Pearl M. Fisher, "English, Democracy, and Color," *High Points* 25 (May 1942): 5–10, 6.

4. Stewart G. Cole, "Culture Patterns in Minority Groups," in *One America*, ed. Francis J. Brown and Joseph Slabey (New York: Prentice Hall, 1946), 564, 468; Murray Eisenstadt, "Total War in the Schools," *High Points* 25 (January 1943): 6–12, 11; Will Scarlet, "Putting the Emotions to Work for Democracy," *High Points* 24 (June 1942): 50–51, 50.

5. Frank H. Paine, "Culture in the Making—What of Our Culture?" *High Points* 27 (June 1945): 25–30, 29.

6. For more on the development and effects of a therapeutic culture, see Ellen Herman, *The Romance of American Psychology: Political Culture in the Age of Experts* (Berkeley: University of California Press, 1995); Eve Moskowitz, *In Therapy We Trust: America's Obsession with Self-Fulfillment* (Baltimore: Johns Hopkins University Press, 2001); Wilfred M. McClay, *The Masterless: Self and Society in Modern America* (Chapel Hill: University of North Carolina Press, 1994); Ann Hulbert, *Raising America: Experts, Parents, and a Century of Advice about Children* (New York: Random House, 2003).

7. Rachel Davis DuBois, *Build Together Americans: Adventures in Intercultural Education* (New York: Hinds, Hayden, and Eldredge, 1945), 108. One of the most influential social science texts for white psychologists was Gunnar Myrdal's *An American Dilemma: The Negro Problem and Modern Democracy* (New York: Harpers and Row, 1944). See also Ralph Ellison's insightful critique of Myrdal in "An American Dilemma: A Review" in *Shadow and Act* (New York: Random House, 1964), 303–17 and Walter A. Jackson, *Gunnar Myrdal and America's Conscious: Social Engineering and Racial Liberalism, 1938–1987* (Chapel Hill: University of North Carolina Press, 1990). For more on the damaged black psyche, see Herman, *Romance of American Psychology* and Daryl Michael Scott, *Contempt and Pity:*

Social Policy and the Image of the Damaged Black Psyche, 1880–1996 (Chapel Hill: University of North Carolina Press, 1997).

8. Rachel Davis DuBois and Corann Okoradudu, *All This and Something More: Pioneering in Intercultural Education* (Bryn Mawr, PA: Dorrance, 1948), 63–84. Throughout this chapter, the name DuBois refers to Rachel Davis DuBois, not W. E. B. Du Bois.

9. For more on the distinction between interculturalists and black ethnic studies movement of the same time, see James A. Banks, "The African American Roots of Multicultural Education," in *Multicultural Education, Transformative Knowledge, and Action: Historical and Contemporary Perspectives*, ed. James A. Banks (New York: Teachers College Press, 1996). For more on the black response to interculturalism, see Darryl Michael Scott, "Postwar Pluralism, *Brown v. Board of Education*, and the Origins of Multicultural Education," *Journal of American History* 91 (June 2004): 69–82 and Jonathan Zimmerman, "*Brown*-ing the American Textbook: History, Psychology, and the Origins of Modern Multiculturalism," *History of Education Quarterly* 44 (Summer 2004): 46–69.

10. DuBois, *Build Together Americans*, 12. W. E. B. Du Bois and Rachel Davis DuBois were friends, but two reformers were not related.

11. Nurnberg, "Children of Freedom," 18.

12. Henry T. Hillson, "The Negro History and Culture Club," *High Points* 25 (November 1943): 21. For a different interpretation of the Negro History and Culture Club at Eastern, see Robert Shaffer, "Multicultural Education in New York City During World War II," *New York History* 77 (July 1996): 301–32, 316.

13. Hillson, "Negro History and Culture Club," 19–23, 21.

14. Mildred Englander, "Homemaking for Boys," *High Points* 29 (June 1947): 67–72, 68.

15. Mary Riley, "American Harmony," *High Points* 26 (March 1944): 15–19, 15.

16. Marie Syrkin, *Your School, Your Children* (New York: L. B. Fischer, 1944), 70–1.

17. Hillson, "The Negro History and Culture Club," 19.

18. Agnes E. Benedict, "Violence in the Schools," *Nation* 156 (January 9, 1943): 51–53, 53.

19. "A City's Shame," *Time* (April 5, 1948): 69. For discussion of some teachers' continuing reluctance to work in black schools see Diane Ravitch, *The Great School Wars* (Baltimore: Johns Hopkins Press, 2000), 255–56.

20. For more on race, poverty, housing discrimination in New York City, and ghettoization, see among others, Robin D.G. Kelley, *Race Rebels: Culture, Politics, and the Black Working Class* (New York: Free Press, 1994); Kenneth T. Jackson, *Crabgrass Frontier: The Suburbanization of the United States* (New York: Oxford University Press, 1985); and Craig Steven Wilder, *A Covenant with Color: Race and Social Power in Brooklyn* (New York: Columbia University Press, 2000): 175–217.

21. Exie Welsch to Thomas J. Patterson, 23 November 1951, folder 2, box 3, Central Harlem Neighborhood Association Records, Schomburg Center for Research in Black Culture, New York Public Library.

22. For more on the relationship between civil rights leaders and the schools

in the 1940s, see Martha Biondi, *To Stand and Fight: The Struggle for Civil Rights in Postwar New York City* (Cambridge, MA: Harvard University Press, 2003), 241–49.

23. Eugene T. Maleska, "White Teacher in Harlem," *High Points* 29 (May 1947): 5–9, 5.

24. DuBois, *Build Together Americans*, 1.

25. DuBois, *Build Together Americans*, 21.

26. Hillson, "The Negro History and Culture Club," 21; DuBois, *Build Together Americans*, 226, 151.

27. DuBois, *Build Together Americans*, xiv.

28. Daniel J. Cahill, "Some Thoughts on Intercultural Education," *High Points* 26 (October 1945): 5–11, 8.

29. Willard Waller, "Revolt in the Classroom," *High Points* 25 (October 1943): 5–12, 8. On claims of anti-intellectualism in curricula generally, see Arnold Bestor, *Educational Wastelands: The Retreat from Learning in Our Public Schools*, 2nd ed. (Urbana: University of Illinois Press, 1985); JoAnne Brown, "'A is for Atom, B is for Bomb': Civil Defense in American Public Education, 1948–1963," *The Journal of American History* 75 (June 1988): 68–90; and Diane Ravitch, *Left Back: A Century of Battles over School Reform* (New York: Simon & Schuster, 2000), 343–52.

30. Charles E. Slatkin, "True Confession," *High Points* 26 (February 1944): 45–49, 47.

31. Syrkin, *Your School, Your Children*, 193.

32. Michael Glassman, "A Practical Intercultural Education Project at Tilden," *HP* 31 (June 1949): 56–63, 57

33. Estella Unna, "The Thrill of Conquest," *HP* 27 (October 1945): 60–64, 63.

34. DuBois, *Build Together Americans*, 89.

35. Sabra Holbrook, "A Study of Some Relationships Between Negro and White Students in New York Public Schools," *High Points* 26 (June 1944): 16.

36. On the ideological limitations of the *Brown* decision, especially in respect to its reliance on social psychology and the theory of the damaged black psyche, see, among others, Scott, *Contempt and Pity*; Richard Kluger, *Simple Justice* (New York: Vintage Books, 1975), esp. 679–747; James T. Patterson, *"Brown v. Board of Education": A Civil Rights Milestone and Its Troubled Legacy* (New York: Oxford University Press, 2001); and Christopher Schmidt, "The Children of *Brown*."

37. See Jonathan Zimmerman, *Whose America? Culture Wars in the Public Schools* (Cambridge, MA: Harvard University Press, 2002).

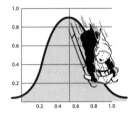

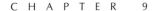

The Children of *Brown*: Psychology and School Desegregation in Midcentury America

Christopher W. Schmidt

OF THE MANY IMAGES that define our memory of the civil rights movement, few are more powerful or more disturbing than a photograph taken of Dorothy Counts on 4 September 1957, the day this fifteen-year-old girl became the first African American to attend Harding High School in Charlotte, North Carolina. The picture captures her as she walks to school, surrounded by her new white classmates. They are jeering and laughing; some make demeaning gestures. The new student's head is held high, although the strain of the situation on her is evident—in her tense body, the apprehension on her face. The foreground of the picture contains two younger white children, each maybe eight years old. One is clearly enjoying the attempts to humiliate Counts. The other glares at her. Although his angry eyes barely reach the height of Counts's elbow, the condescension of his glare is unmistakable.

Counts's experience at Harding High lasted less than two weeks. After being spit on, having things thrown at her, and enduring constant harassment, she withdrew and enrolled in an integrated school in Philadelphia.[1]

THE ASSUMPTIONS BEHIND *BROWN*

In addition to offering a searing portrait of racial hatred, the photograph of Dorothy Counts offers a useful starting point for a critical investigation into the formation of race-related social policy in modern America. Counts's situation was the direct product of the national program of school desegregation that grew out of the Supreme Court's landmark *Brown v. Board of Education* decision of 1954. The picture of Counts's walk to school serves to critique several of the central assumptions of *Brown*, assumptions that were crucial both to the lawyers of the National Association for the Advancement of Colored People (NAACP) who framed the winning argument in the case and to the Supreme Court justices who unanimously supported the decision.

The principles underlying *Brown* can be broken down into three general assumptions. First, racial integration was a desirable and necessary goal for American society and would be pursued even in the face of significant regional resistance. This was the central premise of the entire civil rights movement through the mid-1960s. Second, the schools and children should be at the center of the movement for racial equality. This assumption was found both in the extraordinary effort the NAACP made in its legal campaign against segregated schools and in the willingness of the Supreme Court to redefine its civil rights policy through a school-desegregation decision. And third, a primary rationale for integration derived from the psychological damage segregated schools caused in black children. This argument was found in testimony by expert witnesses; in the briefs and arguments of the NAACP legal team; and, most famously, in the decision written by Chief Justice Earl Warren.

Each of these assumptions, which received broad, almost unquestioned acceptance among liberals in the early postwar era, is challenged, or at least questioned, by the photograph of Dorothy Counts and its surrounding historical context. Juxtaposing the *Brown* decision with this picture raises several questions. How does the "integration" captured in this picture relate to the integration that the NAACP and the Court envisioned? Are the schools really the best place for this to be taking place? Are children the proper group to be dealing with such issues? On the question of psychological damage, who in this picture shows the scars of segregation, the proud Counts, or the raging white children? And what kind of damage, on both white and black children, is being inflicted as a result of the drive toward integration?

By returning to the period in which the assumptions of *Brown*-era racial liberalism took shape, one finds several critical junctures at which these issues were raised; contested; and, to some extent, resolved. Points of contention became, through the process of debate inside and outside the legal system, accepted tenets of liberal reform. Challenges to these assumptions would be viewed as challenges to the entire project of racial progress.

PSYCHOLOGY AND *BROWN*

While each of these assumptions had its own history, a central theme prevailed in all. With remarkable consistency, those lawyers and justices who accepted the assumptions of liberal America and applied them to challenging racial segregation turned to psychology for support. As the NAACP searched for the most effective medium through which to challenge America's system of legalized racial inequality, and as the courts attempted to come to terms with this challenge, psychological treatments of race relations became increasingly prominent. This reliance on psychology went far beyond the controversial footnote 11 of the opinion, in which Warren listed several prominent works of sociology and psychology, and it went beyond Warren's reference to the psychological damage segregation inflicted on the "hearts and minds" of African American children. An awareness of psychology played a central role in the creation of the entire worldview in which the NAACP created their case and in which the justices decided it.

The contribution of psychology to *Brown* was often the product of indirect influence or selective readings. The work of psychology, like all attempts to scientifically study society, is filled with nuances, qualifications, and complexities, characteristics that often make a poor fit in the context of a legal argument. In *Brown*, psychological findings would be adapted to the needs of the legal system. All parties involved—the psychologists who offered expert testimony, the lawyers who interpreted these findings in their arguments, and the jurists who reinterpreted these findings in their opinions— were eager to simplify issues, to emphasize certain facets of an argument over others. Therefore simply working back from Chief Justice Warren's opinion misses the multiplicity of options, the "paths not taken" on the road to *Brown*.

A sense of historical contingency is needed to understand why and how children, psychology, and race collided in the courts in the early 1950s. The famous decision, in its economical, optimistic eleven pages, gave little hint of the eventual ordeals that black and white children would go through as America confronted desegregation. Yet within the record of the psychologists' contributions to the case there were premonitions of these ordeals, even if they were steadily shaved away as the legal argument developed and as the Court neared its momentous decision. For it is in these forgotten premonitions, in the full story of the contribution of psychology to *Brown*, that one is most likely to locate answers to the questions raised by the picture of Dorothy Counts on her way to school in the fall of 1957.

PSYCHOLOGY IN MIDCENTURY AMERICA

Psychology, in academia and in the popular consciousness, achieved unprecedented levels of influence during the postwar period. The decade following World War II was marked by a growing faith among scholars and policymakers in the power of psychology to explain contemporary social problems. The enhanced stature of psychology derived from several factors, including the maturation of the social sciences generally as an academic discipline, the creation of wartime government employment for psychologists in propaganda and morale efforts, and the demand for new explanations of human nature in the wake of Hitler and the Holocaust.[2]

Two fields of psychological inquiry were particularly influential for race relations: social psychology and developmental psychology. Scholars drew on social psychology to explain everything from the "mind" of Nazi Germany to the possibility of harmony among various religious, ethnic, and racial groups in the United States. The alliance of social psychology with efforts to promote intergroup tolerance offered further opportunities for psychology to influence social programs.

Similarly, developmental psychology sought to understand how prejudice and intolerance was first internalized in young people. It played a critical role in highlighting the importance of schools in American society and, more specifically, in solidifying the hold on American society of theories of "progressive education." Since its inception at the turn of the century, progressive education sought to move pedagogy beyond the transmission of specific subject matter and into the realm of individual development through careful structuring of the classroom experience, a project that was strengthened by the findings of developmental psychology. By 1948 psychologist Gardner Murphy approvingly noted that among educators "emphasis is shifting to studies of the personalities of teachers and their pupils; studies of the emotional jamming that makes it hard to learn to read; studies of the social psychology of the classroom."[3] Two years later, a report based on the Midcentury White House Conference on Children explicitly embraced progressive educational theory and developmental psychology, concluding, "The full development of the whole child is the basic philosophy and ultimate aim of all recommendations."[4]

For those involved with the White House conference and for many others interested in developmental psychology, a major barrier to the creation of "healthy personalities" was racial prejudice. By addressing the issue of intolerance in its earliest stages, developmental psychologists hoped to instill in the next generation of Americans a commitment to toleration and national unity. Their efforts were marked by a powerful sense of optimism. They were, after all, focusing on the most malleable of Americans. Like the social psychologists who contributed to intergroup tolerance efforts, developmental psychologists became an essential resource for social reformers interested in demonstrating the damages of racism.

Psychology was central to the growth of racial liberalism in the years leading up to *Brown*. Since the 1920s social scientists had been rapidly abandoning theories of scientific racism and its belief in innate black inferiority in favor of environmental explanations of human development.[5] In this context, an expanding group of racial liberals, both black and white, turned to psychology to explain and address racism in America. Since liberals of this period tended to view racism as the product of unreasoning emotion, which could be treated with carefully formulated social policy, psychology proved particularly attractive. By midcentury, many in the sociological and psychological professions were willing to use their expertise to attack segregation.[6] At the same time, many racial liberals in positions of power and influence were looking to the findings of psychologists to support their attempts to address racial discrimination and inequality.

THE QUESTION OF INTEGRATION

Before the three guiding principles of *Brown*—a commitment to integration, a faith in the schools, and a focus on segregation's harm to black children—became solidified into assumptions, they were issues of debate within the liberal community. Of the three issues, the beneficial nature of integration was the first to move from an issue of contention to a point of widespread agreement among proponents of civil rights. While some disagreement would remain about whether pushing for integration was the best path to progress for African Americans, the debate was largely muted in the 1940s and 1950s. Agreement on the necessity for modern America to be an integrated society was virtually a sine qua non within the liberal community of the early postwar period, even if there was still considerable debate over the best method to achieve it. This agreement, however, was the product of a debate waged by previous generations, a debate that was in part resolved (if only for a time) by the influence of psychologists.

DU BOIS'S CHALLENGE

In one of the last major pre-*Brown* debates within the civil rights community on the advisability of integration, the famous civil rights activist W. E. B. Du Bois made a controversial critique of the drive to desegregate. Separate schools for blacks, Du Bois contended in a 1935 essay, "are needed just so far as they are necessary for the proper education of the Negro race." Considering the existing racial prejudice of white Americans, blacks could not receive an adequate education in white educational institutions. Furthermore, advocating for integrated schools too often entailed a disparagement of the existing black schools, revealing "an utter lack of faith on the part of Negroes that their race can do anything really well." The fundamental problem was not segregation, Du Bois argued, but a lack of "self-knowledge" and "self-respect." In a passage that demonstrated a powerful prescience when read in light of the integration experience of Dorothy Counts, he emphasized the painful challenges that school desegregation would entail for black children:

> I have repeatedly seen wise and loving colored parents take infinite pains to force their little children into schools where the white children, white teachers, and white parents despised and resented the dark child, made mock of it, neglected or bullied it, and literally rendered its life a living hell. Such parents want their child to "fight" this thing out,—but, dear God, at what a cost! . . . We shall get a finer, better balance of spirit; an infinitely more capable and rounded personality by putting children in schools where they are wanted, and where they are happy and inspired, than in thrusting them into hells where they are ridiculed and hated.[7]

PSYCHOLOGY AND THE INTEGRATIONIST CONSENSUS

How were reservations such as these to be overcome? Undoubtedly, the egalitarian ethos that permeated World War II ideology contributed to the rising faith in integration, as did the decline of the Communist Party after the 1930s, which had at times advocated a form of black separatism. Within the NAACP, the defeat of Du Bois's argument was the product of a pragmatic analysis of reform possibilities. Many in the NAACP and other reform organizations assumed that integration and the introduction of the African American community into mainstream American society was simply the most effective way to overcome the vestiges of slavery and racism.

Yet these practical assumptions found significant scientific support in the empirical findings of social psychology. "Contact theory," the idea that increased interaction between diverse groups would lead to improved intergroup relations, largely displaced earlier notions that had assumed unnecessary interactions between different groups risked destabilizing society. Contact theory assumed that prejudice was produced by ignorance and that the best remedy for ignorance was exposure and education. Social psychologists built an entire scholarly literature around this hypothesis, with particular success in the field of residential studies and in studies of military integration.[8]

Discussion of these psychological findings could be heard all over American society, including within the Supreme Court. Before the NAACP forced public school segregation onto the agenda of the Court, the justices considered a case involving whether racially restrictive residential covenants could be constitutionally enforced. Although the 1948 opinion in *Shelley v. Kraemer* made little mention of social science evidence, the justices heard arguments and read briefs that contained sociological and psychological material drawing on contact theory in their critique of residential segregation. The U.S. Justice Department, although not a party in the case, participated in oral argument and filed a friend-of-the-court brief that denounced segregation as "rooted in ignorance, bigotry, and prejudice" and attacked residential segregation as "injurious to our order and productive of growing antagonisms destructive to the integrity of our society."[9]

The Justice Department brief also cited the 1947 report of the President's Committee on Civil Rights, the most prominent civil rights document of the day, which made even more explicit use of contact theory: "Segregation is an obstacle to establishing harmonious relationships among groups. [Experiences] prove that where the artificial barriers which divide people and groups from one another are broken, tension and conflict begin to be replaced by cooperative effort and an environment in which civil rights can thrive."[10] Many involved, including the lawyers for the NAACP, felt that social science played an important behind-the-scenes role in the Court's landmark ruling that restrictive covenants could not be enforced by government action.

The perceived benefits of integration were again highlighted several years later in *Brown*. An appendix to the NAACP brief, titled "The Effects of Segregation and the Consequences of Desegregation: A Social Science Statement" and signed by thirty-two prominent sociologists and psychologists, explained, "Under certain circumstances, desegregation not only proceeds without major difficulties, but has been observed to lead to the emergence of more favorable attitudes and friendlier relations between races."[11] During oral arguments, Justice Stanley Reed pressured NAACP legal counsel Thurgood Marshall on whether segregation laws might still be justified in the name of preserving law and order. Marshall replied these laws were "not necessary now because people have grown up and understand each other. They are fighting and living together."[12]

Within the Court, Justice Felix Frankfurter showed himself conversant in the recent findings of social psychology. "Experience happily shows that contacts tend to mitigate antagonism and to engender mutual respect," he wrote in a personal memorandum that he shared with Warren during the Court's consideration of *Brown*.[13] Although there was still resistance by some of the justices to the integrationist ideal, by the early 1950s most of the justices had come to a conclusion similar to Frankfurter's.[14] Even if the details of the social-psychological literature on contact theory were not known by all the lawyers and jurists involved in *Brown*, its basic, commonsense assumptions—that prejudice was caused by lack of understanding and stereotypes, that these problems could be overcome through interaction and education—pervaded the arguments and deliberations in the court.

SCHOOLS, CHILDREN, AND PREJUDICE

Brown's linkage between integration and education was not inevitable. School desegregation was far from the only area toward which progressive racial reformers directed their energies. A broad-based, locally oriented intergroup-relations movement had made significant gains.[15] There were important efforts to improve race relations within the workforce. The Supreme Court issued landmark decisions in the fields of voting rights and racially restrictive covenants. Truman desegregated the military via executive order. Even the field in which the Jim Crow era defined itself, segregated transportation (*Plessy v. Ferguson*, the case that gave constitutional backing to the policy of separate but equal, was a railroad case), had shown signs of improvement in the 1940s and early 1950s as the Supreme Court issued decisions desegregating interstate transportation. In short, it was far from predetermined that the first major breakthrough of the modern civil rights movement would involve where children went to school. Yet, despite the obvious alternatives and the potential dangers of forcing the civil rights issue with the nation's youth, the campaign for integrated schools captured the imagination of forward-thinking blacks and whites more powerfully than other avenues for racial progress. Part of this can be explained by the newly prominent role of the schools in midcentury American society, a development that was supported by modern psychology.

Tactical and budgetary considerations drove the NAACP's decision in the 1930s to focus on using the courts to promote educational equality, but the organization had other areas of reform interests as well. Most significantly, the organization gave serious consideration to supporting the development of an interracial working-class movement. Yet the prohibitive costs of waging an all-out campaign for equality in the unions and the workplace, in addition to the discomfort some of the NAACP leadership felt with becoming too closely aligned with a leftist-affiliated cause, led to increased attention to the possibilities of a legal campaign aimed at improving the education of blacks, particularly in the South.

The lawyers from the NAACP recognized the potential of the modern school as an object for racial reform. School enrollment for children of both races was growing dramatically. Education for African Americans had always suffered from a chronic lack of resources, but the situation reached crisis levels in the early 1930s, when the NAACP turned its focus to the conditions of black schools. Southern education offered a glaring example of racial inequality, of the failure of the "separate but equal" equation to live up to its name. By the late 1920s, the NAACP initiated a number of investigations into the state of southern schools, and in 1931 it devised an ambitious plan to attack unequal schooling in the South through the courts.[16]

Schools, education, children—all these resonated in the minds of liberals searching for a way to address the racial inequalities that had haunted the nation since its inception. While the education of the nation's youth had been a constant presence in discussions of social reform, in the 1940s and 1950s these discussions took a particular form that made the idea of using the schools to address the problems of race relations increasingly appealing. Influenced by the still-powerful legacy of the progressive-education movement, educational theory turned to psychology to better understand the potential of the schools for reforming society. Psychology proved a particularly powerful resource for those who thought racism could be most efficiently attacked through the schools. Two leading social psychologists described the possibility of "rais[ing] a generation which will be relatively free of ethnic intolerance" as "not only a hope but a real possibility."[17]

THE ROLE OF EDUCATION IN *BROWN*

The rhetorical and symbolic power of children and the schools was clearly evident in the *Brown* litigation. The NAACP's decision to focus its arguments on black children and the damages inflicted by separate schooling was a departure from the approach of plaintiffs in previous Supreme Court cases involving public education, nearly all of which had been argued in terms of parental rights.[18] The NAACP lawyers recognized the symbolic advantage of framing their case on behalf of children as well as the specific psychological damages they could demonstrate with expert testimony. The ideal of black and white children playing together was a common refrain in Thurgood Marshall's oral argument before the Court in *Brown*.[19]

In his attempts to place children and education at the forefront of the segregation issue, Marshall was speaking to a largely sympathetic Court. Frankfurter in particular often praised the role of education in American society. He was himself the inspiring product of public education, having arrived in New York City from his native Austria at age twelve speaking not a word of English. He excelled as a student at PS 25 and City College before going on to Harvard Law School and future fame as a scholar and Supreme Court justice. In a personal memorandum, which he shared with Chief Justice Warren when *Brown* was being argued, Frankfurter praised education as "a powerful instrument for nurturing or counter-acting those feelings and convictions which are essential for the relationship of equality in the discharge of common citizenship."[20] The idea of education as social equalizer and promoter of a more unified nation had support among other justices as well. "It is not reasonable to educate people separately for a joint life," noted Justice Harold Burton in one of the justices' conferences at which they discussed *Brown*.[21]

The language of the *Brown* decision itself reflects the psychologically inflected ideas of childhood and education that pervaded postwar liberal discourse. "Today, education is perhaps the most important function of state and local governments," Warren wrote. It "is the very foundation of good citizenship. Today it is a principle instrument in awakening the child to cultural values, in preparing him for professional training, and in helping him to adjust normally to his environment."[22] This final sentence encapsulates Warren's understanding of progressive educational theories, particularly the psychological aspects of these theories. The wording of this sentence is important: a child is "awakened" to the correct cultural values. If done correctly, the child will grow to be a productive member of society, and, in particular, an effective member of the workforce. In the background lurks the danger that the child may not adjust "normally," that some kind of pathology or neurosis might invade the child's fragile psyche.

As with the support contact theory gave to various integration efforts, developmental psychology's contribution to ending discrimination in education was made more powerful by its element of common sense. Warren did not believe that his reference to childhood development required the reference to scientific studies, just as he did not feel he had to justify the benefits of an integrated society. As a result of a generation of conceptual adjustment within mainstream liberal culture, aided by the work of psychology, these new assumptions about integration and schooling had already taken shape. They required little in the way of elaborate justification. The same could not be said, however, with regard to the third assumption of *Brown*, the argument that segregation inflicted significant psychological harm on African American children.

PSYCHOLOGICAL DAMAGE IN BLACK AND WHITE

Among the most famous phrases in *Brown* are those describing how segregation created in black students "a feeling of inferiority . . . that may affect their hearts and minds in a way unlikely ever to be undone." Similar to the turn to integration and to the schools, this turn to the "hearts and minds" of African American children was the product of the rejection of other options. Yet, unlike the debates over integration and over focusing on education, which the NAACP and its liberal allies had largely resolved before the school-segregation cases came to court, the use of damage arguments to justify the decision was a product of the litigation itself.

There was nothing predetermined in the fact that the psychological damage to black children would be highlighted in *Brown*. There was much work being done on psychology and race on subjects other than children. In fact, most studies of race relations during the 1930s and 1940s were more concerned with the impact of racism on adults. Both the "Chicago School" of sociology and the "self-hate" theories pioneered by Kurt Lewin emphasized that those most affected by discrimination were "marginal" individuals who had the most contact with the dominant group, such as upper- and middle-class adult blacks.

This conclusion was exactly the opposite of that reached by psychologist Kenneth Clark, the NAACP's most important source on matters of black psychological damage. By turning to children, Clark and the NAACP were working on grounds that had been previously studied in a limited manner.[23] Furthermore, the majority of work on racial prejudice focused on its formation within the white majority rather than on its effects on the black majority.[24] Reflecting the dominant trends of scholarship at the time, the testimony and arguments from the lower-court school-desegregation trials created a picture of the psychological damage of segregation in which white children, as well as black children, were the victims.

WHITE DAMAGE

In focusing on the damaged white child, these arguments tapped into the well-developed research of the intergroup education movement, which had taken shape in the interwar years and gained momentum during World War II. The goal of this movement was to reduce prejudice by educating individuals to appreciate difference. While much of the focus of this pluralist movement was on reducing tensions based on ethnicity and religion (where they had their greatest successes), it also sought to address racial antagonism. The dream of the tolerationists was to create a new generation of tolerant American citizens.[25]

The theme of the psychological damage of prejudice on members of the majority achieved new levels of prominence with the publication of studies such as John Dollard's *Caste and Class in a Southern Town* (1937); W. J. Cash's *The Mind of the South* (1941); and, most notably, Gunnar Myrdal's *An American Dilemma* (1944). The dilemma outlined in Myrdal's celebrated examination of race relations was in essence a white psychological condition in which racist actions conflicted with egalitarian ideals. Considering the existing power structure, Myrdal reasoned, racial progress was most likely to come from challenging white racist assumptions.[26] "The Negro problem," he concluded, "is predominantly a white man's problem."

Myrdal's line of argument shaped the lines of liberal debate in the following years. The President's Committee on Civil Rights report made a sweeping case for the psychological damages of segregation: "It is impossible to

decide who suffers the greatest moral damage from our civil rights transgressions, because all of us are hurt. . . . The damage to those who are responsible for these violations of our moral standards may well be greater
[than that of the victims]."[27] Southern writer Lillian Smith offered much the
same characterization of racism in her powerful 1949 book *Killers of the
Dream*. Adorno's *The Authoritarian Personality*, an influential sociological
study of the period, argued that prejudice was antithetical to the democratic
personality. And in 1954 psychologist Gordon Allport published *The Nature of Prejudice*, a comprehensive refutation of the idea of inherited prejudice and an examination of the complex cultural and psychological formation
of intolerance. All these works emphasized that discrimination was not just
a minority problem and that racism damaged all Americans.[28]

PSYCHOLOGICAL DAMAGE ARGUMENTS AND *BROWN*

The written briefs in *Brown* presented the Supreme Court Justices with the
materials necessary to fashion a decision receptive to the notion of racism's
pansocietal impact, a decision that could argue persuasively for the advantages of expanding what was often called the "Negro Problem" into something better approximated by the "American dilemma" Myrdal described.
The American Federation of Teachers contributed an amicus brief in which it
cited a survey of social scientists, 83 percent of whom believed that enforced
segregation psychologically damaged the dominant group.[29] The white-damage
line of argument achieved its fullest development in the appendix to the
NAACP's brief. Although focused mostly on the damage of segregation to
black children, a significant portion of the statement examined what it described as the "more obscure" question of its impact on white children. The
brief cited various sources that described the majority group's "unrealistic
fears and hatreds of minority groups," "distorted sense of reality," "rigid
stereotypes," and "negative attitudes" that resulted from segregation.[30]

   With the prevalence of readily available evidence citing the damage of
segregation on whites, it is striking that the wording of Warren's decision
contained no reference to white psychology. The story the Chief Justice told
in *Brown* was one of the damaged black child. In the Justices' conference in
December 1953 following the second round of *Brown* oral arguments, however, Warren made no reference to concerns about psychological damage at
all. Rather, his primary reasoning was on the basis of equality—segregation,
he stated to his fellow Justices, is based on "the basic premise that the Negro
race is inferior," a premise he rejected.[31]

   Yet when in the spring of 1954 Warren sat down to write the decision, he landed upon the black-damage argument as a primary rationale

for undermining the separate-but-equal fallacy. Although the controversial footnote 11, which listed a number of works of sociology and psychology, was the contribution of his clerks, the crucial line of the opinion regarding the "hearts and minds" of black children was Warren's, added in the margin of the handwritten first draft of the opinion.[32] Despite some passing comments by various Justices expressing uncertainty about the use of psychology in a court opinion, the fact that Warren's black-damage argument made it through the revision process, in which the other Justices offered criticisms and comments, indicates that the Court generally accepted this line of reasoning, or at least did not strongly reject it (in his quest for unanimity Warren was quite sensitive to the concerns of his fellow Justices in drafting the opinion).[33]

THE LOSS OF THE WHITE DAMAGE ARGUMENT

The legal arena is more effective at dealing with specific damages than with constructing a positive vision of social reform, and this factor clearly played a role in strengthening the presence of the black damage argument in *Brown*.[34] In framing the NAACP's case, Thurgood Marshall recognized this fact and planned his argument accordingly. He would later recall his approach to arguing the school-desegregation cases: "I told the staff that we had to try this case just like any other one in which you would try to prove damages to your client. If your car ran over my client, you'd have to pay up and my function as an attorney would be to put experts on the stand to testify to how much damage was done."[35] The NAACP lawyers recognized that the damaged black child, a result of both material inequality and psychological trauma, made a strong case, and they made increasing use of social science as the litigation progressed.[36] Even if the NAACP could have clearly presented the white-damage argument, white children were not their "clients." At the South Carolina trial, psychologist and NAACP expert witness Kenneth Clark presented his doll study, which exemplified the relative clarity of the black-damage argument. Although this study was often maligned on its scientific merits, it had the advantage of being extraordinarily easy to understand. In his experiment, Clark would give young African American children a collection of black and white dolls. He then asked the children to identify the doll they thought was "nice" and the doll they thought was "bad." When he conducted this test among a sample of black children in Clarendon County, South Carolina, the majority preferred the white doll over the black one. From this Clark concluded that the black children had internalized a feeling of black inferiority, a mark of an unhealthy personality.[37] As Marshall recognized, the Clark study perfectly fit his need to prove the damage inflicted on his "clients." In this way, the legal arena in which *Brown* took form contributed to the particular use of psychology in the decision.

Brown was, of course, much more than a legal opinion; it was also a carefully crafted political statement. In this regard, one of Warren's key concerns was selling the decision to the American people, especially in the South. The wording and tone of the opinion contains evidence of this political compromise. Warren sought to craft the opinion to be as conciliatory as possible. The intended audience for the decision, or at least the audience of most concern for Warren, was the white South. It was for this group that the opinion had to be, as he noted in an internal memorandum to the Court, "non-rhetorical, unemotional and, above all, non-accusatory."[38] It was for this group that the opinion avoided a forthright condemnation of segregation as an evil. And, one can assume, it was for this group that Warren avoided a discussion of the ways in which racism psychologically damaged white America. As a political consideration such an analysis of the psychological health of white children might have appeared to be on dangerous, or at least unnecessarily controversial, terrain.[39]

Of the three assumptions of *Brown* highlighted in this essay, the black-damage rationale was the most controversial at the time, even among the supporters of the decision.[40] Long after the NAACP and most of the Court had come to the conclusion that segregation had to go and that the schools were an appropriate place to start, there was still significant debate over how to justify the action. Warren's eventual acceptance of the black-damage argument was not clear until he actually put pen to paper early in 1954. Possibly it is because this argument was used before a broader consensus within the liberal community had taken shape on the issue of psychological damage and segregation that of the three *Brown* assumptions it has fared the worst among future generations of scholars and critics. Yet even in the face of potential criticism, Warren, with the Court's tacit approval, still drew on this argument, a testament to the pervading influence of psychological explanations of racism in postwar liberal discourse.

THE CHILDREN OF *BROWN*

The children of *Brown* are found in many places. They are found among the group of children on whose behalf the litigation was initiated—Linda Brown of Topeka, Kansas, being the most famous of this group. They are found among the ranks of the children who bravely attempted to make the rhetoric of the decision a reality: Dorothy Counts, Autherine Lucy, the Little Rock Nine, Ruby Bridges (age six)—all names that belong at the top of any list of heroes of the civil rights movement. These children drew worldwide attention to the nobility of the project to end racial discrimination in America. They also made clear the profound chasm that separates the formation of social policy from its messy, complex, and intensely personal implementation. For children of *Brown* of a different sort are also found in places that are usually considered the province of adults, in those places where the social policy underlying the school-desegregation effort took shape.

Unlike Linda Brown, Dorothy Counts, and the other children of *Brown*, these children did not have faces or names. They were abstractions designed to serve a specific purpose: to justify that which was quite clear to the socially conscious Americans of the era, that racial segregation was an act of oppression. These children were created in a number of places: the offices of the NAACP, where the ultimately successful litigation strategy was debated and planned; the courtroom of the nation's highest court, where the cases were argued; in the chambers and conference room where the justices worked out the details of the decision; and, not to be underestimated, among the ranks of psychologists who offered up their expertise, sometimes unknowingly, to the services of public policy. The solidification of the assumptions of *Brown* was perhaps a necessary development for such a controversial decision to take shape. Yet the costs that went into the formation of the decision, the potential arguments and lines of analysis dismissed, should not be ignored.

Most notable of the lost paths was the loss of the white-damage argument. The result of this loss was shown most prominently in the debates over implementation following the decision. Missing from this painful conflict was an understanding that, when viewed from the perspective of the damage of racism on *both* races, the interests of white and black children might coincide. Whether a more open acceptance of the white-damage argument by the Supreme Court would have led to a stronger rationale for implementation is, of course, highly debatable. The possibility of appealing to the consciences of southern whites through white-damage arguments might have been hopelessly naive. Yet this was a potential line of attack on segregation that was abandoned at a crucial juncture in the struggle.[41]

The flip side of the loss of the white-damage argument was the increasing reliance on the image of the damaged black. There were clearly benefits to drawing on this imagery, as the NAACP's successful litigation effort in *Brown* demonstrated. But this was also a dangerous theme on which to rely in justifying progressive policy, as Daniel Patrick Moynihan would learn when he undertook his study of the black family in the following decade. Moynihan and others who sought to extend the logic of black damage highlighted in *Brown* to other areas of social policy ran into accusations of "blaming the victim" by a generation of activists and scholars who rejected the idea that the black community was somehow psychologically or culturally damaged by the experience of segregation and racial discrimination. Although oftentimes effective in eliciting white sympathy for racial inequality, the concept of black damage also ran the risk of legitimating paternalistic or even racist attitudes.[42]

While the arguments posed against integration and against pushing social reform through the schools would do more harm than good in the years following *Brown*, they were still able to raise some disturbing questions. The questions were disturbing not only for the potential support they might offer segregationists, but also because of the fact that some of the arguments embedded within them seemed painfully relevant. Perhaps the most formidable criticism of fighting for civil rights through integrating the schools came in an essay from the émigré intellectual Hannah Arendt, whose criticism, like that of Du Bois, had added resonance because of her reputation as a liberal and an advocate of civil rights.

Arendt's essay began as an act of empathy. She wrote it after seeing a photograph, much like the one of Dorothy Counts, of an African American girl going home from the recently integrated Little Rock High School. As Arendt described the scene, the child was "persecuted and followed into bodily proximity by a jeering and grimacing mob of youngsters." Arendt asked herself what she would do if she were in the position of the mother of this girl. To this she concluded, "If I were a Negro mother in the South, I would feel that the Supreme Court ruling, unwillingly but unavoidably, has put my child into a more humiliating position that it had been in before."[43] Why, she asked, should the responsibility for this monumental social transformation be placed on the shoulders of children? Why begin a social revolution in the public schools? Her essay was a striking departure from the liberal orthodoxy on race that had developed following World War II. She cited her frustration at the "dangerous . . . routine repetition of liberal clichés" as her source of inspiration for publishing the controversial piece.[44] Her essay, like the picture of Little Rock that inspired it, like the picture of Dorothy Counts, represented an act of cultural criticism.

It is unclear if *Brown* could have been improved by a more conscious recognition of criticisms such as Arendt's or a more open acceptance of the white-damage argument. Like the work of social scientists, constitutional interpretation by the courts demands the creation of general principles from specific evidence, and this process invariably requires the smoothing out of rough details, the simplification of complexities. In the end, it is the nature of the generalizations and conclusions that are accepted or rejected, whether the specific rationale holds up or not. This is why *Brown* and its central principle of racial equality still stand tall even as some of the decision's underlying rationale, including its reliance on the black-damage argument, has been challenged. The most effective defenses of the decision have reverted to a call to a common sense of moral purpose. From such defenses, one can conclude that the answer to the failures to implement *Brown* is found less in the specific reasoning of the decision and more in the underlying fault lines of American society.[45]

As the trial-by-fire experiences of Counts and other southern black children gradually moved from the front pages of the newspapers as the civil rights movement expired during the 1970s, a new generation of children of *Brown* emerged, this time in the urban North. Here, the battle for integrated schools has taken on a somewhat different appearance. Rather than de jure segregation, the key issues were district lines, busing, and affirmative action—but the personal experience of this new generation of social pioneers was often not much different from that of their predecessors in the South. Again, children were being forced to shoulder the burdens created by America's long history of racial oppression. In many ways, they still do.

The process by which the *Brown* decision took shape is immensely instructive for those interested in integrating psychology and social change. Psychology proved a useful tool for the lawyers and justices, but it was never more than that, a tool. The goal was already set—that segregation would be ended—and psychology entered the legal arena as a way to justify this conclusion. The findings of social psychology and contact theory supported an already powerful movement toward integration, the findings of developmental psychologists made children appear even more inviting as initiators of racial harmony, and the argument of black damage fit particularly well into the arguments demanded by the courts.

What was largely overlooked in this process was that the children who acted as theoretical support for these arguments would eventually have to return to reality. Real children, not abstractions, would have to walk through the schoolhouse doors. And this, an inherent weakness of large-scale social reform, a weakness that is intensified when the subjects are children and the tools are psychological, is what the picture of Dorothy Counts shows in such frightening clarity.

NOTES

1. Davison M. Douglas, *Reading, Writing, and Race: The Desegregation of the Charlotte Schools* (Chapel Hill: University of North Carolina Press, 1995), 72–73.

2. See Ellen Herman, *The Romance of American Psychology: Political Culture in the Age of Experts* (Berkeley: University of California Press, 1995); James H. Capshew, *Psychologists on the March: Science, Practice, and Professional Identity in America, 1929–1969* (New York: Cambridge University Press, 1999); and John P. Jackson, Jr., *Social Scientists for Social Justice: Making the Case Against Segregation* (New York: New York University Press, 2001).

3. Gardner Murphy, "Psychology Serving Society," *Survey Graphic* (January 1948): 12.

4. *Proceedings of the Midcentury White House Conference on Children and Youth* (Raleigh, North Carolina: Heath, 1951), 39.

5. See Herbert Hovenkamp, "Social Science and Segregation before *Brown*," *Duke Law Journal* (1985): 624–72; Carl N. Degler, *In Search of Human Nature: The Decline and Revival of Darwinism in American Social Thought* (New York: Oxford University Press, 1991); and George Fredrickson, *Racism: A Short History* (Princeton: Princeton University Press, 2002), esp. 97–138.

6. For studies on this period that focus on psychology and race, see Daryl Michael Scott, *Contempt and Pity: Social Policy and the Image of the Damaged Black Psyche, 1880–1996* (Chapel Hill: University of North Carolina Press, 1997); Ruth Feldstein, *Motherhood in Black and White: Race and Sex in American Liberalism, 1930–1965* (Ithaca: Cornell University Press, 2000); and Franz Samuelson, "From 'Race Psychology' to 'Studies in Prejudice': Some Observations on the Thematic Reversal in Social Psychology," *Journal of the History of Behavioral Sciences* 14 (1978): 265–78.

7. W. E. B. Du Bois, "Does the Negro Need Separate Schools?" *Journal of Negro Education* 4 (July 1935): 328–335.

8. See Morton Deutsch and Mary Evans Collins, *Interracial Housing: A Psychological Evaluation of a Social Experiment* (Minneapolis: University of Minnesota Press, 1951); Samuel Stouffer, *American Soldier* (Princeton: Princeton University Press, 1949); and Thomas F. Pettigrew, "The Intergroup Contact Reconsidered," in *Contact and Conflict in Intergroup Encounters*, ed. Miles Hewstone and Rupert Brown (New York: Basil Blackwell, 1986), 169–95.

9. The Justice Department brief was published as Tom C. Clark and Philip B. Perlman, *Prejudice and Property* (Washington, DC: Public Affairs Press, 1948), 84.

10. President's Committee on Civil Rights, *To Secure These Rights* (Washington, DC: GPO, 1947), 82–83, 87.

11. "The Effects of Segregation and the Consequences of Desegregation: A Social Science Statement," reprinted in Philip B. Kurland and Gerhard Casper, eds., *Landmark Briefs and Arguments of the Supreme Court of the United States: Constitutional Law*, vol. 49 (Arlington, VA: University Publications of America, 1975), 43–60, esp. 55–60, quotation at 57.

12. Leon Friedman, ed., *Argument: The Oral Argument before the Supreme Court in* Brown v. Board of Education of Topeka, *1952–1955* (New York: Chelsea House, 1969), 67.

13. Felix Frankfurter memorandum, 26 September 1952, Earl Warren Papers, container 571, Library of Congress, Manuscript Division, Washington, DC.

14. On Reed's discomfort with integration, see John D. Fassett, *New Deal Justice: The Life of Stanley Reed of Kentucky* (New York: Vantage, 1994), esp. 555–80. Jackson's reservations about contact theory can be found in Del Dickson, ed., *The Supreme Court in Conference, 1940–1985* (New York: Oxford University Press, 2001), 652.

15. On the intergroup or toleration movement, see Goodwin Watson, *Action for Unity* (New York: Harper & Brothers, 1947); Helen Leland Witmer and Ruth Kotinsky, eds., *Personality in the Making: The Fact-Finding Report of the Midcentury White House Conference on Children and Youth* (New York: Harper & Brothers,

1952), 153–54; Diana Selig, "Cultural Gifts: American Liberals, Childhood, and the Origins of Multiculturalism, 1924–1939" (PhD diss., University of California-Berkeley, 2001); Selig, "The Whole Child," chap. 7, this volume; and Jonna Perrillo, "White Teachers and the Black 'Psyche,'" chap. 8, this volume.

16. Mark Tushnet, *The NAACP's Legal Strategy Against Segregated Education* (Chapel Hill: University of North Carolina Press, 1987), 1–20.

17. Bruno Bettelheim and Morris Janowitz, "Dynamics of Prejudice," *Scientific American* 183 (1950): 11–13, quoted in Witmer and Kotinsky, *Personality in the Making*, 156.

18. Peggy Cooper Davis, "Performing Interpretation: A Legacy of Civil Rights Lawyering in *Brown v. Board of Education*," in Austin Sarat, ed., *Race, Law, and Culture: Reflections on* Brown v. Board of Education (New York: Oxford University Press, 1997), 23–48.

19. Friedman, *Argument*, 67, 239.

20. Felix Frankfurter, "Education," n.d., Warren Papers, container 571.

21. Dickson, *Supreme Court in Conference*, 653.

22. *Brown v. Board of Education*, 347 U.S. 483, 492–93.

23. Scott, *Contempt and Pity*, 124–125.

24. Walter A. Jackson, *Gunnar Myrdal and America's Conscience: Social Engineering and Racial Liberalism, 1938–1987* (Chapel Hill: University of North Carolina Press, 1990), 290; Herman, *Romance of American Psychology*, 178.

25. See Selig, "Cultural Gifts"; and Jonathan Zimmerman, *Whose America? Culture Wars in the Public Schools* (Cambridge, MA: Harvard University Press, 2002); esp. 22–54.

26. Gunnar Myrdal, *An American Dilemma* (New York: Harper & Row, 1944), 1:75–76.

27. President's Committee on Civil Rights, *To Secure These Rights*, 141.

28. Lillian Smith, *Killers of the Dream* (New York: W. W. Norton, 1949); T. W. Adorno et al., *The Authoritarian Personality* (New York: Harper & Brothers, 1950); and Gordon W. Allport, *The Nature of Prejudice* (Reading, MA: Perseus, 1954). See also *Proceedings of the Midcentury White House Conference on Children and Youth* (Raleigh, NC: Heath, 1951), 46, 206, 214; and Witmer and Kotinsky, *Personality in the Making*, 135.

29. "Brief of the American Federation of Teachers as Amicus Curiae," in Kurland and Casper, *Landmark Briefs*, 211–12; citing Max Deutscher and Isidor Chein, "The Psychological Effects of Enforced Segregation: A Survey of Social Science Opinion," *Journal of Psychology* 26 (1948): 259–87.

30. "The Effects of Segregation and the Consequences of Desegregation," in Kurland and Casper, *Landmark Briefs*, 43–61.

31. Dickson, *Supreme Court in Conference*, 654.

32. This draft of *Brown* is found in Warren Papers, container 571.

33. Bernard Schwartz, *A History of the Supreme Court* (New York: Oxford University Press, 1993), 302–3.

34. See Morton J. Horwitz, "The Jurisprudence of *Brown* and the Dilemmas of Liberalism," in *Have We Overcome? Race Relations Since* Brown, ed. Michael V. Namorato (Jackson: University of Mississippi Press, 1979), 185. The inherent

limitations of the courts is a powerful theme of Michael J. Klarman's *From Jim Crow to Civil Rights: The Supreme Court and the Struggle for Racial Equality* (New York: Oxford University Press, 2004).

35. Richard Kluger, *Simple Justice: The History of* Brown v. Board of Education *and Black America's Struggle for Equality* (New York: Knopf, 1976), 316.

36. John Philip Jackson, Jr. "The Transformation of Social Science into 'Modern Authority' in *Brown v. Board of Education,* 1945–1957" (PhD diss., University of Minnesota, 1996), 13.

37. On the doll study, see Kenneth B. Clark and Mamie P. Clark, "Racial Identification and Preference in Negro Children," in *Readings in Social Psychology,* ed. Theodore M. Newcomb and Eugene L. Hartley (New York: Henry Holt, 1947), 169–78; Kenneth B. Clark, *Prejudice and Your Child* (Boston: Beacon Press, 1955); and Richard Kluger, *Simple Justice* (New York: Vintage Books, 1975), 315–21, 353–57.

38. Earl Warren, memorandum to the justices, May 7, 1954, Warren Papers, container 571.

39. I explore the role of psychology in the drafting of *Brown* in more detail in "Postwar Liberalism and the Origins of *Brown v. Board of Education*" (PhD diss., Harvard University, 2004), chap. 7.

40. See James Reston, "A Sociological Decision," *New York Times,* 18 May 1954; and Edmund Cahn, "Jurisprudence," *New York University Law Review* 30 (January 1955): 150–69.

41. See Kenneth Clark, "The Social Scientists, the *Brown* Decision, and Contemporary Confusion," in Friedman, *Argument,* xl–xli.

42. On Moynihan, see Lee Rainwater and William L. Yancey, *The Moynihan Report and the Politics of Controversy* (Cambridge: MIT Press, 1967). For a general discussion of the dangers of psychological damage arguments, see Scott, *Contempt and Pity.*

43. Hannah Arendt, "A Reply to Critics," *Dissent* 6 (Spring 1959): 179.

44. Hannah Arendt, "Reflections on Little Rock," *Dissent* 6 (Winter 1959): 45.

45. See James T. Patterson, Brown v. Board of Education: *A Civil Rights Milestone and Its Troubled Legacy* (New York: Oxford University Press, 2000); Peter Irons, *Jim Crow's Children: The Broken Promise of the* Brown *Decision* (New York: Viking, 2002).

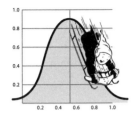

"Training" the Baby: Mothers' Responses to Advice Literature in the First Half of the Twentieth Century

Rima D. Apple

MOTHER AND AUTHOR Ruth Williams Thompson began to toilet train daughter Evelyn Mae at three months of age. The mother placed a "very small toilet, more like a large cup, but easy to handle," on her lap and sat the infant on it, holding her there for ten to fifteen minutes. Sometimes the child would reward her mother's efforts. As Thompson admitted, "Of course at first it was just a game of Luck—or not Luck, and there were times when I felt perhaps it was a waste of time." Perhaps it was a waste of time, but to this modern mother of the 1920s, early training was the best mode of infant care. Therefore she "was determined to give the thing a fair trial, so kept at it day after day." By the time Evelyn Mae was six months old, Thompson was putting the child on the toilet for about forty-five minutes during the day when she was awake and once at night. The mother proudly reported "fewer and fewer diapers to wash."[1]

Although she admitted that her daughter was not completely toilet trained with this routine, Thompson considered the practice thoroughly successful; so successful, in fact, that she embarked on toilet training her second daughter, Dorothy, when Dorothy was six weeks old. However, having learned from her experiences with Evelyn Mae, Thompson modified Dorothy's routine: "It does not pay to hold the baby on the toilet for several minutes at a time and does not make the training any easier," she noted. Instead, "as soon as the baby becomes accustomed to the sitting posture the organs will act immediately if there is a desire to urinate." In the late 1920s, when her children were toddlers, Thompson ignored the many months of patient attention she had lavished on her daughters' toilet training, claiming, "My babies learned to urinate as soon as they touched the toilet."[2]

Thompson's experiences mirror the popular culture of infant care in the early twentieth century. In initiating toilet training early and following stringent routines, Thompson conscientiously followed the directions laid out in a pamphlet from the U.S. Children's Bureau, the highly regarded federal agency that distributed several widely read child-care publications in the early years of the twentieth century. Mothers heard similar advice from their doctors, their friends, and their relatives. They read of the importance of scheduling in state and local government publications, trade books, and women's magazines. Often based on the ideas of the behaviorist John B. Watson, this system of infant care demanded rigid scheduling and regularity.

In contrast to the severity of the behaviorism that characterized the first half of the twentieth century, permissiveness defined the second half of the century. The years following World War II, or the "Spock era," named after the famed pediatrician and social activist Dr. Benjamin Spock, saw the advent of advice givers who admonished the mother to follow the natural rhythms of her child. In the case of toilet training, the mother who read Dr. Spock's books was urged to watch her children carefully and to be alert to signs of readiness, usually between eighteen and twenty-four months, and only then introduce the infant to a potty or toilet seat.[3]

HOW MOTHERS MADE DECISIONS ABOUT THEIR INFANT-CARE ROUTINES

It would be simplistic to conclude that Thompson's adherence to behaviorism meant that mothering practices merely reflected contemporary scientific and medical pronouncements. When we hear the voices of mothers from the first half of the twentieth century, we understand that women often had very specific reasons for instituting specific infant-care routines. Fundamental to their decisions was concern for the health and well-being of their children. Some women anxiously asked for information. Many mothers shared the concerns of A. E. Fenz, of Dallas, Texas, who wrote to the Children's Bureau for information on infant care in 1918, explaining, "We have a baby boy one month of age to whom we wish to do justice in regards to feeding and care to get the best possible results."[4] In other instances, mothers learned about the importance of medically informed infant-care advice from other sources. One study of mothers in rural Montana in the 1910s noted that the women there initially seemed surprised by the suggestion that they should consult a physician about topics such as infant feeding; several even remarked that such visits "seemed an extravagance." The surveyor was pleased to report that when she "made clear that good advice about the feeding and care of a child would probably keep it from getting sick and in the end be a saving of money as well as of suffering," then the mothers were more eager to contact health-care practitioners about infant care.[5] Whether their search was self-initiated or encouraged by others, whether they actually modified their practices or not, mothers wanted to do what was best for their children.

Beyond this common, underlying rationale, mothers' decisions about child care were highly personal, having been shaped by a woman's experiences, beliefs, values, and situations. Consequently, not all mothers of the period rigorously scheduled their infants as contemporary infant care literature and health-care practitioners advised. Mrs. A. J. Johnson's physician had insisted that she feed her infant son "just so much and no more" and at regular hours.[6] Under this regimen, the baby "got cross and fretted a lot more than he should; acted as tho he was hungry, but [according to the doctor's orders,] he shouldn't have any more . . . and not oftener than two hours." This left a crying baby and a frustrated mother. "Then one day his mother thought he can't no more than fuss, so she was going to give him a fill. He had all he wanted to eat, went to sleep and slept like a good boy." Thereafter, Johnson fed her son as much as he wanted when he wanted, and she relates that "he slept and grew like a weed in summer."[7] Mrs. Johnson's doctor suggested one routine, but this mother's lived experience indicated another, one that provided a solution to a hungry infant. From her letter, we sense that she trusted the physician because he was a medical authority, but that she was not so cowed by his expertise that it blinded her common sense and powers of observation.

Other women refrained from rigid schedules for different reasons. Some had little or no contact with advice givers who stressed fixed routines. For others, family practices and traditions were more powerful teachers than were the suggestions of medical practitioners. Other women heard about the importance of scheduling, but either could not or would not accept the practice, often because they could not afford the apparatus demanded by infant-care scheduling or lacked the time to follow the detailed schedules. Or they may have been so confident in their own abilities that they did not bother to listen to the advice of others.[8] The focus of this chapter, however, is the mothers who did believe in scheduling and regularity, who did elect to maintain fixed feeding routines, even to the extent of waking a sleeping infant for a feeding, and who did initiate early toilet training.

Clearly, some women raised their infants in keeping with the directions of child-care experts because as mothers they were convinced that modern medicine offered the best and most healthful counsel. Health-care practitioners advised rigorous scheduling, so these women conscientiously scheduled their infant's lives. But mothers voiced a host of other explanations, demonstrating that women were not blindly following what their doctors told them. Rather, the diversity of these reasons suggests the agency of individual women and their active participation in decision making about their children's health.

The experiences of these mothers illuminates a complex and nuanced picture of everyday life in the first half of the twentieth century and highlights the interaction of material conditions and scientific advice literature that shaped women's lives. Some women heeded medical counsel because of their faith that contemporary medical science would enhance their children's physical and mental health. For some mothers, following fixed schedules increased their confidence in their own abilities; for others, a lack of self-confidence convinced them to adhere to doctor-recommended schedules for the sake of their child's well-being. And for others, scheduling enabled mothers to gain some control over their frenetic lives and the many family and household demands they faced each day. Only by understanding the specificities of their lived conditions can we see the complexity of the decisions mothers made. There is a concrete politics of reception that is a crucial determinant in how messages from experts are received and used.[9] These complex politics are related, but not in any mechanical way, to the realities of class and race in women's lives.

THE TENETS OF SCIENTIFIC MOTHERHOOD

As Thompson's example demonstrates, doctors were not the only sources for information on child care.[10] Newspapers, women's magazines, and books produced by doctors, nurses, and laywomen sought to instruct mothers on the best, most modern health-care advice. The ubiquitous advertising material distributed by manufacturers of baby soaps and infant foods often masqueraded as objective and scientific infant-care advice. And there were less formal sources of child-care information, such as mothers' clubs and traveling lecturers. By the twentieth century, more and more governmental sources, such as city and state health departments and the federal Children's Bureau, focused on maternal education as the most cost-effective means to combat rising maternal and infant mortality and morbidity rates. They, too, distributed literature, held lectures and well-baby clinics, and sent out visiting nurses.[11] Although their advice may have differed somewhat on the specifics of infant care, they were all virtually united in support of what has been termed "scientific motherhood."

Emerging and spreading through the nineteenth and twentieth centuries, scientific motherhood is the belief in the critical role of modern scientific and medical knowledge in the development of healthful and appropriate child-care practices. Good motherhood; healthful motherhood; the best, most modern motherhood, was not seen as a matter of maternal instinct. Mothers needed to be educated. Initially, women were urged to seek out for themselves the most up-to-date information to make decisions on infant care. By the beginning of the twentieth century, however, this ideology had been modified. Modern scientific and medical expertise still provided the basis of proper mothering practices, but now women were expected to learn the critical skills of motherhood directly, from scientific and medical experts.[12] In her 1926 book, *Mothercraft: A Primer for Parents*, mother Mary Whitaker made this point most explicitly. Reminding her readers that "[t]he mere physical fact of motherhood gives us no claim to honor," she insisted that in birthing "we do no more than the brute mothers." To be successful, Whitaker contended, mothers must lift themselves "above the plan of brute creation." The application of scientific advice was what separated the modern mother from the lower animals. Whitaker's modern mother would consult physicians and nurses "and follow their directions intelligently and accurately."[13] Another mother-author, Estelle Reilly, went even further. She insisted that "motherly affection has its seamy side," especially "blind and unintelligent love." Her advice for a prospective mother: "Your first important and most intelligent step is to put yourself in the hands of a good doctor. . . . [B]e sure you understand [his instructions] and do exactly as he tells you."[14] In the first half of the twentieth century, much of this instruction supported the practice of stringent scheduling.

Of course, the existence of literature written by mothers well versed in scientific expertise and even instruction by health-care professionals did not necessarily translate into maternal action. Historians have cautioned against using prescriptive literature as a description of mothers' lives.[15] First of all, was the advice reaching the intended audience? In some cases, such as Thompson's, we have the mother's words: Thompson writes of her search for modern advice and mentions publications of the Children's Bureau, among other sources. Other women also published books, as well as magazine articles. Moreover, women wrote letters to the editors of women's magazines, based on the belief that their own experiences would help other mothers. Still others wrote to agencies such as the Children's Bureau; their correspondence and often the responses to their letters provide critical insights into women's lives and problems.

In addition to this rich, though limited, literature, there is the less personal survey literature. In order to assess the health and welfare of America's mothers and children, the Children's Bureau sent researchers into many different sections of the country, urban and rural, where they conducted close neighborhood surveys, talking with mothers and health-care practitioners. These studies provide a valuable lens through which to view the lives of women who have left few direct records of their own.[16] From such sources, we learn that even in the rural areas of Mississippi, Montana, Wisconsin, and Kansas, many mothers were slowly learning of the ideology of scientific motherhood. This awareness spread through the distribution of books, such as L. Emmett Holt's *Care and Feeding of Infants*; magazine articles; and government publications and through face-to-face encounters with health-conference physicians and visiting nurses. Over the decades as book, magazine, and pamphlet publishing grew and as funds became available to send visiting nurses into more homes across the country, more and more women learned to use these sources in shaping their infant-care practices.

THE SPREAD OF SCIENTIFIC MOTHERHOOD

Arguably the most comprehensive survey of the period was conducted as part of the 1930 White House Conference on Child Health and Protection. Directed by John C. Anderson, this cross-sectional analysis of nearly three thousand families suggests distinctions between and within socioeconomic and racial groups, while highlighting the extensive, though uneven, spread of scientific motherhood across the country. The first striking finding of this study is the extent to which white mothers of all classes read child-care literature. More than half the sample had read a child-care book in the past year, ranging from a high of approximately 80 percent of the "professional class," compared with barely 20 percent of the "laboring class." The contrast between classes was less, though still visible, for other print material. Further, more than one-half of the white mothers in the survey cited pamphlets as an important source for information on child care. In addition to using pamphlets, white mothers took their children to doctors, invited nurses into their homes, and talked with nurses and relatives. Among African American mothers, literature was also an important source of information. Interestingly, blacks were more likely than whites to own the books they read, as widespread segregation denied them access to many of the country's libraries. Many black mothers used health-care providers, although they were more likely to attend clinics and consult with nurses and less likely to confer with physicians than were white mothers.[17]

Anderson interpreted these differences to mean that lower-class mothers needed more training in order to better appreciate the benefits of expert advice. Historian Julia Grant reads the statistics differently, suggesting, "These figures might imply that working-class women had more confidence in their work as mothers because they had not been trained to believe that doctors' expertise in that sphere was superior but trusted instead that raising children was a matter of common sense."[18] These two analyses need not be in conflict. When we look at the studies of the Children's Bureau, the reports of visiting nurses, and letters written to the bureau and other agencies, we see many women from all classes reaching out for modern child-care advice. Class location is clearly not the sole determining factor in decisions about child-care practices. Neither is race nor geography. Although the Anderson survey has its limitations, it suggests the possibility that the majority of mothers across the United States read books and pamphlets, attended clinics, and consulted physicians and nurses.

Given the insistence that women follow the directions of contemporary medical and scientific authorities and the fact that women were reading the prescriptive literature and visiting health-care providers, it is not surprising that many mothers' experiences from the first half of the twentieth century reflect contemporary medical and scientific pronouncements. But the crucial question remains. What was the relationship between this advice and actual practice?[19] In other words, why did some women establish and maintain these stringent schedules?

MOTHERS' REASONS FOR SCHEDULING THEIR CHILDREN

Thompson's book provides some insight into why at least one mother was so scrupulous about scheduling her children. She believed that early training in all areas of child care—eating, sleeping, bathing, and eliminating—would foster her daughters' healthy physical development and lay "the foundation for good habits" that would stand them in good stead later in life.[20] She was pleased to report when her children were toddlers that "the physical and mental happiness which my little girls now enjoy is due primarily to the regularity of eating and sleeping which they learned in infancy."[21]

SCHEDULING IS SCIENTIFIC

But what convinced mothers such as Thompson that training was so important? Thompson explained that a "genetic psychology" course she took in college provoked her belief in the critical importance of regularity to mold the child and teach "the little baby the first lessons of patience." This led Thompson to study a variety of child-care books, including publications of the Children's Bureau. Thus, for Thompson training was firmly grounded in modern medical science. She does not give us a detailed account of the genetic psychology course that inspired her, though it probably was child psychology with Professor George H. Betts at Northwestern University. Typically at this time such courses were influenced by the ideas of psychologist John B. Watson, the name most often linked to the philosophy of rigid infant scheduling.[22]

However, the counsel to stringently train infants, often characterized as "Watsonian" infant care, predates Watson by many decades and was not confined to the medical profession. "I believe that a little care and trouble in earliest infancy would, in almost all cases, save the mother a world of vexation in after-years," advised H.E.W., of Brooklyn, New York, in the popular child-care journal *Babyhood* in 1886. She cautioned that "no time should be lost, for there is nothing more difficult to cure if a child has once become accustomed to the habit." The "habit" in question was bed-wetting; the solution was a routine to train the infant. As H.E.W. relates her experience:

> If a baby of a few days old is held over a vessel at regular periods, say before or after each nursing, there will soon be no need for diapers. I know of one case where, by laying a piece of paper under a babe every morning and evening, he became so regular in his habits that at the end of three months his mother boasted that she had never had a soiled diaper to wash.

Bed-wetting and soiled diapers were, to H.E.W., a sign of moral weakness on the part of the infant in the form of stubbornness or, worse yet, resulted from the "laziness of its elders." The benefits of rigorous attention to this early toilet training routine was a "nice and dry" infant and none of the "extra and disagreeable work" of diapers.[23]

H.E.W. does not say where she learned of the importance of early training her children but her letter implies that this was simply common knowledge and that she learned it independent of the advice of physicians. Women of the late nineteenth century may have considered scheduling the most appropriate infant care practice because it had a long tradition and they were familiar with it. Although training could be time-consuming and tedious, its compensations were great. In other words, a mother should carefully train her child both for the good of the child's future and to ease her own labor.

Women other than H.E.W. were clearer about their sources. By the end of the nineteenth century and the beginning of the twentieth, one of the most often cited was Dr. L. Emmett Holt, a New York pediatrician. In the 1890s, Holt wrote a four-page catechism for nursery maids training at New York's Babies' Hospital. Students carried the booklet into the private homes of their patients, and mothers soon requested copies of their own. In 1894, Holt published the catechism as a sixty-six-page book, *Care and Feeding of Children*, which went through seventy-five printings and twelve revisions by the mid-1920s and was translated into several foreign languages.[24]

Holt's message was clear: the infant must be trained early, most especially in the areas of feeding, sleeping, and eliminating. Physicians did not differentiate between routines that a mother could impose upon the child, such as feeding, and routines that entailed the direct involvement of the child, such as toilet training. Instead they lumped the various child-care routines together, insisting on the importance of regularity in all. If bowel training were begun early, Holt maintained, the infant could be trained by the second month. The doctor demanded scheduling because its benefits were clear to him: "It formed the habit of having the bowels move regularly at the same hour, which is a matter of great importance in infancy and makes regularity in childhood much easier. It also saves the nurse much trouble and labour."[25]

Echoing H.E.W.'s point of view, Holt's perspective on scheduling married the moral and the practical. Other physician-authors also called for careful scheduling, employing rationales that were similar to Holt's. Oftentimes they spoke in defense of the infant's health, claiming that irregular feedings could upset a baby's sensitive stomach, lead to indigestion and loss of appetite, would "also tax the mother's vitality," Dr. A. C. Eastman insisted in the *Boston Medical and Surgical Journal* in 1907. So much so that the infant be fed "by the clock. Five or ten minutes in leeway in either direction soon grows to a half hour and in a short time the whole schedule is upset." To avoid this calamity, Eastman counseled that if the baby awakened early and cried, "make him wait, and if he is asleep wake him during the day, and before many weeks he will awake approximately at the time for his feeding."[26] Although published in a medical journal, Eastman's claims were identical to those published in magazines for mothers. Dr. Maria M. Vinton believed that "[a] well-regulated baby needs only to be kept clean and warm, to be fed regularly and allowed to sleep between his feedings." She warned readers of *Babyhood* in 1893 that if the infant "learns to cry for coddling and holding whenever he is awake, [he will] give his mother no rest or quiet except with him in her arms."[27]

Frequently, mothers interviewed for the Anderson and Children's Bureau surveys and women writing into contemporary magazines referred to the advice that they read in Holt's *Care and Feeding*. F.B.S., of Atlanta, Georgia, wrote to *Babyhood* because she was puzzled by something she had found in Holt. When F.B.S.'s daughter was almost one year old, her mother knew that it was time to incorporate more substantial items in her daughter's diet. She also knew that she needed to change her feeding schedule. Holt, she explained, "considers five meals a day proper for a one-year old, but insists that there be no night feedings after 9 months." Yet, if she dropped the 11:00 p.m. nighttime feeding, her daughter would have only four meals a day. Is that not "too little for her age?" she queried the magazine's editors. F.B.S. was asking for clarification, not questioning the need for a feeding schedule. In the late nineteenth century, even before the popularity of Watsonian psychology, feeding schedules and rigid training were widely endorsed and evidently widely instituted.[28]

SCHEDULING EASES MOTHERS' WORKLOAD

The idea of strict training dates back at least to the early nineteenth century in American child-care literature. In her *Maternal Physician*, the first infant-care book published in the United States, mother Mary Palmer Tyler urged women to focus on training their infants to ensure their development as healthy, morally upright citizens of the new nation.[29] Later in the century, H.E.W. and other mothers of her generation looked to scheduling as a boon because it gave them some control over their hectic lives and helped to reduce their workload. In the 1880s and 1890s, many of the correspondents to *Babyhood* voiced their concerns over sleep schedules. Although it took many months of persistent efforts, I.A.H. had taught her son by age five months to expect to be put "in his bed at six, warm, dry, and fed, and left there in a dark room to coo himself to sleep." I.A.H. believed that with this routine, "his sleep is sweeter and sounder than ever," and her health had improved, "for I am not strong and need all the rest I can get to be able to nourish my child."[30]

The pragmatic needs of everyday life continued to influence mothers' perspectives on scheduling into the twentieth century. Mrs. Max West, author of the 1914 first edition of *Infant Care*, a widely read pamphlet put out by the Children's Bureau, had such a practical approach. West considered a system of schedules "not only one of the greatest factors in keeping the baby well and in training him in a way which will be of value to him through life, but . . . also [an aid that] reduces the work of the mother to a minimum and provides for her certain assured period of rest and recreation."[31] West noted examples of her own experiences that demonstrated her practices and belief in the benefits of scheduling. Moreover, she offered the same advice when answering letters written to the Children's Bureau. Mrs. N.W., of Seattle, wrote in 1920 of her troubles with her three children, ages three months, twenty months, and three years. She was exhausted all the time and surrounded by unfinished housework. She understood the importance of "all these scientific and hygienic duties for babies," but how could she accomplish everything? West sent two pages of detailed practical advice that included feeding and nap schedules and, most particularly, a fixed bedtime of 6:00 p.m. As she explained to Mrs. N.W.:

> If you have not tried putting away your children at six o'clock, you have no idea what a relief it will be to you. It can be done: I have done it myself with

three boys, and no mother who knows the satisfaction of having the care of her children cease before her own evening meal, and the quiet comfort of a still household in the evening, would fail to immediately begin the training necessary to make it possible.[32]

In later editions of *Infant Care*, as a panel of physicians replaced West as author, the pamphlet continued to advocate scheduling, but its rationale shifted. Now, as in Watson's behaviorism, mothers became the obstacle to the scientific care of children, even a threat to their health and well-being. Scheduling not only trained the infant but also, the revisions implied, kept the mother's potential harmful influences in check by giving her detailed rules to follow.[33]

In the writings of many mothers, though, the idea of training the baby was often understated; foremost in these mothers' minds was the belief that scheduling eased their burdens of infant care. Author Kathleen Norris considered it important to release women from the drudgery of child rearing in order to eliminate their dread of child raising. From her experience, modern motherhood eliminated such fears. The prescriptions for scientific motherhood "with regular hours, baths and meals on schedule," had changed mothers' tasks and had actually made motherhood "fun."[34]

SCHEDULING BUILDS MOTHERS' SELF-CONFIDENCE

Many mothers had other reasons to follow the rigorous timetables of feeding, sleeping, and eliminating. For Thompson, West, and others, the practice of scientific motherhood with its carefully timed regimens enhanced their self-confidence. For others, the detailed instructions that brooked no exceptions led mothers to doubt their own observations and sapped their self-confidence. Mrs. L.J.R., of Anaconda, Montana, reported to the Children's Bureau that she dutifully followed the infant-care practices outlined in the agency's pamphlet. She wrote that her year-old son appeared "in excellent health." Still, she felt insecure enough to visit a well-baby clinic, where the nurse gave her a diet schedule suitable for the infant. Despite her close adherence to an approved schedule, and her observation that her son was healthy, she needed further confirmation. Consequently, she had her son "examined by a baby specialist here simply to assure myself that there is nothing wrong with him."[35] Mrs. L.J.R. had confidence in the advice she was given, but that advice undercut her trust in her own observations. Diet schedules and the like would ensure the child's healthful upbringing, but Mrs. L.J.R. needed medical experts to verify her results. Mrs. L.J.R. believed in the medically sanctioned rules on regularity, but doubted her ability to carry out the program without outside confirmation.[36]

Still other mothers found that following the strict scheduling was empowering. In her study of Montana in the 1910s, Viola Paradise discovered that despite, or perhaps because of, the lack of physicians and nurses, the mothers in that rural area reached out for and embraced medically sanctioned information on infant care. Some used physician-authored books, such as Holt; others depended on brochures and booklets distributed by federal and state agencies; still others turned to advertising material. One mother told Paradise that "she had followed exactly" a government booklet. Another reported that she had raised her child according to physician advice printed in a women's magazine. She did this despite the opposition and "the prejudices of grandparents and neighbors."[37] Having the most up-to-date medical advice gave her the strength to resist tradition and local practices.

SCHEDULING AS THE MODERN FORM OF CHILD-CARE

This last example suggests another very important reason that some mothers gave for religiously adhering to fixed schedules for their infants: it was the modern way. Lois Waggoner received a one-hundred-page booklet at a lecture on infant care in rural Indiana. She called it "my baby 'Bible.'" Before having children of her own, she had lived with a family and cared for their children. Despite this experience, which some other women often found increased confidence in their own abilities, Waggoner remembered that "I wanted to learn some new ways of caring for my baby."[38] Upwardly mobile women who had attended college, journalist Lenore Pelham Friedrich reported in 1939, "were scientific, even if it was expensive."[39] Contemporary infant-care advice enhanced mothers' status as modern women.

For some immigrants and their children, modernization often went hand in hand with Americanization. In her interviews with Jewish American daughters of immigrants from eastern Europe, who birthed in the 1930s and 1940s, Jacquelyn Litt also found that "the faith in modern medicine and the desire to become modern mothers were taken for granted, commonly accepted and understood." These women used medicalized mothering practices to distance themselves from their parents' immigrant culture and to move visibly into the American middle class. Among Litt's informants were highly motivated women who actively sought out the best infant care they could find for their children. Having identified that "best care," they diligently followed its prescriptions. For them, best care was modern, and that meant medicalized. As one of Litt's informants expressed it: "I was a modern mother and the modern way was to go to a specialist." Another recalled vividly the contrast between her mother's way and the modern, scientific way. When her daughter awoke before the next scheduled feeding time, she would let the baby cry.

This behavior horrified her mother, but the informant reported to Litt that she would not feed her daughter before the scheduled time. "This was the way it had to be," she said. "If [the doctor] said every four hours, every four hours. It was the right thing to do."[40] In their study of a population similar to that of Litt's informants, Cowan and Cowan found that these mothers also did not argue with medical experts and expertise. Moreover, those who departed from "expert practice" were regarded by their contemporaries as hopelessly barbaric.[41] The practice of modern infant care with its fixed scheduling served to separate this generation from previous immigrant generations—it made them modern; it made them American.

HOSPITAL SCHEDULES

Increasingly through the first half of the twentieth century, "modern," "American" mothers entered the hospital for childbirth, where the birthing environment induced them to follow fixed routines.[42] The hospital's structured, controlled schedules gave them a measure of security, but at the same time contributed to a lack of self-confidence, which many women were articulating by the 1940s. Their newborns were safe, cared for by medical professionals in a sterile, sanitary environment. When mothers received their infants, they were instructed in appropriate methods of feeding and healthful infant-care practices. But the mode of this instruction and the arrangement of this security could lessen the self-assurance of all but the most confident of mothers. Typically, newborns were immediately whisked away to a closed nursery where they were bathed, changed, and displayed by white-uniformed nurses in face masks. Mothers received their infants on a fixed feeding schedule, usually every four hours, but sometimes every three hours. On the one hand, these new mothers enjoyed the privilege of having their newborns delivered and cared for by medical professionals. Today new mothers are released from the hospital forty-eight or twenty-four hours, or even sooner, after delivery. In the interwar years and into the 1940s, however, women stayed two weeks or more in the maternity ward before returning home. As new, very nervous mothers, cut off from alternative infant-care advice and convinced of the efficacy and appropriateness of hospital-offered medical direction, they gratefully absorbed the routines and schedules they observed in those early weeks.

A 1942 *Parent's Magazine* article typifies the hospital experience for mothers and its aftereffects. Lois Huntington's infant spent most of her days and all her nights in the nursery; consequently, during her last week in the hospital, Lois "spent a good deal of time peering through the nursery windows." In her peering, she "gained useful knowledge of changing, bathing, and so forth." She learned more about these techniques through demonstration classes given by the nurses. When the infant was brought to her for feeding, she "practiced picking her up and putting her down, bubbling, and so forth." Armed with this information and detailed instructions from the doctor telling her "exactly how to make the baby's formula," which she wrote down carefully, "it all seemed too simple and we [she and her husband] patted our selves on the backs for being such good planners."[43]

It did not take long for reality to rear its ugly head. Huntington found her first day home "pretty hectic and my husband returned after a hard day to find me in a state of physical and mental exhaustion." Having been insulated in the hospital from the mundane tasks of bottle making and baby bathing, she had had no idea of how intense modern mothering was. Moreover, she had not "realized how very much on my own I was and how little I really knew about babies." Her solution was to work out a meticulous schedule with her husband in which they shared tasks such as nighttime bottle feedings. Gradually, caring for her daughter grew to be enjoyable. Yet throughout the trauma of homecoming, the exhaustion, and the worry, Huntington never doubted the medical directions under which she organized her life. The rules and routines she had learned while observing in the hospital and consulting with her physician defined her motherhood practices. In the end, Huntington appreciated the control that scheduling gave her.[44]

INDIVIDUALIZING SCHEDULES

Viewing fixed schedules as a pragmatic solution to their maternal workload, mothers could and would modify schedules, or parts of schedules, if it meant that their homes would run more smoothly without compromising the health of their children. Thompson's balancing of expert advice and familial and personal needs is clear as she adjusted the feeding schedules for her growing girls. She conformed to every other aspect of dietary advice advocated by contemporary medicine. But when it came to feeding schedules, she tempered medical directions with experience. On the one hand, contemporary advice books advocated establishing a four-hour schedule for infants five to six months old. On the other hand, Thompson believed that to "have changed to a four hour schedule then would have meant a complete disruption of my earlier schedule, and I felt that it would be very unwise to do that." Once again, she did not reject modern medical and scientific advice. She studied the topic and decided that the regularity of a fixed three-hour schedule slowly modified to a three-meal-a-day plan was superior when compared with merely following the recommended schedule. In other words, she accepted the general philosophy of regularity and found the best way to fit that into her daily life.[45]

Mother-authored literature and surveys and studies of mothers' infant-care practices all demonstrated that through the first half of the twentieth century, many women continued to follow infant care based on fixed scheduling of feeding and sleeping, with early initiation of toilet training. Why was scheduling considered the best? Because women believed that it ensured the development of a healthy child with healthful habits. Especially in the second quarter of the century, rigid routines were considered modern, so modern mothers scheduled their children. At the same time, there was a long tradition of establishing feeding schedules and the like, dating back to at least the early nineteenth century. While some mothers chose scheduling because it was modern, other women continued because it was a tradition, it was familiar. For some immigrant populations, modern medical routines were a part of Americanization. Moreover, such adherence enhanced their confidence in their mothering practices. Ironically, while confident women often found comfort in scheduling, many women with low self-confidence did as well. Women concerned about their abilities to develop healthful mothering practices took solace in these medically sanctioned routines because scheduling promised to maintain and protect their child's health.

Although the weight given to each of these reasons varied over the historical period and varied by mother, mothers consistently cited two overriding explanations for following strict infant-care schedules. One was the health of the child. Underlying a mother's decision was her conviction that she was ensuring her child's health, well-being, and future. The second was more utilitarian: scheduling enabled the mother to cope with the stresses, strains, and sheer workload of infant care. For Thompson, scheduling was the practical choice because it promised fewer diapers, as H.E.W. had decided four decades earlier, and West had advised in the 1910s and 1920s. For Norris, scheduling transformed the drudgery of child care into play; for Huntington, scheduling enabled her to get through her hectic day. In each of these cases, advice from scientific and medical experts served as solutions to problems that mothers faced every day.

SCHEDULING BABIES TODAY

Mothers today facing the issue of scheduling continue to hear from scientific and medicine experts. As with mothers of the earlier period, their advice is shaped by available contemporary technology. But now there is a greater diversity of contradictory opinion being played out in the popular

press. An article in the *New York Times Magazine* in 1999 epitomizes the
dilemma mothers face, confronted as they are with wildly different advice
that itself is informed by differing philosophies and shaped by technological
and commercial interests.

The article, titled "Two Experts Do Battle over Potty Training," pits
the stringent training recommended by John Rosemond, a family psychologist, syndicated columnist, and author of many parenting advice books,
against the more relaxed training advocated by T. Berry Brazelton, a leading pediatrician and professor emeritus of pediatrics at Harvard Medical
School. Since the 1960s, Brazelton, along with Spock, had been instructing
mothers in a flexible approach to toilet training. It was counterproductive,
they argued, to force toilet training. The attempt to establish regular routines would merely set up a power struggle between mother and child and
potentially injure the child psychologically. When children were ready to be
potty trained, they would use the toilet, the doctors instructed.[46]

There is some evidence that mothers took the advice of Spock and
Brazelton; certainly, practices mirrored their recommendations. In 1957,
at the age of eighteen months, 92 percent of U.S. children were toilet trained.
By the end of the 1990s, at the age of twenty-four months, only 4 percent
were toilet trained. Studies show that a majority of children, 60 percent, were
diaper free by thirty-six months and as many as 2 percent remained in diapers at the age of four years. Late toilet training became practical because of
technological advances. A multibillion-dollar industry of training pants and
oversized disposal diapers designed for children over the age of two relieved
the mother of laundry problems, and modern washers and driers took some
of the drudgery out of the use of cloth diapers.[47]

Rosemond contended that delayed toilet training was "a slap to the
intelligence of a human being that one would allow him to continue soiling
and wetting himself past age 2." The psychologist complained that it was
inspired by "Freudian mumbo jumbo." Moreover, he criticized Brazelton for
serving as a consultant to Pampers, a popular disposal diaper, and for ap-
pearing in its advertising. Rosemond designed a simple routine for training
a child in a few days, and for a mere seventy-five dollars, rather than the
many dollars parents spend for years on cloth diapers, disposal diapers, or
diaper service. As he advised: "You stay home from work with your child
for a few days. . . . You let the child walk around the house naked all day
long." You put a potty or child's toilet in the room in which the child spends
a majority of the time, moving it when required from room to room. Once
in a while, you remind the child to use the potty. As he explained:

> Children at this age do not like urine and feces running down their legs. When
> they have an accident, they stop and start to howl, and the mother comes along

and says, "Well, you forgot to use the toilet." She puts him on the toilet, wipes him off, speaks reassuringly to him. And within three days, or five days, he is doing it on this own.

The seventy-five dollars, by the way, is to clean the carpet, another advantage of modern technology. No mother could confuse these two methods, and the author of the article concludes that mothers are pragmatic: they use "whatever works."[48] Still how to decide between these two opposing views? How to determine what works? Such is the dilemma of the modern mother.

This study of scientific infant-care advice and its appropriation and use provides us with an important instance of how women then, and now, strategically deal with the material conditions of their lives. Women who rigorously and religiously followed strict infant-care schedules were not mindlessly following the directions of their doctors. Rather, they understood the benefits of medical counsel *and* the need to gain control over their frantic lives. In making their decisions, they considered both the medical and the pragmatic. It was the conjunction of these forms of counsel that molded mothers' practices, a conjunction that continues to influence mothers' lives today.

NOTES

1. Ruth Williams Thompson, *Training My Babes* (Boston: Richard G. Badger/Gorham Press, 1929), 44–47.

2. Thompson, *Training My Babes*, 44–47.

3. For more on the psychological underpinnings of advice literature from the first half of the twentieth century, see Martha Wolfenstein, "Fun Morality: An Analysis of Recent American Child-Training Literature," in *Childhood in Contemporary Cultures*, ed. Margaret Mead and Martha Wolfenstein (Chicago: University of Chicago Press, 1955), 169–71; Benjamin Spock, *The Common Sense Book of Baby and Child Care* (New York: Duell, Sloan, and Pearce, 1945), 193–202; Nancy Pottisham Weiss, "Mother, the Invention of Necessity: Dr. Benjamin Spock's *Baby and Child Care*," *American Quarterly* 29 (1977): 519–46 and "The Mother-Child Dyad Revisited: Perceptions of Mothers and Children in Twentieth-Century Child-Rearing Manuals," *Journal of Social Issues* 34 (1978): 29–45; Julia Grant, *Raising Baby by the Book: The Education of American Mothers* (New Haven: Yale University Press, 1998), esp. chap. 5, 137–60. In addition to the readiness of the child, late twentieth-century editions of Spock talk about readiness of the parents. See Benjamin Spock and Steven J. Parker, *Dr. Spock's Baby and Child Care*, 7th ed. (New York: Pocket Books, 1998), 506–7.

4. A. E. Fenz, 24 May 1918 letter to the Children's Bureau, and the bureau's reply dated 29 May 1918, National Archives, Children's Bureau Collection, folder CB 4-4-0.

5. Viola I. Paradise, *Maternity Care and the Welfare of Young Children in a Homesteading County in Montana* (Washington, DC: GPO, 1919).

6. For more on changes in infant feeding over the twentieth century, see Rima D. Apple, *Mothers and Medicine: A Social History of Infant Feeding, 1890–1950* (Madison: University of Wisconsin Press, 1987).

7. Mrs. A. J. Johnson, "How I Raised My Baby," *Farm, Stock, and Home* 33 (1 October 1917): 602.

8. For some preliminary analysis on the reasons why women rejected contemporary advice, see Rima D. Apple, *Reaching Out to Mothers: Public Health and Child Welfare*, Evening Lecture Series (Sheffield, UK: European Association for the History of Medicine and Health Publications, 2002).

9. Richard Johnson, "What Is Cultural Studies Anyway?" *Social Text* 16 (1986–87): 38–80.

10. For more on these sources, see Rima D. Apple, "Constructing Mothers: Scientific Motherhood in the Nineteenth and Twentieth Centuries," *Social History of Medicine* 8 (1995): 161–78; Apple, *Mothers and Medicine.*

11. Apple, *Reaching Out to Mothers*; Richard Meckel, *"Save the Babies": American Public Health Reform and the Prevention of Infant Mortality, 1850–1929* (Baltimore: Johns Hopkins Press, 1990).

12. Apple, "Constructing Mothers."

13. Mary C. Whitaker, *Mothercraft: A Primer for Parents* (Cleveland: Judson, 1926), 65–67.

14. Estelle M. Reilly, *Common Sense for Mothers on Bringing Up Your Children from Babyhood to Adolescence* (New York: Funk & Wagnalls, 1935), 1–2.

15. Jay Mechling, "Advice to Historians on Advice to Mothers," *Journal of Social History* 9 (1975): 44–63; Weiss, "Mother-Child Dyad"; Jacquelyn S. Litt, *Medicalized Motherhood: Perspectives from the Lives of African-American and Jewish Women* (New Brunswick: Rutgers University Press, 2000); Grant, *Raising Baby by the Book*; Lynne Curry, *Modern Mothers in the Heartland: Gender, Health, and Progress in Illinois, 1900–1930* (Columbus: Ohio State University Press, 1999).

16. Helen M. Dart, *Maternity and Child Care in Selected Rural Areas of Mississippi* (Washington, DC: GPO, 1921); Paradise, *Maternity Care*; Frances S. Bradley and Margaretta A. Williamson, *Rural Children in Selected Counties of North Carolina* (Washington, DC: GPO, 1918); E. Moore, *Maternity and Infant Care in a Rural County of Kansas* (Washington, DC: GPO, 1917); and F. B. Sherbon and E. Moore, *Maternity and Infant Care in Two Rural Counties in Wisconsin* (Washington, DC: GPO, 1919). For a similar study conducted two decades later during the Depression, see Margaret J. Hagood, *Mothers of the South: Portraiture of the White Tenant Farm Woman* (New York: W. W. Norton, 1977).

17. White House Conference on Child Health and Protection: Section III, Education and Training, Committee on the Infant and Preschool Child, *The Young Child in The Home: A Survey of Three Thousand American Families* (New York: D. Appleton-Century, 1936). See also John E. Anderson, "The Clientele of a Parental Education Program," *School and Society* 26 (6 August 1927): 178–84; Ruth W. Washburn and Marian C. Putnam, "A Study of Child Care in the First Two Years of Life," *Journal of Pediatrics* 2 (1933): 517–36.

18. Grant, *Raising Baby by the Book*, 84.

19. The examples in this chapter are drawn from my book *Perfect Motherhood: Science and Childrearing in America* (New Brunswick: Rutgers University Press, 2006). On psychology and the relationship between mothers and expert advice, see also, among others, Grant, *Raising Baby by the Book* and Litt, *Medicalized Motherhood*.

20. Thompson, *Training My Babes*, introduction, n.p.

21. Thompson, *Training My Babes*, 16.

22. Thompson is probably referring to her study of child psychology with Professor George H. Betts of Northwestern University. Thompson, *Training my Babes*, preface.

23. H.E.W., "Bed-Wetting," *Babyhood* 2, 19 (1886): 255–56. For a similar analysis of sleeping routines, see I.A.H., "Another Mother's Experience in Putting Her Babies to Sleep," *Babyhood* 2, 16 (1886): 145.

24. The second half of the twentieth century had so-called Spock babies, whose mothers had read and followed Spock's *Baby and Child Care*; the late nineteenth and early twentieth centuries had "Holt babies." Holt's book was listed in 1946 as one of the one hundred books that "influenced the life and culture of the American people." There were only three medical books on the list, the other two being clinical/research volumes. David A. Randall, "Books That Influenced America," *The New York Times Book Review*, 21 April 1946, 7, 22. On Holt, see R. L. Dufus and L. E. Holt, Jr., *L. Emmett Holt: Pioneer of a Children's Century* (New York: D. Appleton-Century, 1940), 115–18; Edwards A. Parks and Howard H. Mason, "Luther Emmett Holt (1855–1924)," in *Pediatric Profiles*, ed. Borden S. Veeder (St. Louis: C. V. Mosby, 1957), 37–38.

25. L. Emmett Holt, Jr., *The Care and Feeding of Children: A Catechism for the Use of Mothers and Children's Nurses*, 8th ed. (New York: D. Appleton, 1915), 165.

26. A. C. Eastman, "The Physician's Responsibility in the Training of Infants," *Boston Medical and Surgical Journal*, 156, 23 (1907): 738–41.

27. Maria M. Vinton, "The Mother's Nursery Guide: Baby's First Month," *Babyhood* 9 (1893): 69–71. See also Henry L. Coit, "Brief Paragraphs Concerning Artificial Feeding and Nursery Hygiene," *Babyhood* 11 (1895): 229–23.

28. F.B.S., "Various Points of Diet," *Babyhood* 10 (1894): 56–57.

29. "An American Matron" [Mary Palmer Tyler], *The Maternal Physician: A Treatise on the Nature and Management of Iinfants* (New York: Arno Press, 1972 [reprint of 1818 edition]); Marilyn S. Blackwell, "The Republican Vision of Mary Palmer Tyler," *Journal of the Early Republic* 12 (1992): 11–35.

30. I.A.H., "Another Mother's Experience in Putting Her Babies to Sleep," *Babyhood* 2 (1886): 145.

31. Quoted in Weiss, "Mother, the Invention of Necessity," 522–27.

32. Letter from Mrs. N.W., Seattle, Washington, to Julie Lathrop, 4 March 1920, and the response by Mrs. Max West, 16 March 1920, quoted in Weiss, "Mother, the Invention of Necessity," 525–26.

33. For more on the revisions of *Infant Care*, see Weiss, "Mother, the Invention of Necessity."

34. Kathleen Norris, *The Fun of Being a Mother* (Garden City, NY: Doubleday, Page, 1927).

35. Mrs. L[eonard] J. R[ice] to Grace Abbott, 4 November 1923; letter and the agency's response from Ethel M. Watters, M.D., dated 9 November 1923, are located in the National Archives, Children's Bureau Collection, folder CB, 4-5-3-0.

36. For another example of this scenario, see "Narrative Report, Monroe and Jackson Counties: June 1938," June 9, Fairchild, Wisconsin Bureau of Maternal & Child Health Series 2253, located in Wisconsin Bureau of Maternal & Child Health, "Programs & Demonstrations, 1922–61," State Historical Society of Wisconsin, Madison, box 13, folder 3.

37. Paradise, *Maternity Care*, 73.

38. Quoted in Eleanor Arnold, ed., *Voices of American Homemakers* (Bloomington: Indiana University Press, 1985), 103.

39. Lenore Pelham Friedrich, "I Had a Baby," *Atlantic Monthly* 163 (1939): 461–65.

40. Litt, *Medicalized Motherhood*, 13, 52, 55–56. Litt also found a similar phenomenon among African American mothers, though it was expressed somewhat differently in that culture; her informants defined themselves as mothers in relationship to the "scientific motherhood" that permeated U.S. culture in the period. See also Litt, "Mothering, Medicalization, and Jewish Identity, 1928–1940," *Gender and Society* 10, 2 (1996): 185–98; Litt, "American Medicine and Divided Motherhood: Three Case Studies from the 1930s and 1940s," *Sociological Quarterly* 3, 2 (1997): 285–302.

41. Neil M. Cowan and Ruth S. Cowan, *Our Parent's Lives: The Americanization of Eastern European Jews* (New York: Basic Books, 1989), 182.

42. Judith W. Leavitt, *Brought to Bed: Child-Bearing in America, 1750–1950* (New York: Oxford University Press, 1986).

43. Lois Huntington, "Schedule for a New Baby's Mother," *Parent's Magazine*, September 1942, 24–25, 61.

44. Huntington, "Schedule for a New Baby's Mother," 61.

45. Thompson, *Training My Babes*, 23–25.

46. Erica Goode, "Two Experts Do Battle over Potty Training," *New York Times Magazine*, 12 January 1999, A1, A17.

47. Goode, "Two Experts Do Battle," A1, A17.

48. Goode, "Two Experts Do Battle," A1, A17.

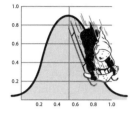

C H A P T E R   1 1

Bringing Up Boys: Science, Popular Culture, and Gender, 1890–1960

Julia Grant

WHETHER THEY ARE SITTING around a playground bench watching their kids navigate the monkey bars or clustering around the kitchen counter at a party, when mothers of young children talk, the conversation often turns to the differences between little boys and girls. Many feminist mothers claim to be taken aback at the typically "boyish" characteristics they observe in their sons—despite their attempts to practice gender-neutral parenting. Meanwhile, mothers who do not identify as feminists may perceive gender differences as reflecting essential laws of human nature. Mothers from both camps commonly view common sense as a more reliable guide than science for understanding the nature of children. When science finds that little boys are different from little girls, some wonder why research dollars are going to fund studies that merely confirm what people already know to be true.

Both common sense and science as frameworks of knowledge have their virtues and vices, yet neither is a fail-proof guide to understanding children. Our explanations of children's behaviors and characteristics are embedded in particular worldviews that become more apparent the further removed we are from their historical or cultural origins. Additionally, common sense and science are not as disparate as they may at first appear. While science sometimes appears to be nothing more than common sense ornamented with statistics, common sense may often be nothing less than science with a patina of folk wisdom. In other words, it is not always easy to tell where one explanatory system leaves off and the other begins.

The story of ten-year-old Maurice, who was profiled as a "sissy" in a 1928 child guidance textbook, exemplifies the difficulty in distinguishing between scientific expertise and popular wisdom. Maurice had a "soft, feminine face" and an unathletic build and was relentlessly bullied at school. He had suffered from many physical maladies, which had strengthened his bond with his mother. Maurice's physician referred him to a child guidance clinic for help in overcoming the "over-solicitude of his mother." The clinicians portrayed Maurice's mother as obsessed with her son's health. Moreover, they deemed his father to be ineffectual.

This inauspicious combination had produced a timid, nervous child whose prognosis for healthy adulthood was poor. The neighbors observed that the mother "used to skip down the street with her son when he was seven or eight years old, pick him up in her arms and cover him with kisses in full view of the entire neighborhood." Both the neighbors and clinicians agreed that Maurice was not a "real boy." In the words of the case history: "This 'perfect little gentleman,' this 'carefully nurtured flower' . . . needs more than anything else to be helped to become a real boy."[1]

Nearly thirty years later, the charge of "sissy" resounded even more powerfully as the concept of the "real boy" became the standard for measuring boys' normalcy. In his study *Patterns of Child Rearing* (1957), Robert Sears asked mothers of preschoolers how important it was to them to raise "real boys." One of the mothers interviewed admitted that she wanted a "real boy" and "not a sissy," elaborating, "I wouldn't want him otherwise— I would give him boxing lessons if I had to." In many respects, for individuals in both eras, sissies and real boys were made and not born.[2] Boys were not boys by nature alone, but became real boys through proper upbringing and socialization. With the help of male role models, unprotective mothers, and exposure to same-age peers and typical boys' activities, little boys could be helped to become real boys.

In this chapter I trace the convergence of social and psychiatric conceptions of sissies and "real boys" during the twentieth century. My focus is on young boyhood, when masculinity is in the making, when the transition from babyhood to boyhood and adolescence is in process, and when gender boundaries are somewhat more fluid than in later years. During the first half of the twentieth century the behaviors, characteristics, and temperaments of young boys were placed under a microscope for manifestations of gender deviance. In fact, just as the traditional gender roles of adult men and women were being challenged by the politics of women's rights and the transformations in work and leisure that accompanied urbanization during the early twentieth century, young boys were being more closely monitored for gender-appropriate behavior by both parents and professionals.[3]

By the late nineteenth century, scholars in the newly minted disciplines of the human psyche—sexology, psychology, sociology, and psychiatry— were investigating the cultural underpinnings of personality, gender, and sexuality. These experts sought to describe the trajectory of normal child and sexual development, as well as to prescribe it.[4] They used the language of pathology rather than sin and sought medical rather than religious cures for deviations from the norm. The norm, rather than the good, became the standard for assessing children's development as a whole and children's gender roles in particular. In many ways, norms of behavior were set by peers rather than parents and were used by parents and professionals alike for assessing boys' masculine gender development.

Concerns about effeminacy in little boys ebbed and flowed throughout the twentieth century. Fears about the feminization of boys were a predominant theme at the turn of the nineteenth century, with many decrying the diminishing masculine influence in schools and churches as a threat to America's imperial mission and institutions.[5] These strident proclamations were tempered in the 1920s, but experts still warned that "too much mother love" could have dire consequences. Child guidance was a new profession in the 1920s, with little in the way of a theoretical or research base for understanding gender-role socialization. In their everyday practices, however, clinicians drew on popular conceptions of typical male behavior in diagnosing their clients.[6] Boys who failed to partake in the typical pranks and escapades of boyhood—who were fastidiously dressed and overly obedient and clung to their mothers—were scorned and stigmatized by peers and labeled as abnormal by professionals. While the charge of effeminacy had been leveled at adult men for centuries, by the twentieth century the label was applied to little children, carrying both clinical and political meanings.

This rhetoric evolved throughout the interwar period, as researchers built a body of literature on the acquisition of gender roles and as psychoanalysis became increasingly mainstream. As the century progressed boys were expected to embody masculine attributes at earlier and earlier ages, and boys' organizations and athletic teams steadily lowered the age at which boys could join. When the Boy Scouts were first established in 1910, only boys twelve and older could join. It was not until the early 1930s that the Cub Scouts were organized for boys ages nine through eleven. Prior to 1939, when the Little League was organized for eight- to twelve-year-olds, organized athletics had been the purview of teenagers. These developments indicate an emerging belief that peer-centered activities were needed to induct even very young boys into the masculine fraternity.[7]

In the 1940s and 1950s, social science and psychoanalysis were invoked, both in tandem and separately, to warn of the consequences of boyhood effeminacy. This nearly hysterical rhetoric of pathology and deviance arose in response to wartime and political anxieties, concerns about sexual diversity, changing gender roles, and masculine discontent in the workplace and the family.[8] The British anthropologist Geoffrey Gorer saw these fears as central to the American character, pronouncing in 1948 that "the overriding fear" of all American parents was that of raising a sissy.[9]

GENDER AND CHILDHOOD IN THE NINETEENTH AND EARLY TWENTIETH CENTURIES

In the eighteenth- and early nineteenth-century United States, gender was perceived primarily as a social category that was acquired in stages as children matured. Babies were somewhat gender neutral, according to this view, which their treatment and dress reflected. The donning of trousers, for instance, a ritual that symbolized the emergence of boyhood, had occurred in the nineteenth century between the ages of five and seven, but steadily moved downward to ages two or three by the turn of the century. It was not until the 1930s that the custom of dressing infants in pink and blue, to establish unmistakably a child's gender, gained popular currency.[10]

Middle-class Victorians sought to isolate young children from the forces of sexuality and the demands of gender-role socialization. Mothers bore the major responsibility for rearing children of both genders up through ages six or seven and were often ambivalent about the transformation of their male youngsters into "boys."[11] They cherished the long curls of toddlers of both sexes, and boys and girls alike wore similar, although not identical, frilly frocks. Boyhood did not commence as a stage of life until boys were outfitted in their first set of trousers, an event sometimes regarded ambivalently by their mothers.[12] According to one mother, writing about the day her five-year-old donned trousers: "'He will be a noisy, shouting, out-of-doors boy and not a dear little house boy any more at all.'"[13]

During early childhood, boys' identities as babies overshadowed their identities as boys, although class and race could foreshorten this moratorium from masculinity. As boys aged, donned trousers, and entered the peer culture of other boys, boy culture played a role in helping to patrol gender boundaries.[14] In the peer culture, boys valorized personal characteristics that were in many ways antithetical to Victorian ideals, but the qualities of tenderness, self-control, and self-sacrifice were celebrated for both genders in children's literature and prescriptive advice.[15]

The late nineteenth and early twentieth centuries proved to be a crucial period in the forging of modern manhood.[16] The question of how to define manhood for those middle-class males who no longer exercised their manly muscles in order to maintain home and hearth underlay many reform efforts to simultaneously restrain and cultivate masculine qualities. In their writings and speeches, figures such as Theodore Roosevelt and G. Stanley Hall spoke of the perils that overcivilization posed for American manhood. The class- and race-biased overtones in this discourse were unmistakable. Middle-class boys were thought to suffer from overcivilization and nervousness because of the repression of their masculine impulses, whereas working-class, immigrant, and non-Caucasian boys needed to have their masculine impulses directed into productive activity.[17]

Beginning in the 1890s, G. Stanley Hall proposed a framework of boys' development that would guide those who worked with boys for several decades. Hall contended that boys' development reenacted the various stages of civilization, beginning with savagery. Boys, he argued, had been stunted by mothers' and teachers' attempts to foist feminine notions of niceness and refinement on boys whose developmental trajectory required them to pass through a "savage" phase. Early nineteenth-century educators believed that their task was to tame the savage impulses thought to be the basis of boy nature; Hall called on educators to capitalize upon the "barbarism" of boy nature along the route to civilization.[18]

BUILDING BETTER BOYS

The phrase "the boy problem" arose in the late 1800s in response to the perceived threat posed by working-class and immigrant boys who idled about the street, seemed neither to be attending school nor working, and engaged in petty crimes. These boys appeared to suffer from a paucity of legitimate outlets for the expression of their masculine impulses. Sociologists and social workers vigorously tackled this problem, creating the occupation of "boy worker," that is, a counselor who would develop programs that would serve both at-risk and feminized boys by simultaneously stimulating and harnessing masculine impulses. The emerging masculine fraternity of the Boy Scouts, boys' clubs, summer camps, and athletic organizations embodied these ideas and aspirations.[19]

Boy workers conceived of little boys as having many of the qualities associated with girls. They imagined masculine identity as developmental, maintaining that gendered attributes and instincts emerged at specific ages. In 1912, J. Adams Puffer speculated: "Little girls and little boys, as they emerge from babyhood, are not so unlike. But somewhere around the age of ten, the little boy begins to undergo a transformation, which in the girl never takes place at all."[20] In other words, girls remain the same as they age (or never grow up), while boys become increasingly masculinized.

Eighteen years later, Paul Hanly Furfey, a Catholic boy worker and student of Hall, argued that prior to age eight or ten, boys were apt to play with girls, were uninterested in team sports, and shared with girls an "effeminacy of disposition," which drew them to girls as playmates. Shortly after boys started school they ceased being gender-neutral children and began to become men.[21] When the "gang age" approached at about age ten, boys became obsessed with group sports and began to make the final transition to real boyhood.[22] By taking advantage of the natural proclivities and impulses of boys at different ages, boy workers hoped to properly direct these tendencies into acceptable channels.

Boy workers sought to make use of the "gang spirit" to cultivate leadership and manliness. In *The Boy Problem* (1907), William Byron Forbush contended that in the peer group boys gained "the masculine standpoint which his mother, his nurse, and his school-teacher cannot give."[23] Twentieth-century experts put a positive spin on peers, viewing them as ameliorating the potentially deleterious effect of mothers and female teachers—even civilization itself—on the development of boys' masculinity. Although boy workers were less than explicit about the relationship between the development of masculinity and heterosexuality, their colleagues in psychology would vigorously analyze the topic in the years to come.

THE ACHIEVEMENT OF HETEROSEXUALITY

By the close of the nineteenth century, a recognizably twentieth-century masculine ideal was conceived of as being in opposition to effeminacy. Homosexual men were identified by their sexual behaviors and were apt to be viewed as unmanly; effeminate men were likely to have their sexuality questioned.[24] For late nineteenth- and early twentieth-century scientists, the concept of sexual inversion, or gender-role reversal, was central to understanding homosexuality. The evolving case study approach to psychological pathology lent support to the idea that the seeds of sexual inversion could be found in the experiences of early childhood.

Initially, many scientists targeted adolescence as the period of life during which sexual instincts first manifested themselves, as Hall himself stated in his famous volumes on the subject of adolescence in 1905. Hall described the "reproductive instinct" as vague even in adolescence, not associated definitely with either sex, and prone to give rise to "sexual perversions" if not appropriately directed.[25] There was an important role for society in enabling the transition to healthy heterosexuality. Frankwood Williams, a champion of mental hygiene, warned an audience in 1926 that "[e]verything in the future depends upon" the "establishment of hetero-sexuality" in adolescence. Heterosexuality "does not just happen; it is a development and growth that is nourished and contained by what it feeds upon."[26]

Critics such as Williams argued that heterosexuality was imperiled by the tendency to segregate boys from girls during the critical period of adolescence. Prudery, the double standard, and misplaced sex antagonism all contributed to the social disease of homosexuality. Adjustment to one's proper sex role as an adult was dependent not only on the psychodynamics of family life but also on social practices conducive to heterosexuality.[27]

Freudian conceptions of childhood sexuality contributed to changes in ideas about the timing of gender and sexual development. Some Freudian ideas fit quite nicely with boy workers' concepts about the "effeminacy" or gender neutrality (although Freud would not have thought of it this way) of early childhood. Psychologist Leta Hollingworth claimed in 1928 that young children were not particularly heterosexual, while reiterating the emerging view that childhood was not a sexless time: "Previous to the onset of puberty, the child is not definitely heterosexual. Its sex life has been vague but incipient. Its longings for human contacts have been vague and unlocalized; its affections attachable to persons of either sex somewhat equally."[28]

In her widely cited book on children and sexuality, published in 1934, Frances Strain took a more contentious stance: "The pre-adolescent age is naturally homosexual, which is merely saying that the bond is strongest between those of the same sex." Because young children were essentially bisexual, the transition period from homosexuality to heterosexuality was uncertain and could to lead to protracted homosexuality.[29] Cross-sex identification was seen by some as both a prelude and a potential obstacle to heterosexuality.

By the 1930s, most experts agreed that sexual orientation was established in infancy. In a standard child psychology text Anna Freud made a claim that would become orthodoxy within much of the psychological establishment: "The normality of the entire later life of the child, its ability to love and procreate," is "dependent on the fate of infantile sexuality."[30] In a more popular vein the prolific sociologists Ernest and Gladys Groves argued that "heterosexuality . . . is an end-product of the normal growth of impulses that appear first in infancy and early childhood." The Groves admitted that all people share masculine and feminine characteristics but "the degree to which we swing to our normal pole or its opposite is in part determined by the happenings of early childhood."[31] The father who taught his daughter to hunt and play baseball because he had always wanted to have a son was not a twentieth-century phenomenon. However, these kinds of social practices took on new meanings as scientists sought to determine the genesis of homosexuality and other disorders of heterosexual desire and the human psyche.

The newly established *Parents' Magazine* published a slew of articles on sex education and family life in the 1930s.[32] In "Mothers Make Sissies," published in *Ladies' Home Journal* (1938), Charles Drake located the genesis of the sissy in young childhood. He reported the findings of a survey of young boys who were asked to name the characteristic traits of a five-year-old sissy. The boys described sissies as fastidiously dressed crybabies, who liked to play with girls and had "peculiar hair cuts." Drake blamed mothers for babying their young sons and failing to reinforce their masculinity. He warned of "future social ostracism or criminality" if sissy boys were left unchecked.[33]

During the late 1930s academics began serious research on the development of sexual orientation and gender roles. The most important projects were Lewis Terman and Catherine Cox Miles's study of masculinity and femininity and George Henry's study of homosexuality, published in 1936 and 1941, respectively.[34] Both studies used homosexuals as a means of distinguishing "normal" from "abnormal" patterns of masculinity and femininity and identified early warning signs of homosexuality. Terman and Miles's recipe for homosexuality in boys is quite familiar: "Too demonstrative affection from an excessively emotional mother, father who is unsympathetic, autocratic, brutal, much away from home, or deceased, treatment of the child as a girl, coupled with lack of encouragement or opportunity to associate with boys and take part in the rougher masculine activities; overemphasis of neatness, niceness, and spirituality."[35]

George Henry's extensive study of homosexuals led him to similar conclusions. Ultimately, these studies underscored the importance of careful surveillance of both the gender dynamics of the family, as well as boys' budding masculinity, in order to offset the dangers of homosexuality. The studies of Terman, Miles, and Henry did not break new ground in the science of sexuality; rather, they lent clinical weight to widely held conceptions about the development of gender identity and the genesis of homosexuality.[36]

MAKING SISSIES AND REAL BOYS

In the nursery schools, kindergartens, child guidance clinics, and newspaper advice columns that were sprouting in the 1920s experts implemented and disseminated their ideas about children. They sought to educate parents and steer children toward normalcy using science as a guide. Professionals drew on a range of authorities, from behaviorist John B. Watson, G. Stanley Hall, and Sigmund Freud, to writers such as newspaper advice columnist Angelo Patri—who at the time was quite influential. Assumptions about gender underscored much of the work of all these writers, so much so that they rarely felt the need to spell these assumptions out explicitly. Yet in assessments of little boys with "mother complexes," a shared understanding of the causes and treatment of sissy boys emerged.

Psychologist Helen Thompson Wooley was ahead of her time in 1922 when she explicitly drew connections between maternal overprotection and gender identity in her notes on a nursery school child. She described three-year-old Johnny as "spoiled" and the victim of the "unwise affections" of his mother. The mother's relation to him was "merely an indulgence of her own emotional nature." By contrast, his father was a severe disciplinarian and Johnny feared men intensely. Wooley reported that Johnny wished he was a girl and liked to wear dresses and play the role of bride. He was "very much disgusted when it proved to be impossible to make the old lace curtain which was used as a bridal veil, stick to his short, stubby hair."[37]

The idea that mothers were both "unwise" and "indulgent" in their affections for their sons suggests a double edge to these worries: mothers lacked both the knowledge and the emotional control to rear their sons effectively. Such mothers were simultaneously seductresses and parasites. In the process of tearing apart the myth of the self-sacrificing Victorian mother, the culture was producing a new and more pernicious myth of motherhood.

The idea that "smother-love" was directly related to gender-inappropriate behavior is implied in this account of a five-year-old at the Philadelphia Child Guidance Clinic: "He did not play with other boys—in fact he was distinctly not a boyish boy. . . . He never wants to leave his mother."[38] The fact that these connections were so commonly drawn in the case literature, with little in the way of research to support them, suggests that workers and theoreticians drew on a causal analysis that was widely shared among the general public. Psychology would buttress—but not invent—this explanatory logic.

Concerns about sissy boys in case records rarely directly alluded to the dangers of homosexuality. Grace Caldwell, the director of a nursery school for Italian immigrant children in Boston—who characterized one of her young charges as a "homo-sexual in the making" in 1928—was an exception.[39] As boys grew older, their feminine mannerisms and proclivities were linked more explicitly to aberrant sexuality. A day nursery report described an eleven-year-old whose mother was "exaggerated in her affection for the boy, whom she overprotected. . . . The boy was distinctly effeminate, and last spring showed marked symptoms of homo-sectuality [sic]."[40] Overprotective mothers were the ubiquitous culprits in clinical accounts. Missing, distant, and punitive fathers also played a role, but as in real life, their role was defined mainly by their absence. Clinicians just did not have that much to say about fathers.

Parents' perspectives on the real boy and his antithesis, the sissy, are illuminated by the correspondence of Angelo Patri, a New York City public school principal who wrote a newspaper advice column for parents in the 1920s and 1930s.[41] Patri was an exponent of Hallian theories of boyhood and, as such, perpetuated the theory of the inherent savagery of little boys. Patri's advice exemplified ideas about boyhood shared by many boy workers and educators; although Hall's influence was diminishing in the rarified atmosphere of the academy, he had legions of followers among those working with children.

A description of a real boy and Patri's analysis of his mother's plight demonstrates the new light in which typical boyhood behaviors were being cast. M.H. from Oakland, California, wrote in 1925 about her unruly, pugilistic, and spiteful seven and a half year old son. Patri's response was very reassuring: "You have a real boy. He has very unpleasant qualities. All little boys have. . . . At seven years of age a little boy enters upon a stage of what is akin to savagery. . . . [W]hen he reaches the age of twelve or thirteen he approaches another stage of growth where he drops some of the savage characteristics and takes on the instability of adolescence."[42] Many of the disagreeable traits associated with boyhood—which many parents strove to eradicate through stern discipline—were recast as embodiments of boyhood's natural development.

Patri valiantly defended the real boy to parents, but parents themselves also appropriated the phrase in defense of their sons. Parents often prefaced their letters with testimonials of their sons' credentials as real boys. J.G.C. described her son as a "bright, lively boy; what folks call a real boy," before recounting his conflicts with his teachers. R.M. confided, "My boy is one of the real boy types, normal in every way," in spite of his severe temper tantrums. Other letter writers claimed that their sons were "all boy" or "every inch a boy"—using these phrases to inoculate their sons against the charge of pathology.[43]

Sissies, by contrast, did not have recourse to this normalizing rhetoric. It was in the context of middle school, which immersed children in the society of their peers, that boys were most likely to be identified as sissies and to suffer from the victimization of other boys. However, younger boys were also subject to taunting and had to contend with parents who confronted them with their lack of virility. J.M. of Buffalo, New York, lamented that her timid six-year-old was big for his age yet silently withstood bullying. She and her husband used physical punishment and shame as mechanisms for instilling masculinity: "We've talked to him and got mad and spanked him for not taking his own part but it doesn't seem to help. . . . Once I got so provoked I called him a coward." The mother also wondered whether her son's timidity was caused by the intensity of her mothering.[44]

Parents and professionals often equated certain body types with effeminate or sissy temperaments. A father wrote in 1924 about his nine-year-old, whom he described as "delicate looking . . . extremely slender and small boned." The boy loved to dance and act and would rather play with girls than with boys. The father complained that his son was regarded by his peers as a "sissy," and editorialized: "He is one. . . . His lack of physical strength, as well as his disinclination to fight makes him the butt [of teasing] all the time." The father regarded this configuration of qualities with great fear, worrying that the trouble might be "the forerunner of some desperately serious future condition."[45]

Boys who enjoyed typical feminine pursuits and who failed to take "their own part" in battles with other boys were being inadequately socialized into the peer culture of other boys. Psychological or sexual pathology might await the boy who failed to exhibit the requisites of manhood. If boys were unable to hold their own in this peer society, parents and professionals were apt to view them as physically and mentally unhealthy.[46]

"TROUSERED MOTHERS AND DISHWASHING DADS": THE 1940S AND 1950S

From Rosie the Riveter to Christine Jorgensen and homosexual government employees, there seemed abundant evidence of gender reversals and transgressions during the 1940s and 1950s. In "Trousered Mothers and Dishwashing Dads" (1957), Dorothy Barclay argued that boys and girls had a difficult time learning gender roles when their dress and play was interchangeable: "Today in some circles the tree-climbing, marble-playing, ball-batting boy is just as likely to find a short-haired and betrousered girl beside him as another lad."[47] Antifeminist Marynia Farnham echoed this complaint in *Parents' Magazine*, claiming that children were brought up "as if there were no fundamental differences between girls and boys."[48] The fear that children were not being socialized into their appropriate sex roles was confirmed by many studies of young children, which concluded that the middle class, in particular, was doing a poor job of inculcating conventional gender roles.[49]

The omnipresent overprotective mom who emasculated her sons informed a spate of popular psychological works, including Edward Strecker's explanation of shell-shocked veterans, *Their Mothers' Sons* (1946); Philip Wylie's jeremiad about the dangers to American civilization of a mollycoddled generation of men, *Generation of Vipers* (1942); and David Levy's psychoanalytic account of the dangers of mother love, *Maternal Overprotection* (1943). Sissy boys despoiled the image of a strong, masculine, virile America that could stand up to Nazis and Communists alike and remain untainted by feminine influences. Psychiatrists played a major role in World War II, and studying homosexuals was no small part of their work.[50] The status they gained during the war helped to sustain their influence over family life and sexual behavior in the 1950s.[51]

Popular writings about overprotection and the feminization of boys of the earlier period were largely silent or evasive on the issue of homosexuality. This silence was irrevocably shattered by the publication of Alfred Kinsey's

Sexual Behavior in the Human Male, published in 1948, which shocked the public with its claim that a large percentage of American males had engaged in homosexual behaviors. Popular social-scientific writings highlighted the connection between sissies and homosexuals. An article in *Science Digest* titled "Homosexuals Didn't Play Baseball" (1956) revealed that boys who grew up to be gay were also more likely to play with dolls.[52] Parents, however, were still loath to give voice to their fears of homosexuality in their children. An anonymous writer for *Parents' Magazine* (1951) confessed that the realization that there was something "sissy" and "downright girlish" about her seven-year-old son was a thought that "a mother can hardly face."[53] Yet this mother did not need to invoke the word *homosexual*: she could assume that her audience would understand the implicit meaning of her grim pronouncements.

In the midst of these dire warnings about the implications of cross-gender behavior, there were also calls for a more relaxed approach to raising girls and boys. *Parents' Magazine* published an article with the ironic title "That's What Little Boys Are Like!" (1951), which included a caption, "Nobody spoiled this cowboy's fun by saying boys don't play with dolls. He knows they do, and girls play cowboys, too." Doris Guilford concluded that little boys have the same interests as girls in the house and family life and that "if we become too intent on our small sons being 'all boy,' we may deny them some of the tenderness and the help that they need in these early years."[54] Researchers such as Kinsey and Margaret Mead, who had studied individual differences in gender and sexuality both cross-culturally and in the United States, called for greater tolerance of those who deviated from the norm.[55]

Strict gender-role socialization was also associated with an undemocratic ethos. In a wartime article titled "Boys and Girls Together," Joseph Folsom queried: "Is it not more democratic to encourage both boys and girls to play the games of both boys and girls?" Not coincidentally, he observed that the Nazi rise to power was accompanied by a reinforcement of traditional gender roles.[56] Popular child psychologists Louise Bates Ames and Frances Ilg contributed to the democratic rhetoric, arguing that differences in degrees of masculinity and femininity were biologically based and that it would be undemocratic to seek to eradicate such differences.

Yet most psychologists of the period focused on a "social-learning" approach to gender roles. While many scholars acknowledged that there were biological differences between boys and girls, there was little clinical evidence of these differences, and behavioristic research was in vogue. Scientists sought to describe and quantify the gender characteristics of parents and children and the connections between child-rearing practices and degrees of masculinity and femininity, using problematically the Freudian concept of identification with the same-sex or opposite-sex parent in their project designs.[57]

Researchers creatively made use of toys, stick drawings, and doll play as a means of assessing children's gender-role identification. Doll play and stick drawings afforded researchers the tools for gaining perspective on children's understandings of gender roles and the children's attitudes toward their parents. Researchers also assessed parents' attitudes toward gender-appropriate behavior in children and its relationship to their children's degree of gender compliance.[58] The widely used "toy preference" test allowed children to choose their preferred toys from a mix of "boys'" and "girls'" toys. Their choices were measured against the choices of a typical sample of boys and girls to see what degree of masculinity or femininity they possessed.[59]

Explanations for those boys who were failing to acquire the trappings of the typical male role increasingly emphasized social learning and conditioning. Now psychologists focused on parents who failed to provide explicit instruction in gender-appropriate behavior.[60] Psychologist Meyer Rabban theorized that father absence combined with a lax approach to gender roles could produce an effeminate boy. Five-year-old Norman chose girls' toys over boys' and "would just as soon cook as do carpentry." His mother remarked that he "doesn't seem to recognize boy and girl differences in activities," but she seemed unconcerned about the matter. Rabban determined that the low masculinity score resulted from a minimal identification with his father and parents, who were lackadaisical about the enforcement of "sex-appropriate" behavior.[61]

In contrast, four-year-old Danny was quite knowledgeable about the differences between boys' and girls' toys. When his mother was asked what she would say if her son wanted to play with girls' games, she said: "Dolls are for girls, not for boys. Everybody will think you are a sissy. You should play with cars and trucks."[62] These findings seemed to support the notion that socially acceptable behavior could be fostered by a system of rewards and punishments.

Although social learning theorists were predominant in academic circles, psychologists who equated body build with temperament were popularized in the mass media. William Sheldon's works, published in the early 1940s, purported that body type could be correlated with masculine or feminine personality characteristics. Boys with narrow shoulders and minimal facial hair were less masculine, while girls with small breasts and broad shoulders were less feminine, according to the theory. Louise Bates Ames and Frances Ilg furthered this perspective in their syndicated newspaper columns in the 1950s and 1960s.[63] These competing ideas about the biological and environmental basis of personality and gender roles were mirrored in mothers' letters to experts and in research on maternal attitudes. Parents, especially mothers, who downplayed the significance of gender-role socialization were clearly on the defensive.

MOTHERS AND EXPERTS

Writing in 1957 to "Parents' Ask," Ames and Ilg's popular advice column, a mother asked whether she should be concerned about a seven-year-old who liked to play with girls and disdained sports: "Does it mean that he's growing up to be a sissy or effeminate because he is not a mean and rough boy like so many of them are and that I'm not doing the right thing to make him more masculine or should I respect his personality—that he'll never be one of those rough boys and let him hang around girls and do what he wants?"[64] Despite her worry that her son would be labeled as "sissy" or "effeminate," the mother's ambivalence was manifested in her characterization of so-called normal boys as "mean and rough." She wondered whether she should "respect" his personality" or "make him more masculine."

Ames responded that parents were largely unable to alter children's individual temperaments: "It is most difficult to make a boy more masculine than he actually is. To a large extent, this kind of thing is, in our opinion, inborn."[65] Ames contended that there were many varieties of constitutions and temperaments within each gender—most of which could be subsumed under the category of "normal."

Another mother was similarly confused about an eleven-year-old who did not enjoy typical boys' activities, and consequently she asked the doctors: "Is this a natural thing for boys of Alan's type? Should we simply ignore it and let him go his happy, unstimulated way without any effort to help him fit himself into a tough masculine world? Or should we suggest and then press until he does some of these things?"[66] Both mothers were perplexed about the respective roles of biology and child rearing in their sons' temperaments and unsure about their own responsibilities for inculcating masculinity.

In each of these cases one thing was clear: masculinity was not a given in little boys. The idea that one becomes rather than is born a boy is evident in this excerpt from Sears's text: "I would want him to be a real boy. . . . Last week he came home and climbed a fence and ripped a brand new pair of grey flannel pants. His father was very proud of him. He at last had become a boy." Clearly, boys did not become boys only by their genetic endowments. Their actions counted too.[67]

There were also mothers who evinced skepticism about the need to instill masculinity in little boys. While many girls were allowed a "tomboy" phase through their elementary school years, some boys were permitted a "sissy" stage, although its outer limits were generally younger than that of girls. And some other mothers were more philosophically inclined to gender neutrality, as a mother cited in Sears's study revealed: "I think that boys and girls have many similar likes and dislikes in play. . . . Oftentimes he plays house with her [his cousin], and she often plays cowboys with him. And I don't think there's too much difference in what boys and girls play at that age. And just to be a regular boy, because he is a boy, I don't think is all that important."[68] This mother's differentiation between the concept of the "regular boy" and her own child's sex membership suggests her awareness of the social context of the "regular boy" and her resistance to this cultural mandate.[69]

Sissy boys sometimes seemed immune to the social pressure to conform to their assigned gender roles.[70] One mother wrote to Drs. Ames and Ilg about a four-year-old who enjoyed dressing up in women's clothes: "He went outside today with my old hat, shoes, bag, earrings, necklace and bracelet. His brother and father have [sic] a fit." But the child was apparently unabashed by the negative reactions he evoked: "People make fun of him, but he doesn't mind. He sings constantly and quite well and is a terrific 'ham.'" Another little boy stole dolls and strolled about with them in his wagon in spite of the disapproval of his distraught father. Ames and Ilg applauded the boy's willingness to resist social pressures and enjoy his doll play.[71] A range of explanations might be offered for boys' flouting of gender conventions: desire, resistance, rebellion, and confusion, among others. Yet whether they consciously flouted gender conventions or not, they displayed autonomy in the face of the prescriptions of peers and parents alike.

CONCLUSION

There have been many shifts in professional expertise and parental wisdom regarding the meaning of masculinity in little boys in the past hundred years. Feminists of the 1970s and 1980s turned the social-learning theories of gender-role conditioning on their head, arguing that such conditioning was inherently damaging to little girls, an argument that would eventually extend to little boys, at least in some quarters. Writers such as psychologist William Pollack contend that boys have been emotionally scarred by socialization for masculinity, with little boys being dissuaded from openly expressing their feelings of pain and affection. More conservative writers contend that the opposite is true: that boys have been damaged by educators who have tried to instill traditional female virtues in them.[72] Few challenge, however, the idea that boys are genetically programmed to be boys. Even so, an array of toys, clubs, and classes exist to accommodate and ensure the development of boys' burgeoning masculinity at earlier and earlier ages. Simultaneously, challenges to the gender and sexual regimes abound, with the transgendered perhaps posing the most radical challenge to both bio-logical and social scientific conceptions of gender differences. Yet main-taining a skeptical humility about the possibility of encapsulating boys' psyches into a scientific theorem or a folk saying such as "boys will be boys" seems to be still outside our grasp.

NOTES

1. Mary Buell Sayles, *The Problem Child at Home: A Study in Parent-Child Relationships* (New York: Commonwealth Fund, 1928), 285, 287.

2. Robert R. Sears, Eleanor E. Maccoby, and Harry Levin, eds., *Patterns of Child Rearing* (Evanston, IL: Row, Peterson, 1957), 398.

3. Gail Bederman, *Manliness and Civilization: A Cultural History of Gender and Race in the United States, 1880–1917* (Chicago: University of Chicago Press, 1995).

4. Jennifer Terry, *An American Obsession: Science, Medicine, and Homo-sexuality in Modern Society* (Chicago: University of Chicago Press, 1999); George Chauncey, *Gay New York: Gender, Urban Culture, and the Making of the Gay Male World, 1890–1940* (New York: Basic Books, 1994).

5. David Tyack and Elisabeth Hansot, *Learning Together: A History of Co-education in American Schools* (New Haven: Yale University Press, 1990).

6. Elizabeth Lunbeck, *The Psychiatric Persuasion: Knowledge, Gender, and Power in Modern America* (Princeton: Princeton University Press, 1994), 237; Kathleen Jones, *Taming the Troublesome Child: American Families, Child Guid-ance, and the Limits of Psychiatric Authority* (Cambridge, MA: Harvard Univer-sity Press, 1999).

7. David I. MacLeod, *Building Character in the American Boy* (Madison: University of Wisconsin Press, 1983); Clifford Putney, *Muscular Christianity: Man-hood and Sports in Protestant America* (Cambridge, MA: Harvard University Press, 2001).

8. Edward Strecker, *Their Mothers' Sons: A Psychiatrist Examines an Ameri-can Problem* (Philadelphia: Lippincott, 1946); David M. Levy, *Maternal Overpro-tection* (New York: Columbia University Press, 1943); Philip Wylie, *Generation of Vipers* (New York: Farrar and Rinehart, 1942).

9. Geoffrey Gorer, *The American People: A Study in National Character* (New York: W. W. Norton, 1948), 85.

10. See Jo B. Paoletti, "Clothing and Gender in America: Children's Fashions, 1890–1920," *Signs* 13 (Spring 1987): 136–43; Care Rose, *Children's Clothing Since 1750* (London: B. T. Batsford, 1989); Henrietta May Thompson and Lucille E. Rea, *Clothing for Children* (New York: John Wiley & Sons, 1949); Jacqueline S. Reinier, *From Virtue to Character: American Childhood, 1775–1850* (New York: Twayne, 1996).

11. Karin Calvert, *Children in the House: The Material Culture of Early Child-hood* (Boston: Northeastern University Press, 1992); Stephen M. Frank, *Life with*

Father: Parenthood and Masculinity in the Nineteenth-Century American North (Baltimore: Johns Hopkins Press, 1999), 33.

12. John Tosh, *A Man's Place: Masculinity and the Middle-Class Home in Victorian England* (New Haven: Yale University Press, 1999), 4, 103.

13. Calvert, *Children in the House*, 109.

14. Calvert, *Children in the House*, 99. See also Anthony Rotundo, "Boy Culture: Middle-Class Boyhood in Nineteenth-Century America," in *Meanings for Manhood: Constructions of Masculinity in Victorian America*, ed. Mark C. Carnes and Clyde Griffin (Chicago: University of Chicago Press, 1990).

15. Claudia Nelson, *Boys Will Be Girls: The Feminine Ethic in British Children's Literature* (New Brunswick: Rutgers University Press, 1991), 2.

16. Bederman, *Manliness and Civilization*; Anthony Rotundo, *American Manhood: Transformations in Masculinity from the Revolution to the Modern Era* (New York: Basic Books, 1993).

17. Bederman, *Manliness and Civilization*.

18. See G. Stanley Hall, "Feminization in School and Home," *World's Work* (May 1908): 10237–44; Hall, *Adolescence: Its Psychology and Its Relations to Physiology, Anthropology, Sociology, Sex, Crime, Religion, and Education* (New York and London: D. Appleton, 1905); Dorothy Ross, *G. Stanley Hall: The Psychologist as Prophet* (Chicago: University of Chicago Press, 1972).

19. MacLeod, *Building Character*; Putney; Kenneth Kidd, *Making American Boys: Boyology and the Feral Tale* (Minneapolis: University of Minnesota Press, 2004).

20. J. Adams Puffer, *The Boy and His Gang* (Boston and New York: Houghton Mifflin, 1912).

21. See Paul Hanly Furfey, *The Growing Boy: Case Studies of Developmental Age* (New York: MacMillan, 1930), 65–66. See also Furfey, *The Gang Age: A Study of the Preadolescent Boy and His Recreational Needs* (New York: MacMillan, 1926); and Puffer.

22. Furfey, *The Gang Age*.

23. William Byron Forbush, *The Boy Problem* (Boston: Pilgrim Press, 1907).

24. See Terry, *An American Obsession*; Chauncey, *Gay New York*.

25. Hall, *Adolescence*, 1:286.

26. Frankwood Williams, "Confronting the World: Adjustments of Later Adolescence," in *Concerning Parents: A Symposium on Present Day Parenthood* (New York: New Republic, 1926), 152

27. Williams, "Confronting the World," 152.

28. Leta S. Hollingworth, *The Psychology of Adolescence* (New York: D. Appleton, 1928), 117.

29. Frances B. Strain, *New Patterns in Sex Teaching* (New York: D. Appleton, 1934), 182–83.

30. Anna Freud, "Psychoanalysis of the Child," in *A Handbook of Child Psychology*, ed. Carl Murchison (Worcester, MA: Clark University Press, 1931), 562, 566.

31. Ernest R. Groves and Gladys Hoagland Groves, *Sex in Childhood* (New York: Macaulay, 1933).

32. Roy E. Dickerson, "New Approaches to Sex Education," *Parents' Magazine* 10 (May 1935): 65.

33. Charles A. Drake, "Mothers Make Sissies," *Ladies Home Journal* 55 (March 1938): 114.

34. Lewis M. Terman and Catherine Cox Miles, *Sex and Personality: Studies in Masculinity and Femininity* (New York: Russell & Russell, 1936); George W. Henry, *Sex Variants: A Study of Homosexual Patterns* (New York: Harper and Brothers, 1941).

35. Terman and Miles, *Sex and Personality*, 320.

36. Terry *An American Obsession*; Joseph H. Pleck, *The Myth of Masculinity* (Cambridge: MIT Press, 1981).

37. Helen Thompson Woolley, "The Pre-kindergarten Child," paper given to the Michigan Teachers Association, 3 November 1922, box 117, file 5, Merrill-Palmer Institute Papers, Walter Reuther Library, Wayne State University.

38. Gerald H. J. Pearson, "What the Preschool Child Needs," *Parents' Magazine* 6 (January 1931): 13.

39. Grace Caldwell, "The Play School for Habit Training," 10 March 1925, North Bennett Street School for Industrial Training Papers, series II, box 103, file 80, Schlesinger Library on the History of Women.

40. "Survey of Mather Families," 1934, Cleveland Day Nursery Papers, box 6, file 32, Western Reserve Historical Society.

41. Ralph LaRossa, *The Modernization of Fatherhood: A Social and Political History* (Chicago: University of Chicago Press, 1997).

42. M.H to Angelo Patri, Oakland, CA, 15 September 1925; Angelo Patri to M.H., 10 October 1925, Angelo Patri Papers, Library of Congress.

43. M.H. to Angelo Patri, Oakland, CA, 15 September 1925, Patri Papers.

44. Mrs. James Miller of Buffalo, NY, to Angelo Patri, n.d., circa 1926, Patri Papers.

45. H.S.B. of Washington, DC, to Patri, 9 October 1924, Patri Papers.

46. Paula S. Fass, *The Damned and the Beautiful: American Youth in the 1920s* (New York: Oxford University Press, 1977); and John Modell, *Into One's Own: From Youth to Adulthood in the United States, 1920–1975* (Berkeley: University of California, 1989).

47. Dorothy Barclay, "Trousered Mothers and Dishwashing Dads," *New York Times Magazine*, 28 April 1957, 48.

48. Marynia F. Farnham, "Helping Boys to be Boys . . . Girls to be Girls," *Parents' Magazine* 28 (January 1953): 34.

49. Lydia Boyce Fauls and Walter D. Smith, "Sex-Role Learning of Five-Year-Olds," *Journal of Genetic Psychology* 89 (1956): 106.

50. Allan Berube, *Coming Out under Fire: The History of Gay Men and Women in World War II* (New York: Free Press, 1990), 149–74; Elaine Tyler May, *Homeward Bound: American Families in Cold War America* (New York: Basic Books, 1998).

51. Ellen Herman, *The Romance of American Psychology: Political Culture in the Age of Experts* (Berkeley: University of California Press, 1995).

52. "Homosexuals Didn't Play Baseball," *Science Digest* 40 (September 1956): 37; John D'Emilio, "The Homosexual Menace: The Politics of Sexuality in Cold War America," in *Passion and Power: Sexuality in History*, ed. Kathy Peiss and Christina Simmons (Philadelphia: Temple University Press, 1989).

53. Quotation from Gorer is cited in Michael Kimmel, *Manhood in America: A Cultural History* (New York: Free Press, 1996), 243; A Mother, "Was Our Boy a Sissy?" *Parents' Magazine* 26 (April 1951): 45.

54. Doris F. Guildford, "That's What Little Boys Are Like!" *Parents' Magazine* 26 (July 1951): 42–43.

55. Margaret Mead, *Male and Female* (New York: William Morrow, 1949); Alfred Kinsey, *Sexual Behavior in the Human Male* (Bloomington: Indiana University Press, 1948).

56. Joseph K. Folsom, "Boys and Girls Together," *National Parent-Teacher Magazine* 38 (February 1944): 6.

57. Walter Mischel, "A Social-Learning View of Sex Differences in Behavior," in *The Development of Sex Differences*, ed. Eleanor E. Maccoby (Stanford: Stanford University Press, 1966), 56–81.

58. Fauls and Smith, "Sex-Role Learning," 109–10.

59. Fauls and Smith, "Sex-Role Learning," 110; B. G. Rosenberg and B. Sutton-Smith, "The Measurement of Masculinity and Femininity in Children," *Child Development* 39 (1959): 372–80; Lenore A. DeLucia, "The Toy Preference Test: A Measure of Sex-Role Identification," *Child Development* 34 (1963): 107–17; D. G. Brown, "Sex-Role Preference in Young Children," *Psychological Monographs* 70 (1956); Fauls and Smith, "Sex-Role Learning," 109–10.

60. Paul Mussen and Luther Distler, "Masculinity, Identification, and Father-Son Relationships," *Journal of Abnormal and Social Psychology* 59 (1959): 350–56.

61. Meyer Rabban, "Sex-Role Identification in Young Children in Two Diverse Social Groups," *Genetic Psychology Monographs* 42 (1950): 132.

62. Rabban, "Sex-Role Identification," 130–31.

63. Frances L. Ilg and Louise B. Ames, *Child Behavior* (New York: Harper, 1955); W. H. Sheldon, S. S. Stevens, and W. B. Tucker, *The Varieties of Human Physique* (New York: Harper, 1940); and W. A. Schoncence, "Deficient Development of Masculinity: Psychosomatic Problem of Adolescence," *American Journal of Diseases of Children* 79 (January 1950): 17–29.

64. Mrs. N.N. of Raleigh, North Carolina, to Louise Bates Ames, 9 December 1957, Parents Ask Letters, Louise Bates Ames Papers, Library of Congress.

65. Louise Bates Ames to Mrs. N.N. of Raleigh, North Carolina, 17 December 1959, Parents Ask Letters, Louise Bates Ames Papers.

66. M.J.D. of Hamden, CT, to Louise Bates Ames and Frances Ilg, 14 September 1955, Louise Bates Ames Papers.

67. Robert R. Sears, Eleanor E. Maccoby, and Harry Levin, *Patterns of Child Rearing* (Evanston, IL), 404.

68. Sears et al., *Patterns of Child Rearing*.

69. Rabban, "Sex-Role Identification," 133.

70. See Matthew Rottnek, *Sissies and Tomboys: Gender Nonconformity and Homosexual Childhood* (New York: New York University Press, 1999).

71. These letters and the authors' responses were published in Louise Bates Ames and Frances L. Ilg, *Parents Ask* (New York: Harper, 1962), 222–23.

72. William Pollack, *Real Boys: Rescuing Our Sons from the Myths of Boyhood* (New York: Random House, 1998); Christina Hoff Summers, *The War Against Boys: How Misguided Feminism Is Harming Our Young Men* (New York: Simon and Schuster, 2000).

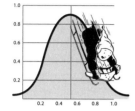

The Sciences of Childhood

Barbara Finkelstein

THE CHAPTERS IN THIS VOLUME reveal what was intellectually thinkable, economically valuable, professionally defensible, and institutionally practical in the important half century when psychology, pediatrics, and sociology came of age as disciplines of expertise in the United States. It was during this fifty-year period that universities incorporated the social sciences; legitimized the power of medical, social, and psychological sciences and scientists; and amplified an evolving therapeutic theology that was to inform the practices of child health, education, and welfare; professional intervention; and the delivery of social services. It was during this period that psychologists, physicians, pediatricians, sociologists, professional educators, child guidance professionals, truant officers, social workers, child therapists, and special educators discovered adolescence and delinquency. It was during this period that schools served ever larger and more diverse groups of students and that social service agencies extended their reach into families, schools, clinics, and early learning settings. It was during this period that newly minted experts convinced legislative and judicial bodies to articulate standards of child care, regularize child-rearing practices, secure the rights and interests of children, and solidify the legitimacy of child-care workers, including physicians, psychologists, and parent advice givers, among others. And it was during this half century that a cadre of expert authorities refined traditional constructions of childhood and the regulatory policies that ought to govern the lives of the young. In short, cadres of academic specialists began to do battle for the minds and hearts of children, youth, and families, as they have continued to do to this day.

Each of the chapters in this book, whether focused on the intersections of knowledge, pedagogy, and the curriculum; the professionalization of child study; the outcomes of public policies; the effects of parent education; the politics of expert authority; or approaches to the construction and implementation of education reform, reveals a consistent pattern and trajectory. Each documents the perdurability of particular approaches to child welfare and education, the importance of tutorial environments, the roles of women as responsible agents for the rearing of the rising generation, and the ambitions and passions of social scientists and medical authorities seeking to advance the authority and language of science. Taken together, these themes complement, if not substitute for, the authority of religion and families as guides to childhood nurture and social policy.

As actors in the forming of social arrangements and practices, psychologists, physicians, social workers, and school reformers owed as much to the power of tradition as they did to the power of scientific thinking in their formulations of what was proper, useful, and effective for children. In their scientific zeal and commitments to social betterment, they amplified the importance of childhood as a stage of life and generated bodies of medical knowledge that have made important differences in the quality of life of children. But they neither acknowledged continuities with the past nor recognized the constructed, contextually bounded nature of their own work as scientists, failing to understand the contingent nature of the truths they sought to advance or the way their own expert roles were politically as well as intellectually embedded. Nor it seems, did they quite understand the limitations and possibilities, the dilemmas and contradictions, that would be imposed by the organizational silos that they helped to create.

Without quite meaning to, they parsed children into measurable parts and pieces, and then, in order to help them, they classified, assessed, and labeled them. Whether through the construction of IQ tests, indexes of abnormality, taxonomies of disadvantage, or measures of difference, they created labels that, while intended to help, in the process organized new forms of status degradation that reproduced and gave new names to the kind of social and cultural hierarchies and stereotypes that had dominated social and education thinking in the nineteenth century. One need only attend to contemporary achievement gaps between rich and poor students, the predominance of socioeconomically privileged students in classrooms for the so-called gifted and talented, the demographics of school tracking, the race-based assessments of student capacity, or an accountability structure that emphasizes technical rather than moral and social matters of learning—to understand the ways that scientific thinking has intruded into the practices of everyday pedagogical life and rationalized an array of social policies.

Not only did twentieth-century scientists parse children into measurable bits and pieces, they contributed to the enactment of public policies that parsed children into distinct and isolated policy enclaves: departments of health and human services, education, labor, and defense, to name just a few. Over the course of the twentieth century, departments of health, education, and welfare emerged as distinct agencies of government with responsibility for distinct aspects of child development and public policy. As government agencies multiplied, so, too, did the array of experts who claimed scientific legitimacy and sought to shape the forms that public regulation ought to take. Not surprisingly, an array of turf wars emerged and, along with them, a series of structured tensions and contradictions that have bedeviled child advocates ever since.

There are tensions among the relatively uncommunicating caregivers—psychologists, physicians, social workers, psychiatrists, pediatricians, early childhood educators, teachers, special educators, community leaders—who ply their trades in diverse institutions, among them hospitals, schools, welfare offices, nonprofit organizations, colleges, universities, think tanks, private offices, and local neighborhoods. It is no surprise that holistic childhood policies emerge only atypically—as prescriptions of advocacy organizations such as the Children's Defense Fund; as the province of a specialized group of school reformers seeking to combine health, education, and social services in traditionally specialized institutions in local communities; in community-based health facilities that deploy teams of cooperating professionals to deliver health, education, and welfare services; and in specific education experiments. One thinks of charter schools such as the Maya Angelou and Seed Schools in Washington, DC, as examples of experimental boarding schools that combine services and model holistic approaches. Looked at as a whole, however, the classification of students according to distinct categories of need constrains the capacity to view and to treat children holistically. So, too, does the specialized role of government agencies, which inevitably deliver services in a piecemeal, nonholistic fashion.

Finally, there are tensions between the complexity of the problems that beset children, youth, and families, and the capacity of science and scientists or, for that matter, any single group of professionals or community members to identify and address them fully. There are problems of poverty and the unequal distribution of material resources across sectors of the population. There are traditions of political practice that cultivate sharp divisions between public and private life; contractual and personal relations; the rights and needs of children; and the relative authority of family, church, and state. There are powerful constructions of normality and difference that bedevil attempts to identify, discover, and organize collaborative and holistic approaches to problems that are social, economic, political, and transcultural, as well as simply psychological and individual.

When the chapters of WHEN SCIENCE ENCOUNTERS THE CHILD are taken together, they document the emergence of concepts of professionalism that have disjoined scientific thinking from the political, economic, and social contexts which gave rise to them and shaped their development. The chapters demonstrate a certain quality of incoherence between scientific method and social improvement, while at the same time suggest the omnipresence of humanitarian impulses. Finally, the eleven chapters suggest the magnitude of the social, political, economic, cultural, and psychological task of nurturing the good of each child and of the communities that help to shape what each can know, do, and be.

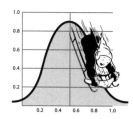

About the Editors and the Contributors

RIMA D. APPLE is a Professor at the University of Wisconsin-Madison in the School of Human Ecology and Women's Studies. She has published extensively on the history of medicine and of women's health and is the author of *Perfect Motherhood: Science and Childrearing in America*.

BARBARA BEATTY (Editor) is Associate Professor of Education at Wellesley College. She is the author of *Preschool Education in America: The Culture of Young Children from the Colonial Era to the Present* and other publications on the history of preschool education, educational psychology, and teacher education.

CARLOS KEVIN BLANTON is an Assistant Professor of History at Texas A&M University. He is the author of *The Strange Career of Bilingual Education in Texas, 1836–1981* and other publications on the history of Mexican Americans, Texas, and the Southwest.

EMILY D. CAHAN (Editor) is Associate Professor of Psychology at Wheelock College. She is the author of *Past Caring: A History of U.S. Preschool Care and Education for the Poor, 1820–1965* and other publications on the social, intellectual, and institutional history of developmental psychology.

BARBARA FINKELSTEIN, Professor and Founding Director, International Center for Transcultural Education, University of Maryland, College Park, explores the history of children, youth, and teachers in schools and has published widely on the intersections of childhood and education, student-teacher relations, the meaning of adolescence, the constructions of child abuse, and the comparison of teaching and learning in several nations.

JULIA GRANT (Editor) is Associate Professor of History at James Madison College, Michigan State University. She is the author of *Raising Baby by the Book: The Education of American Mothers* and other publications on the history of childhood, education, and motherhood.

JONNA PERRILLO is Assistant Professor of English and Director of the Writing Project at the University of Texas at El Paso. She is currently revising her dissertation, "Reforming Teachers: The Politics of Professionalism in the New York City High Schools, 1919–1969," for publication and is the author of other publications on the history of teachers and teaching.

ROBLYN RAWLINS is Assistant Professor of Sociology and Director of Women's Studies at the College of New Rochelle. Her research and publications focus on childhood precocity; prescriptions for mothering; and the relationship of child-rearing advice, popular conceptualizations of parents and children, and parenting practices.

STEVEN SCHLOSSMAN is Professor of History at Carnegie Mellon University. He is the author of *Love and the American Delinquent, Transforming Juvenile Justice,* and numerous articles on the history of childhood, education, and juvenile justice.

CHRISTOPHER W. SCHMIDT earned his doctorate in the History of American Civilization at Harvard University, where he wrote his dissertation on the origins of *Brown v. Board of Education.* He has taught at Phillips Academy and Dartmouth College and is currently completing a law degree at Harvard Law School.

DIANA SELIG is Assistant Professor of History at Claremont McKenna College. The recipient of a grant from the Spencer Foundation, she is working on a study of education against prejudice in the United States in the 1920s and 1930s.

DAVID WOLCOTT earned his PhD at Carnegie Mellon University and currently teaches U.S. history at Miami University of Ohio. He is the author of *Cops and Kids: Policing Juvenile Delinquency in Urban America, 1890–1940.*

STEPHEN WOOLWORTH is an Assistant Professor in the School of Education at Pacific Lutheran University. He teaches in the areas of social foundations, diversity, equity, and educational leadership and is the author of publications on medical authority in the public schools.

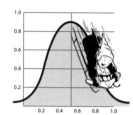

Index